# The Formation of National Party Systems

# The Formation of
# National Party Systems

---

## FEDERALISM AND PARTY
## COMPETITION IN CANADA,
## GREAT BRITAIN, INDIA,
## AND THE UNITED STATES

*Pradeep Chhibber*
*Ken Kollman*

PRINCETON UNIVERSITY PRESS

PRINCETON AND OXFORD

Library of Congress Cataloging-in-Publication Data

Chhibber, Pradeep K., 1956–
The formation of national party systems : federalism and party competition in Canada,
Great Britain, India, and the United States / Pradeep Chhibber and Ken Kollman.
p. cm.
Includes bibliographical references and index.
ISBN 0-691-11931-7 (alk. paper) — ISBN 0-691-11932-5 (pbk. : alk. paper)
1. Political parties—History—Case studies. 2. Federal government—History—Case studies.
3. Comparative government. I. Kollman, Ken, 1966– II. Title.

JF2011.C53  2004
324.2—dc22        2003064676

British Library Cataloging-in-Publication Data is available

This book has been composed in Sabon

Printed on acid-free paper.∞

www.pupress.princeton.edu

Printed in the United States of America

1  3  5  7  9  10  8  6  4  2

*To Anuka*

---

*To Kathleen and Patrick*

# CONTENTS

# FIGURES AND TABLES

## FIGURES

## TABLES

# ACKNOWLEDGMENTS

THIS BOOK IS the product of close to seven years of work. Scores of people have contributed to this project, and many assisted in the research that supports our findings. Through their efforts, they helped shape our own thinking. We are grateful for the terrific colleagues and students who have made their mark on this book.

We are indebted to Brian Gaines for allowing us to build upon and use his data set on Canadian constituency elections. He has been very forthcoming at various stages of this project. Financial support from the National Science Foundation and our home universities made this research possible. We would like to acknowledge the support of the following institutions or centers at the University of Michigan: Center for Political Studies, Department of Political Science, International Institute, Horace H. Rackham School of Graduate Studies, Office of Vice President for Research, and the College of Literature, Science, and the Arts. At the University of California, Berkeley support received from the endowment of the Indo-American Community Chair was critical in the final stages of the project.

We received outstanding research assistance from talented and hardworking graduate students, including Won-ho Park, Junghwa Lee, David Backer, Richard Agin, Jae-Jae Spoon, Dulcey Simpkins, Kris Miler, Sarah Nicolet, Sang-Jung Han, Ben Bowyer, and Caroline Arnold. Several diligent undergraduates helped us as well, including Marian Dixon and Jamie Armitage.

Our greatest intellectual debt is to those who have commented on previous papers we have written on the subject, the research project as a whole, or on the book manuscript. We particularly thank Terri Bimes, O. N. Chhibber, Paul Gargaro, Ken Greene, Simon Hug, Orit Kedar, Hanes Walton, and two anonymous referees for reading the entire manuscript and offering helpful suggestions. A large number of scholars also provided insightful critiques on parts of the research. In particular, the suggestions and comments of Richard Johnston, William Carty, Donald Blake, Fred Cutler, Scott Mainwaring, Roy Pierce, Elisabeth Gerber, Scott Page, Jenna Bednar, Gary Cox, Tim Feddersen, Chuck Myers, Brian Gaines, Gary Jacobson, Arend Lijphart, John Aldrich, David Samuels, Burt Monroe, Nancy Burns, Don Kinder, Karen Long, Rob Franzese, Rob Mickey, Rob van Houweling, Allen Hicken, Andre Blais, Jay Dow, Mike McDonald, Jacqueline Stevens, Rein Taagepera, Mariano Torcal, Chris Achen, Ben Page, Ted Brader, Jake Bowers, Cara

Wong, John Campbell, Bill Zimmerman, Samuel Eldersveld, Richard Hall, Vincent Hutchings, Ronald Inglehart, John Jackson, Arthur Lupia, Doug Lemke, Dan Levine, Ann Lin, Robert Axelrod, Mark Tessler, Ashutosh Varshney, Jennifer Widner, Eric Schickler, Jim Robinson, and Ruth Collier were useful. We would also like to acknowledge the role of participants at seminars at the University of Minnesota, University of Notre Dame, University of California, San Diego, University of California, Berkeley, University of Iowa, University of Rochester, Harvard University, MIT, Northwestern University, University of North Carolina, and the University of British Columbia.

We thank Chuck Myers at Princeton University Press for his support, and Paul Gargaro and Brian MacDonald for help in editing of the final manuscript.

This book would never have been completed without our families' patience and love.

# The Formation of National Party Systems

*Chapter 1*

# INTRODUCTION

THE SAME POLITICAL PARTIES dominate contemporary American politics at the national level and in nearly every state. Despite a few well-publicized independent candidates and politicians and, in recent years, a smattering of celebrities from the Reform Party or Independent Party, such as Ross Perot, Patrick Buchanan, and Jesse Ventura, the Democratic and Republican parties control congressional delegations from all the states, majorities in the state legislatures, and governorships in all but a few states.[1] Since the early twentieth century, the United States has displayed a pattern of virtually complete two-partism—that is, two national parties compete and win seats in every major region in the nation. Two-partism, however, has not always been characteristic of the United States, at least not for congressional and state elections. Throughout most of the nineteenth century, electoral support was spread across more than two parties, and some parties were competitive only in a few states. In certain regions, such as the South from the 1890s to the 1970s, one party predominated for long periods.

Compared with the contemporary era in the United States when two major parties compete and win seats in every major region in the nation, the 1850s marked a more highly regionalized, fractious, and turbulent decade in American party politics. After the collapse of the Whig Party early in the decade and subsequent attempts by various competitors to win cross-regional support, it was not clear whether another national party would emerge to compete with the Democrats for control of the national government. For a time the Know-Nothings, a shadowy political group dedicated to anti-immigrant and anti-Catholic principles, sought to be that party. But the Know-Nothings foundered by mid-decade, not only because their northern and southern factions split over the slavery issue but also because they could not agree on a national policy program to deal with issues that were essentially local in American society to that time: regulation of liquor, authorizations for Catholic schools, and legal tolerance of immigrant laborers (Gienapp 1987). Because these issues were addressed either by state or local governments,

---

[1]Exceptions include governors in Minnesota and Maine in the 1990s and early 2000s, and a small number of members of Congress from Minnesota and Vermont in the 2000s.

party politics for several elections was characterized by electoral competition among state-level or regional parties.

By creating an intraparty consensus around a national policy program opposing the expansion of slavery into new territories, the Republicans ultimately forged a national party. Republican leaders came to recognize that electoral success required presenting to the electorate *national* policy solutions to the great questions of the age. As a result, the young party won the presidency and dominated the congressional elections in 1860. It was a humiliating loss for the Democrats and for the political leaders in the South, leading to southern secession and civil war.[2]

In the 1990s politicians and voters in India and Canada faced difficulties in forming national coalitions not unlike those of nineteenth-century Americans. Numerous political parties fielded candidates in India, but in 2002 none had been able to craft a national majority to replace the Congress Party, which had lost its dominant status in the late 1980s. As of this writing, only two parties since 1991 have contested for national power, the Congress Party and the Bharatiya Janata Party (BJP), a right-wing Hindu nationalist party. Neither party, however, has been successful in articulating a national policy program that unites disparate regional factions within its party or absorbs enough regional or state parties to form a winning national party. And neither party can overcome the most difficult obstacle to national power—namely, the perception that the delivery of public goods and services such as electricity and clean water are the perview of state governments.

Canadian voters faced a loss of a national opposition to the Liberals in the 1990s. The Conservatives went from the position of majority party in one election to a party with only three seats in the House of Commons after the 1993 elections. By the turn of the millennium, few could predict which party, if any, would coordinate enough voters across the provinces to provide a serious challenge to the Liberals for national control. Ideological and regional divisions among former Conservative voters prevented them from rallying behind a single national leader or party label, and attempts to build national coalitions by other parties of the right such as Reform and Alliance parties foundered. As a result, for the first time since World War II, a Canadian prime minister, Jean Chrétien from the Liberal Party, won a third consecutive parliamentary majority in 2000.

In Britain, two national parties competed to form majorities in the House of Commons for much of the twentieth century. Nevertheless, unlike the situation in the United States, there has nearly always been the persistent presence of a third party, which draws a substantial share

---

[2]For an excellent discussion of the party politics leading to the Civil War, see Holt (1999), and a comprehensive survey of the rise of the Republican Party appears in Gienapp (1987).

of the vote away from Labour and the Conservatives. At times, it was the Liberals or the Social Democrats. Today, it is the Liberal Democrats. In Britain, minor party strength has fluctuated. During World War I, for example, British politics was in dramatic flux, and as many as five parties won at least ten seats to the House of Commons in 1918.

The current U.S. phenomenon of two national parties competing everywhere in the country does not exist in Canada, Great Britain, and India, even though they share many of the same electoral rules. Two-partism did not even exist in previous eras in the United States, although its electoral rules have stayed relatively constant. In the three other countries, the national legislatures seat politicians from parties that are strong only in particular provinces, regions, and states. In Canada and India, provincial and state politics are often dominated by parties that have little or no national standing. In contemporary Britain, after the 1997 devolution and creation of independent assemblies in regions, regional political parties such as Plaid Cymru and the Scottish Nationals have gained prominence.

Modern American two-partism not only looks unusual in comparison with party politics in other countries with similar electoral laws but also when compared with party politics in other eras in American history. Why is it that two national parties dominate the American political landscape in modern times? And why does this pattern not exist in other countries such as Canada, Great Britain, and India? In this book we seek to explain not only such differences across these countries but also to explain within each country why and when national parties emerged and why regional parties have drawn significant vote shares.

We show that, although these four countries have similar electoral systems—single-member, simple-plurality voting systems for the lower houses of parliament—party systems vary not only across these countries but also over time within these countries. Using historical data, we attribute changes in the party systems in these nations to the changing role of the state. In particular, we examine the relationship between the national (federal) and provincial (state) governments. Our claim that the nature of federalism influences the dynamics and stability of a party system differs from previous party system theories that stress the significance of social cleavages, electoral laws, and other constitutional features.

## PARTY SYSTEM CHANGE IN CANADA, GREAT BRITAIN, INDIA, AND THE UNITED STATES

Political parties and party systems are vital to the functioning of modern democratic politics. We define a political party in this book as a group of candidates running for election under the same label. (We acknowledge, though, that parties accomplish far more than that. A more extensive discussion appears in chapter 3.) Parties provide a means to organize and coordinate voters, candidates, political donors, legislators, executives, and interest groups around common goals.

A party system is an enduring pattern of electoral competition between parties for public office. There are marked differences in party systems across countries, including the number of parties that compete regularly at the national and lower levels, the stability of the governing coalitions and opposition, the durability of party loyalties within electorates, and the frequency of new-party formation.

Our primary interest in this book is the formation of national party systems. We define a *national party system* as one in which the same parties compete at different levels of vote aggregation. In practice, this means that party systems at the constituency level, or at the state or provincial levels, look similar to national party systems. Our understanding of the nationalization of party systems is similar to that of Carmani (2000; 2004), Cox (1999), and Jones and Mainwaring (2003). According to Jones and Mainwaring (2003, 140), a party system is "highly nationalized . . . [when] the major parties' respective vote shares do not differ much from one province to the next. In a weakly nationalized party system, the major parties' vote shares vary widely across provinces."

One widely studied component of party systems is the number of parties. The number of parties contesting seats in lower-house elections in Canada, Great Britain, India, and the United States has differed over time. In Britain, for example, twelve parties won seats to the House of Commons, and five parties won at least ten seats each in the 1918 elections. In 1992, five parties won seats, and three parties won at least ten seats. For elections to the Canadian House of Commons, the number of parties winning more than 10 percent of the national vote has fluctuated from as low as two (in 1925, for example) to as high as four in 1979 and 1993, while the number of parties seated in Parliament has ranged from two to as high as twelve.

In most political systems with free and fair elections, there can be dozens, if not hundreds, of parties competing in elections, most of which have little or no bearing on governments and policy outcomes. There are often hundreds of independent candidates who avoid party labels altogether. This is especially true for single-member district systems such as in the four countries examined here. In the United States, for example, the Prohibition Party ran candidates in hundreds of districts across the country from the 1870s to the 1950s. For a thirty-year stretch, from the 1880s to the 1910s, it won between 0.5 and 3.0 percent of the national vote in congressional elections, and fielded candidates in approximately half of the nation's congressional districts, although it never elected a single member to Congress. While still fielding hundreds of candidates into the 1950s, it won no more than 0.5 percent of the national vote in any decade after the 1910s. And this is a party that actually may have had some bearing on national policy during its peak in the early part of the twentieth century, especially in pressuring the major parties to adopt the policy goal of prohibition.[3] Far more numerous, and less consequential, are the candidates who have run under obscure or humorous labels, such as the Umoja Party, the Miller High Life Party, or the Politicians Are Crooks Party, to give some examples from congressional elections in recent years.

Similar examples exist in most countries, and as these parties have little bearing on either the vote share of major parties or who governs, political scientists do not simply count the number of parties that contest elections as indicative of how many parties are competitive in a party system. Instead, political scientists use measures that calculate how many parties actually influence political outcomes. The most commonly used measure is Laakso and Taagepera's (1979) "effective number of parties" index, or N, which gives increasing weight to parties that get higher proportions of the vote. The formula is the inverse of the sum of the squared proportions of the vote or of the seats. For n parties receiving votes, and for $p_i$ representing the proportion of popular votes received by party $i$,

$$N = \frac{1}{\sum_{i=1}^{n} p_i^2}.$$

If one is using votes to calculate proportions, as we do throughout this book, when 2 parties share 98 percent of the vote equally between them, and 100 tiny parties win the remaining 2 percent, the measure will be very close to 2. When 2 parties each win 44 percent of the vote and a third party wins 12 percent of the vote, however, the measure will be close to 2.5.[4]

Figures 1.1–1.4 show the fluctuations in the effective number of national parties competing in national lower-house elections in Canada, Great Britain, India, and the United States. First notice the United States in Figure 1.4. Prior to the New Deal, and most certainly throughout the nineteenth century, more than 2 parties regularly won substantial portions of the vote in elections to the House of Representatives. In Canada (Figure 1.1) the effective number of parties getting votes in national elec-

---

[3]The influence of the Prohibition Party is examined in detail by Kleppner (1987).
[4]There are other measures of the number of parties, and we justify our use of N in chapter 2.

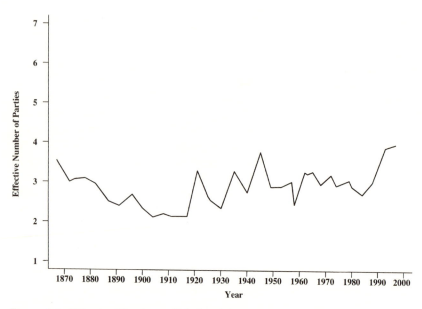

Figure 1.1. Effective Number of National Parties in Lower-House Elections in Canada

tions was 3.5 in the first national elections held in 1867. In 1917 only 2 parties competed in elections for the lower house, whereas in 1995 the effective number of parties getting votes was approximately 4. In India (Figure 1.3) the number of parties competing in national elections also has fluctuated, although there has been a steady increase since the 1970s with the effective number of parties rising from 3 in 1977 to almost 7 for the 1996 and 1999 elections. In Britain (Figure 1.2) the effective number of parties receiving votes in 1885 (after the Second Reform Act and the adoption of single-member districts for much of Britain) was 2.17, increasing to 4.43 in 1918, and then settling to about 2.5 for much of postwar period before rising above 3 in the 1990s.

There are also significant differences across the countries in the number of parties. The United States has had the fewest number of parties in the contemporary period, although in the first half of the nineteenth century the party system in the United States resembled party systems in the other countries. India and Canada have more parties on average than either the United States or Great Britain. India in recent decades has had an unusually large number of parties receiving votes for the Lok Sabha (the lower house).

The fact that these countries have not experienced consistent two-partism at the national level represents a departure from well-known

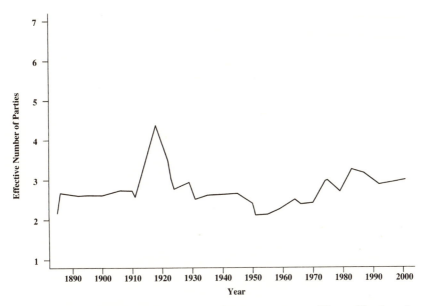

Figure 1.2. Effective Number of National Parties in Lower-House Elections in Great Britain

assertions made about the number of parties in countries with single-member district systems. Duverger ([1954] 1963) wrote that countries with single-member districts tend to have two dominant national parties, and a large volume of literature has followed his original book. All four of these countries had single-member, simple-plurality electoral systems for lower-house elections during the periods represented in Figures 1.1–1.4. Yet the effective number of parties has varied over time in each of these nations. Although many qualifications and addendums have been made to Duverger's "Law"—such as William Riker's (1982) revised version, which seeks to explain why Canada and India did not conform to the prediction of two-partism, or Sartori's (1976) version that links the number of serious competitors to the ideological differences among the major parties—none has explained successfully both the changes over time in the number of parties in such systems and the variation in the number of parties across these countries.

We show in chapter 2, however, that two-partism continues to be a robust phenomenon at the district or constituency level. If the effective number of national parties is considerably above 2 while the average effective number of district or constituency level parties is near 2—a common occurrence in these countries—it follows that the same parties

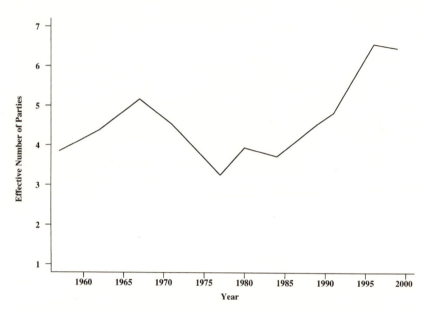

Figure 1.3. Effective Number of National Parties in Lower-House Elections in India

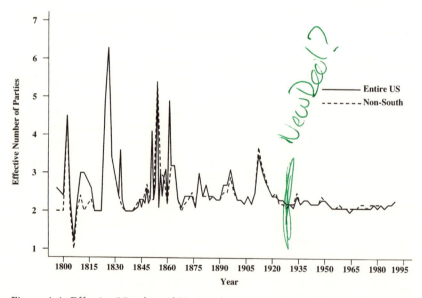

Figure 1.4. Effective Number of National Parties in Lower-House Elections in the United States

do not compete across local levels. In recent elections in India, for example, the effective number of national parties has been near 7, while the average effective number of parties at the constituency level is much lower, near 2.5. This suggests that different parties are getting significant shares of votes across constituencies and that many parties get votes only in particular locales. By our definition of a national party system, the degree to which the gap between national and local party systems exists is the extent to which the party system deviates from a pure national party system.[5]

In the remainder of this book, we offer an explanation for when a national party system will be formed and detail conditions under which the party system may not be national. We also suggest reasons for why we do not find the same number of national parties across these countries. In the remainder of this introductory chapter, we discuss previous explanations for changes in party systems, provide an introduction to our explanation, and lay out the plan for the book. We also describe the electoral data we use.

## Approaches to the Study of Parties and Party Systems

Party systems have real consequences, affecting the quality and nature of democratic representation, economic policies, and the stability of governments and political systems.[6] There is evidence, for example, that the number of parties in governing coalitions—which is related to the number of parties in the party system—affects the ability of governments to respond to economic shocks (Franzese 2002). Likewise, voter turnout across countries is positively correlated with various aspects of party systems, including the number of parties (Blais and Dobrzynska 1998). And some scholars have linked the success of regional parties to secessionist pressures (Filippov, Ordeshook, and Shvetsova 2004).

One could cite evidence that party systems are shaped to some extent by electoral systems and other features of governmental institutions and that the consequences of having national parties or a certain number of parties are not nearly as important as the consequences of having in place a parliamentary, majoritarian, or presidential system of government (see Powell 2000 for a summary of these arguments). In other words, party system differences could be merely epiphenomenal, reflect-

---

[5]There are different measures and notions of the nationalization of a party system, and we discuss these in chapter 6.
[6]See, for example, Alesina, Roubini, and Cohen (1999); Powell (2000); Persson and Tabellini (1999); Chhibber and Nooruddin (2004).

ing other differences in institutions that are more important in determining political outcomes and policies.

We believe that it is valuable to study the causes and consequences of party system change because these changes are themselves consequential. Cross-national research on a variety of topics often includes the number of parties in the parliament—an imperfect measure of the nationalization of the party system in cross-national studies—as a proxy for the degree of difficulty in introducing significant policy change, and these variables often are statistically significant in predicting policy outcomes, even when controlling for whether the country has one chamber of the legislature or two, has an elected president, or is federal (Persson and Tabellini 2003).

Although national party systems may not be inherently more desirable than party systems with regional parties, we agree with Sartori (1976; 1986) that having national parties, as opposed to fragmented, localized parties, tends to channel the choices of voters and politicians into a smaller number of coalitions and to force governments to confront national-level problems. Few would deny, for example, that if recent Indian governments had consisted of single-party majorities, such as in Britain, economic reforms arguably necessary for development would be easier to pass into law. Instead, Indian policy making was hampered in the early years of the twenty-first century by the constant struggle by the prime minister to keep in place his governing coalition, the National Democratic Alliance (NDA), which had well over a dozen parties (Bardhan 2002; Nayar 1999; Saez 2002).[7] In contrast, it would have been very difficult for Tony Blair, as prime minister of Britain, to pursue reforms if he had not had a single-party majority but rather had had to contend with leaders of diverse leftist and center leftist parties to maintain a majority. Further, it is hard to disagree with Schattschneider's ([1960] 1975) view that national, organized political parties are the most important countervailing powers to wealthy special interests in modern democracies.

Because parties and party systems are so central to democratic politics, their features and behavior have been the subject of research across many subfields in political science, including the study of voting, elections, legislatures, presidents and executives, bureaucracies, courts, elec-

---

[7]Witness the difficulty faced by the government in its attempts at economic reform, especially the privatization of state-owned enterprises (the public sector), which has often been held up because of pressure from coalition partners. Granted, in a country like the United States, where party discipline is relatively weak, there are similar pressures on party leaders from factions in Congress. The apt comparison is of both of these countries to most other democracies where governing coalitions can rely on at least party discipline (though not necessarily government coalition discipline).

toral systems, and international relations. Scholars have used various methodologies and theoretical paradigms to analyze parties and party systems. Among these, three general approaches have dominated the literature.

### Party Systems as Reflections of Social Cleavages

The first approach in analyzing party systems, and by far the most prominent in comparative politics, focuses on the nature of social cleavages that manifest themselves in party politics. Scholars seek to understand which groups in society political parties represent. Lipset and Rokkan (1967) offer a well-known thesis in this research tradition. They argue that deeply rooted, stable social cleavages lead to stable party systems. Mid-twentieth-century voting patterns in Europe reflected the economic, social, and religious divisions that arose as a result of the national and industrial revolutions many decades earlier (Caramani 2004; Katz and Mair 1994). It takes major social changes, such as postindustrialization (Inglehart 1997), civil war, depression, or massive population shifts, to alter those patterns significantly (Burnham 1970). Caramani (2004) demonstrates how pre–World War I electoral cleavages remained relatively stable throughout the twentieth century in Europe.

In this approach, social cleavages shape party systems in an almost axiomatic way. While political leaders can try to shift groups of like-minded voters into and out of parties to serve partisan or political ends, these efforts can be difficult. For some scholars, whom Torcal and Mainwaring (2001) term as the "objective" social relations interpreters, parties represent societal interests, and these interests are ontologically prior to partisan debates. Numerous country studies use this perspective to account for the nature of the party system. Often political scientists will either use or control for a set of social categories when attempting to explain developments in party politics.[8]

The literature on party systems in Canada, Great Britain, India, and the United States is predominantly rooted in this tradition. British electoral politics typically are described in terms of the class and regional cleavages that exist in Britain (Crewe, Fox, and Day 1995). Class forms the basis of the party system with the working class voting overwhelmingly for the Labour Party, whereas regionalism stokes the success of the Scottish and Welsh parties (Butler and Stokes 1970; Mughan 1986; Rose 1974a). In Canada, region and language also have been the dominant factors used to explain the number of parties and the fluctuations in

---

[8]Rose (1974b) offers the most comprehensive analysis of the influence of social cleavages on the party system across Western democracies.

partisan fortunes. Ethnic divisions began to play a large role in Canadian party politics in the 1890s and were, according to some, critical in explaining the first electoral success of the Liberals (Schwartz 1974; Martin 1974). Regional parties, such as the Social Credit of Alberta and the Progressives of Saskatchewan, emerged because of the ostensible neglect of farming issues by the industry-centered politics of eastern Canada (Martin 1974; Blais 1997; LeDuc 1985). The rise of linguistic separatism in Quebec also has reshaped the Canadian party system with the Parti Quebecois and later the Bloc Quebecois emerging as powerful electoral forces in Quebec. For Canada, as a result, a host of scholars continues to stress the continuing role of ethno-religious divisions such as Catholics and Protestants, French versus English, and urban-rural divisions in structuring the Canadian party system (see, for instance, Johnston et al. 1992, chap. 2).

Indian electoral politics, because of well-known social divisions in language, religion, and caste, have been analyzed largely in terms of the role played by existing social cleavages. Despite some notable exceptions (Kothari 1964), analysts have focused on the impact of caste in structuring much of the party system (Brass 1965; 1984; Rudolph and Rudolph 1987; Yadav 1996). Religion and "religiosity" have been regarded as a major social cleavage in contemporary Indian politics insofar as they lie at the base of support for the BJP (Jaffrelot 1995). Regionalism has been long present in Indian party politics, and the contemporary Indian party system is seen as following regional patterns rather than divisions based on ideologies or different preferences over national policies (Wallace 2000).

Multiple lines of research on American party politics also place social cleavages at the center of many analyses. Kleppner (1970) and Holt (1999) use the "objective" social cleavage of ethnicity—especially national origin—to account for developments in U.S. party politics in the nineteenth century. The study of party realignments, influential not only in research on the United States but also in research on politics in many countries, traces the changing nature of partisan coalitions back to preceding social and political crises that disrupt formerly stable alliances among social groups (Key 1949; Schattschneider [1960] 1975; Burnham 1970; Petrocik 1981; Sundquist 1983). For example, the Great Depression severed the long-standing allegiance of many northern whites and southern blacks to the Republican Party, allowing Franklin Roosevelt to forge a national Democratic coalition that endured for at least four decades. Research into partisan attachments among voters emphasizes the stability of voting patterns among large social groups in the United States (Campbell et al. 1960; Converse 1964). The voting patterns of a vast majority of southerners, Catholics, Jews, African Americans, urban residents, and suburban whites are predictable over many elections and change slowly, if at all. (The similarity of conclusions between the microlevel study in *American Voter*, by Campbell et al. [1960], and the macrolevel study in Lipset and Rokkan's [1967] research on European partisan coalitions is striking.) A relatively antiquated tradition in the study of the American two-party system explains the weakness of third parties on the cultural dualism of American society, and the lack of a strong labor movement in the late nineteenth and early twentieth centuries (Lipset, Trow, and Coleman 1956; Charlesworth 1948; Hartz 1955). This line of research in American politics emphasizes how social cleavages, while malleable, are mostly durable and tend to shape the American party system.

The inverse effect, namely the impact of the machinations of party competition on recognizable and salient social cleavages, has been less emphasized (see Riker 1986; 1993). Some argue that political considerations have an influence on the party system somewhat independent of social cleavages, or that the cleavages themselves are formed as a result of party competition or interelite politics (Torcal and Mainwaring 2001; Bartolini 2000; Bartolini and Mair 1990). While social cleavages shape party systems, political leaders can try to shift groups of like-minded voters into and out of parties to serve partisan or political ends, although these efforts can be difficult. Voters develop strong loyalties for parties, politicians, and ideological labels, and they develop habits in partisan voting that are difficult to change. Accordingly, social cleavages can become politicized in interrelated ways that affect party systems (Bartolini 2000; Katz and Mair 1994; Kirchheimer 1966; Pederson 1979; Webb 2000). Politicians who seek public office campaign and form party coalitions that shape the partisanship of the electorate, which in turn solidifies party coalitions. Recent studies of Chile and Spain show that the role of political elites is indeed critical to cementing a relationship between political parties and social cleavages (Mainwaring and Torcal 2001). More generally, studies point to interelite politics as the cause of party systems based on social cleavages (Chhibber and Torcal 1997; Torcal and Mainwaring 2001). These recent inquiries that offer more autonomy to the "political" in structuring the relationship between social cleavages and the party system mostly stress the role of political elites in politicizing some cleavages over others; hence, interelite conflict lays the basis for the party system.

Government policies and the development of state bureaucracies also can create winners and losers that form or solidify partisan alliances (Kitschelt 1999; Maravall 1997). These policies interact with other social factors to form cleavages that remain durable over decades. Bartolini (2000), in a detailed analysis of the political mobilization of the left in European electoral politics for the twentieth century, suggests that the relationship of class to the party system is not axiomatic. Rather, the politicization of the class cleavages was determined by many features of European society and politics. The consolidation of external boundaries, the bureaucratization and centralization of the state, the degree of cultural heterogeneity, the educational level of the population and the extent of intrastate communication, the role of the church, economic transformation, and democratization all played roles in determining whether class was a partisan cleavage in particular countries. For Bartolini, the "economic-functional conflicts tended to prevail over other divisions with the formation and consolidation of the economic and administrative center. It was only with the development of the modern state and with the integration of different groups . . . [that] conflicts between these groups . . . [were] centralized" (18–19).

### Parties as Solutions to Collective Dilemmas

The second approach, which has much in common with recent literature in many of the social sciences on the origins of institutions (North 1990), is relatively new and is by far the smallest of the three in terms of the number of published articles and books that rely on it. The approach begins with the fundamental question, Why have parties at all? Scholars seek to explain the origins and existence of political parties in the self-interested behaviors of voters, candidates, or legislators. For most scholars writing in this literature, parties have their origins in legislatures (Aldrich 1995; Cox and McCubbins 1993). Collective dilemmas such as cycling majorities and collective action problems are inherent in democratic politics, especially in legislatures. As a result, entrepreneurial politicians have strong incentives to set up long-term commitment devices. Such devices could take several forms, but as Aldrich (1995, 186) writes, "there are more or less continual incentives for ambitious politicians to consider party organizations as means to achieve their goals. In the most general terms, these incentives flow from the very nature of liberal democracies in an extended republic, and in an immediate sense that means the ability to fashion and hold majorities."

Demonstrating that parties will be stable over time is a theoretical challenge for these scholars. Within the framework adopted by these authors it is possible to conclude that parties will eventually unravel. Individual, self-interested legislators may want to defect from any short-term agreement made to support the goals of their party. What binds politicians over the long term to parties? To explain the persistence of political parties in this approach, parties must be presented as "equilibrium solutions"—that is, organizational solutions from which legislators would rather not defect continuously.[9]

We discuss some of these theories in more detail in chapter 3. For now we note that theories stressing the role of elites, whether they focus on the politicization of social cleavages or party formation, leave unanswered a series of questions about the nature of the party system. How many parties will be competitive? Will these parties be national or regional? The next approach offers some answers to these questions.

### Party Systems as Reflections of Institutional Rules

The third approach, of which Duverger ([1954] 1963) and Cox (1997) are two major bookends, focuses attention on the influence of electoral laws on party systems (Rae 1971; Riker 1982; Lijphart 1994; Taagepera and Shugart 1989). This literature is vast, and we address it in greater detail in later chapters. The approach tends to be prominent in cross-national comparative studies of party systems. (The more sociological approach that we summarized first tends to be used in single-country studies, although seminal works such as by Lipset and Rokkan and by Inglehart are cross-national.) For this third, more institutional approach, the main aspect of party systems to be explained is number of political parties that contest either for seats in the national parliament or for executive power in presidential systems, or for both. The many ways in which votes are counted and seats are allocated affect the number of parties. Likewise, different methods for choosing presidents affect the number of serious presidential contestants (Shugart and Carey 1992; Lijphart 1994).

Recently, this approach has become enriched by recognition of the importance of other factors, such as the nature of social cleavages (Amorim and Cox 1997; Ordeshook and Shvetsova 1994), the role of presidential elections (Cox 1997), the relative timing of presidential and parliamentary elections (Mainwaring and Shugart 1997), and the degree of fiscal centralization (Chhibber and Kollman 1998). Nevertheless, researchers typically begin from the premise that electoral rules go a long way in explaining the number of parties and the nature of party competition, and that other factors, especially those highlighted in the sociological tradition, can help to explain exceptions, or interact with electoral rules to play a causal role.

---

[9]Not surprisingly, then, the goal of researchers in this tradition is to demonstrate the equilibrium properties of partisan loyalties among politicians or voters. As one example, a recent paper by Levy (2004) argues that legislators need to bargain simultaneously among

This approach complements the other two approaches, although it is more methodologically compatible with the second, microeconomic perspective on party formation. The second and third approaches are strongly related in that they both emphasize the importance of formal institutions that constrain the self-interested behavior of politicians, voters, and legislators. Both see parties as solving collective dilemmas; however, the second approach emphasizes how parties solve n-person prisoner's dilemma problems or voting cycle problems within legislatures, whereas the third stresses how parties solve coordination problems among politicians and voters trying to decide which candidates or parties to support. Cox's *Making Votes Count* (1997) is an attempt to combine these two approaches, although more attention is paid to the latter than the former.

The first and third approaches are also related, but more in terms of their conclusions than in their underlying premises. A major theme of these two approaches is the durability of party systems. Following Lipset and Rokkan (1967), many researchers have studied the variability in party strength over time in democratic systems all over the world. The relative *lack* of significant fluctuations in party strength has been a consistent finding (e.g., Bartolini and Mair 1990; Caramani 2004). In the political-institutional tradition, fixed formal institutions lead to stable party systems because the particular electoral system, first-past-the-post or various kinds of proportional representation or multimember districts, leads to an equilibrium number of parties (Lijphart 1994; Sartori 1986).

## Some Omissions in the Literature

All three approaches highlight certain features of social and political life and leave out other features. Significantly, none of these approaches seeks to explain how party systems change over time within a country that has not changed its electoral system or has not undergone significant social changes commensurate with changes in the party system.

Several other minor shortcomings of the existing literature deserve some mention. Although the social cleavage approach to the study of party systems has a long and distinguished lineage and has proved valuable in analyzing some aspects of party systems, noticeably absent is a theory of social action underlying much of the research. Which cleavages will become salient enough for political leaders to exploit? How do voters and candidates decide among alternative strategies for winning repre-

---

multiple policy dimensions in order to sustain agreements among themselves and maintain the loyalties of voters in periodic elections.

sentation and political power? How many parties will form in response to social cleavages? The conceptual tools used in this literature offer little leverage for answering these questions.

More specifically, in Britain and Canada, although race and the national origin of naturalized immigrants conceivably could lead to voting blocs that split along ethnic lines—for example, specific Asian immigrant communities developing new parties in western Canada or in London, England—these cleavages actually have small, direct influences on the party systems. In India, with literally thousands of castes, only a few large agglomerations have any bearing on the party system (more on this in chapter 2). Similarly, in the United States there are many more social cleavages than there are political parties. In none of our four countries can the number of social cleavages explain the number of parties or predict when a new party based on a social division will come into existence.

Almost all explanations of the rise of parties based on social cleavages are "after the fact." No theory emphasizing the primacy of social cleavages can link all potential political cleavages based on social cleavages to existing political parties. In fact, research on the origin of parties based on new social divisions by Kitschelt (1989), Kalyvas (1996), Rudig (1990), and Rosenstone (1983) shows that one needs far more than a social cleavage to form a party, much less a party system. As Bartolini (2000) argues, the influence of class cleavage—the cleavage that structured European party politics for almost a century—on the party system was a result of the confluence of a multitude of factors, and the cleavage itself did not automatically form the basis of the party system. Similarly, Hug (2001) demonstrates the interactive effects of new social cleavages and institutional factors, including ballot access laws and electoral rules, in explaining the rise of new parties.

The research linking electoral systems to party systems does, in contrast, have an underlying theory of individual choice, although researchers have had a notoriously difficult time matching the theories to real data. Witness all the amendments to Duverger's Law to improve the track record of the argument (Riker 1982; Sartori 1986; Cox 1994). The correlations between district size and the number of parties across long-standing democracies are reasonably tight, but they improve considerably when scholars include social cleavages in the analyses (Amorim and Cox 1997; Ordeshook and Shvetsova 1994; Golder 2003). Ironically, when incorporated into cross-national studies that control for electoral system factors, social cleavages end up having important effects and enhance the correlations between electoral system factors and the number of parties. This begs the question of whether these researchers in the electoral institutions tradition have assessed the causal relationship accurately. An alternative hypothesis—that electoral systems are chosen by political leaders to reflect or even deflect social cleavages, and that the formal rules are determined by, rather than determine, political or partisan alliances—is always present (Stokes 1963; Boix 1998; Jones-Luong 2002; Robinson 2002). In Canada, Great Britain, India, and the United States electoral rules have been more or less the same in the period under consideration, while the party systems have changed (Figures 1.1–1.4). Therefore, to explain the dynamics of party systems, one must focus some attention on factors that change over time as well.

Our concerns are similar for the second approach on parties as solutions to collective action problems. The approach does not do well (and, in fairness, it does not seek to) in explaining variations in party systems. The argument can generally explain the existence of one governing party or perhaps the existence of two parties in a legislature, a majority and an opposition, but it has so far provided little leverage in explaining the existence of more than two parties. For this reason it has focused almost exclusively on American-style political systems (Aldrich 1995). When it has been applied, it has been used to explain the existence of parties in the United States.

These are sins of omission by the literature on parties, not deep flaws that require us to start anew. The literature on parties and party systems is vast, diverse, and valuable. Admittedly, our research here does not escape all of these criticisms.

To explain variation in party systems, we draw on concepts from all three approaches. Party systems, we suggest, are shaped by social cleavages, electoral rules, political entrepreneurs, and a fourth element that interacts with all three of these others and creates incentives for candidates and elected officials to link voters in disparate geographic locations under common party labels. That element is the distribution of authority across different levels of government.[10]

## Federalism, Centralization, and Party Systems

Developing the logic of our argument and providing empirical support for it constitute much of the content of this book. For now, we offer a brief overview. The argument begins with a focus on electoral competition within a single electoral district. As mentioned, in all four of our countries members of the lower house of the national parliament are

---

[10]Like Bartolini (2000) we focus on the role of government policy and governmental structures, but we emphasize those features of policies and structures that make some social cleavages political.

elected in single-member, simple-plurality districts.[11] Only the candidate with the most votes from a districtwide election attains a seat in the legislature, and there are no runoff elections.

In predicting the number of candidates or parties at the district level under single-member, simple-plurality systems, Duverger's Law has considerable bite (Cox 1994; 1997; Feddersen 1992; Palfrey 1989). Duverger's Law holds that this type of electoral rule leads to two-partism. Theoretically, the most compelling arguments in favor of the law rely on the premise that voters in a single election tend to vote for the candidates who have a chance of winning. This not only reduces votes for candidates expected to finish third or worse but also diminishes the incentives for candidates to join the contest for election if they do not think they can finish in the two top positions. Likewise, it reduces incentives for funders to provide money or other resources to candidates who are unlikely to finish near the top of the heap. Empirically, the evidence for the existence of two parties (or two candidates winning nearly all the vote) in district elections under this electoral system is quite strong (Chhibber and Kollman 1998; and see chapter 2), although there are noticeable exceptions, as shown in the next chapter. Even when districts are remarkably heterogeneous socially, as in India, in a vast majority of district elections to the national parliament two candidates receive nearly all the votes.

Whether national party systems will resemble the predictions in Duverger's Law is entirely another matter. It depends on the degree to which candidates and parties make linkages across districts to establish larger political groupings or organizations based on common party labels. While there may be two parties or two candidates receiving most of the votes in district elections, if there are D districts in the country, there could be as many as 2D parties at the national level if each candidate uses a unique party label on the ballot. Candidate Francine Jones could herself become the sole representative of the Francine Jones Party, and Gerry Smith could be the sole representative of the Gerry Smith Party, and so on.

Of course, since the beginning of modern representative democracy, there have been local, regional, and national parties. Regardless of electoral rules, politicians have always seen it in their collective and individual interests to establish linkages across district lines, to aggregate their votes across districts to create regional or national parties that can influence policy or run the government. We call this process *party aggregation*. Cox (1997) has called it linkage. Even in those countries with an

---

[11]This is true today, anyway. In all three countries there have been some two-member districts at various times in history, a topic we take up in the next chapter.

unusually high number of parties, such as the Netherlands or Israel (with the purest forms of national proportional representation and low thresholds), there are vastly more candidates winning seats to the parliament than national parties, indicating that most candidates prefer to aggregate their votes into party totals. However, the number of national parties is a function, to a large degree, of the incentives for candidates and politicians to coalesce around the same labels as politicians from different regions who have different ideologies and have different loyalties to previous and current government policies and leaders.

Consider two situations. It could be the case that politicians feel it necessary to join parties that represent only their particular region or particular narrow slice of the ideological spectrum. Or it could be the case the politicians feel it necessary to join parties that link districts across the entire country or across a very wide range of the ideological spectrum. Which kind of situation prevails—whether minor parties can survive because politicians are comfortable in alliances with less-than-national groupings, or whether minor parties cannot survive because politicians are only comfortable in national groupings—in turn depends on which level of government controls resources that voters care about.

In the first situation, if local governments make most decisions that affect voters, then it may be relatively unimportant to politicians that party labels communicate to voters the national party group that the politician will work with once in office. In fact, it may be crucial that the party label communicate the local or regional group that the candidate will work with once in office. The national label and the local or regional label may coincide, but they don't have to. Under decentralized political or economic systems, candidates will have fewer pressures to join broad, national parties because voters will know that local or regional governments make the important decisions anyway.

In the second situation, if national governments make most decisions that affect voters, then it becomes important for candidates to communicate to voters the policy position of the candidate relative to national government policies, and also the possibility that the candidate, once elected, could become part of the government. For both functions, national-party labels, especially labels of parties that may be expected to become part of the government, will be valuable.

This discussion so far has presented the possibilities starkly, as though only two scenarios are possible. In one, politicians are comfortable with minor-party labels; in the other, politicians want to have the label of a major, national party in nearly every case. These are extremes, of course, and the degree of political and economic centralization and, by extension, the incentives of candidates to adopt only major-party labels can vary by matters of degree. For example, as we argue in later chapters, the United States in the current era represents the one extreme, where serious candidates for the House of Representatives feel compelled to take either the Republican or Democratic label almost without exception. In the nineteenth and early twentieth centuries, however, candidates often felt comfortable adopting minor-party labels. This comfort level, judging by the proportion of competitive candidates who ran as neither Democrats, Republicans (or Whigs in the earlier era), fluctuated in tune with the degree of political and economic centralization. Over time, the number of parties competing for House seats changed, sometimes gradually, sometimes suddenly, but always in keeping with the notion that the incentives of politicians respond to which level of government was responsible for the policies that voters cared about.

To summarize our argument in brief, electoral system effects are most prominent in district elections, but party aggregation depends on the policies and role of the national government in relation to subnational governments. Federal policies of the national governments hinder or help minor, regional-based parties to survive on the national scene and, therefore, affect the nature of party coalitions and the party systems. Party systems become more national as governments centralize authority; in contrast, there are more opportunities for regional, state, or provincial parties to thrive as provincial or state governments gain more authority relative to the national government.

It could be argued that political parties, which control governments, are actually the instruments of centralization and decentralization, and that the party system has a bearing on which level of government has more influence rather than the other way around. We address this issue of reciprocal causation explicitly in the final chapter. For now, we merely note that the evident trends toward centralization and decentralization (or the level of government at which most decisions are made, central versus provincial or state) are actually the consequences of larger forces that work mostly independently of the party system.

We shall leave our theoretical arguments there for now and develop them in more detail in the third chapter. Let us now turn to a description of our data and summarize the chapters that follow.

## DATA

We have collected data on electoral returns for lower-house contests going back to the beginning of democratic elections in Canada, India, and the United States, and going back to 1885 in Great Britain. For Canada the data begin in 1867, for India in 1957, and for the United States in 1789. (Details on data collection and organization are in the appendix.) The data report district-level election results, with the generic term "district" referring to ridings in Canada, constituencies in Great Britain and India, and congressional districts in the United States. When we measure national party totals, we aggregate vote totals for parties across districts.

For the most part, the party label information of candidates in our data is quite good. Party labels from early elections in Canada and especially in the United States are spotty, and so our inferences from these data are less confident than from later eras. Party labels are missing for nearly 90 percent of U.S. House candidates in decades before the 1830s, for example. Beginning in the 1840s, however, we have labels for nearly every candidate.

The treatment of independent candidates (i.e., independent of party label), especially in India, deserves some comment. The orientation we adopt is that candidates join a party when they adopt the party label on the ballot. If a candidate chooses to run as an independent, then he or she is running under a party label, but the label is his or hers alone. In other words, an independent candidate is a party, albeit a degenerate one. It only has one member. To see where this becomes relevant, consider the process of counting the number of parties in a national party system. Let us say that across all district elections in a given year, party A receives 45 percent of the national vote, party B 20 percent, and party C 15 percent. The remaining 20 percent of the national vote is split among dozens of independent candidates. This is similar (in spirit) to what occurred in India in the early elections following the advent of democratic elections after independence. In the elections for the Lok Sabha in 1957 and 1962 there were hundreds of independent candidates who did well in district elections. When we count the number of parties, using the measure N, for example, we consider each independent candidate to be a party. Thus, if in our hypothetical example the 20 percent of the remaining votes were split among nine candidates, then the formula for the number of parties will have vote counts of the three top parties, plus the nine other parties. In other words, the vote proportions of nine parties will be entered into the formula. (We shall just make the obvious point for clarity: the formula does not imply that there are twelve parties in the party system; the formula weights the parties by their vote share.)

Besides election results (measuring our main dependent variables), to measure our major explanatory factor—the relative authority of central governments and subnational governments—we collected and analyzed original data and analyzed voluminous secondary literature on a variety of government activities related to federal relations in our four countries. A summary of our collection and coding criteria is contained in chapter

5, and we discuss many of our sources in the appendix. Briefly, our most complete information includes data on changes in constitutional or legal authority between levels of government, threats to the integrity of the nation-state from secession or other nations, alterations in the relative economic role of the national and/or provincial governments, and fluctuations in the size of national and provincial governments.

## CASE SELECTION

We have selected Canada, Great Britian, India, and the United States for this study mostly because of their similar electoral systems. Each country has a single-member, simple-plurality electoral system in the period under study, and so for cross-national comparisons we are able to control for the effects of formal, electoral rules, especially the one variable that has loomed large in studies of party systems, the district magnitude or size. The size of the district in this literature refers not to population size but to the number of legislative seats awarded from the district. These four countries have district magnitudes (or sizes) of one. Three of the countries—Canada, India, and the United States—are federal, meaning that, by constitutional mandate, they grant significant powers to states or provinces. Britain, in contrast, is not federal under this definition, at least not for the period under study.

Since our concern is how voters and candidates link across geographic regions, single-member district systems arguably offer the hardest cases of coordination or vote aggregation across districts. In our four countries of interest, no national districts or party lists automatically pool party votes to award extra seats to parties or majorities. The closest institutional device that accomplishes this kind of pooling is the U.S. presidential election. But for lower-house elections in all four countries, voters, candidates, or regional parties have to combine their votes themselves by using party labels, without any built-in features of the electoral rules. This is in contrast to systems in Germany, Russia, or South Korea, which have special portions of their legislatures reserved for pooled party votes. Coordination mechanisms in those countries are written into law, whereas in our four countries aggregation has to occur without the aid of national districts or bonus seats.

Our set of cases includes the two largest democracies in the world (India and the United States), the clearest example of a long-standing democracy facing constant threats of secession (Canada), and probably the countries with the most developed and richest party systems at the state or province levels (Canada, India, and the United States; the only country that comes close to these three from among long-standing democracies is Germany). The countries span a range of party systems found among long-standing democracies, from nearly the largest number of parties represented in a national legislature anywhere (India) to the smallest number among democracies (the United States), to somewhere in between (Britain and Canada).

There are other single-member, simple-plurality countries, including the Bahamas, Barbados, Belize, Botswana, Dominica, Ghana, Grenada, Jamaica, Kenya, New Zealand, St. Kitts-Nevis, St. Lucia, St. Vincent, Trinidad, and Zimbabwe. None of these has had a lengthy history of democratic elections under single-member, simple-plurality rules (New Zealand is an exception) and, as far as we know, offers available data on electoral returns at the lowest level spanning more than a few years. It is fortuitous that our four countries keep excellent election statistics.

Although the electoral systems for national parliamentary elections are virtually identical for our four countries, some caveats on case selection are in order. Differences across these countries may make it easy to challenge our claims that cross-national variation is caused by different degrees of centralization. Most glaring, perhaps, is the fact that the United States has a presidential system with separation of powers, whereas Canada, Great Britain, and India have parliamentary government. This is no minor difference according to research in comparative politics. Various scholars, including Cox (1997), Samuels (2002), Shugart and Carey (1992) , and Jones (1994), have pointed to the existence of a presidential system as having a large effect on a party system, and most often the claims are that presidentialism reduces the number of parties. So, for example, one explanation for the persistence of a highly nationalized two-party system in the United States, when other single-member, simple-plurality countries have had more fractionalized party systems on a regular basis, is that presidential elections encourage politicians at other levels of government or in other branches of government to link themselves to one of the candidates who has a chance to win the grand prize. Because the presidential election system is, in effect, a contest within a single, national district, the number of serious contestants—following the logic of Duverger's Law—will generally be two. Therefore, if politicians are going to link themselves to one of the serious presidential candidates, they will typically have two options (e.g., Republican or Democrat). Without this linkage, the argument goes, it leaves more room for other parties. It is worth noting, however, that while the number of parties competing for seats to the U.S. House of Representatives has fluctuated over time—in the first half of the nineteenth century, for example, many parties received votes in elections to the House of Representatives—there have always been presidential elections in the United States. So, although the presidential system may explain some cross-national differences, it can hardly explain the over-time variance in the number of parties getting votes in elections to the House of Representatives.

Changes in the *significance* of the presidential office may explain changes in the party system, and this corresponds to the main argument in this book. As the presidential office becomes more significant and powerful, something that leads to increased centralization of authority in the country, it, in turn, may lead to greater incentives for politicians across the country to link themselves to presidents or presidential candidates. McCormick (1975) makes the argument that this is what occurred in the 1830s in the United States. As the presidency became more prominent under Andrew Jackson, congressional candidates increasingly adopted national-party labels. Our data bear this out. While more congressional candidates linked themselves to the party labels of presidential candidates after 1832 than they did in the previous two decades, they did not confine themselves to two party labels right away. Early in the decade, they linked to various party labels, making the all-important distinctions on party ballots between Democrats, Jackson Democrats, and Democrat-Republicans. Yet over the course of the 1830s, as shown in Figure 1.4, the Democrats aggregated into a truly national party.

Presidentialism in the United States is not the only noticeable difference among our four political systems. One could focus on a number of other differences. For example, the United States has a stronger, more independent judiciary and a stronger upper house of parliament than the other three, and India is larger (in population) and has more diverse electoral districts than the other three countries. Canada and the United States grew gradually, with westward expansion appending new local party systems onto the national systems piecemeal. As many of these states and provinces applied to become part of the nation, perhaps this gave incentives for local politicians to adopt party labels that mimic national-party labels, in order to win over national parliamentarians and encourage them to vote in favor of statehood or admission to the Canadian nation.

As noted, by our definition, Britain was not federal prior to 1998. We include Britain in the study because it provides some small leverage to examine the effects of federalism among countries with similar electoral systems. The British cases allow us to explore whether patterns discovered in the electoral data occur in spite of federalism, because of federalism, or because of some interaction between federalism and other factors. For example, fluctuations over time in the strength of regional, ethnic-based (or nationalist) parties are less abrupt in Britain in comparison with those in Canada or India. We suggest later that these differences can be attributed to the fact that, for example, in Canada, provincial assembly elections provide a platform for nationalist parties to operate prior to competing for national seats, whereas such opportunities for lower-level parliamentary election victories did not exist in Britain when it did not have regional assemblies prior to 1998. The city council elections that did exist in Britain gave small boosts to minor parties in some instances. As Margaret Thatcher's actions in the 1980s proved, however, when she abolished several of the councils, those councils were not sovereign governments protected by constitutional laws in the same way that American and Indian state parliaments and Canadian provincial parliaments are protected.

Despite these caveats, we believe that our four countries effectively illustrate our arguments. Moreover, we actually have more than four cases. The "cases" in our data are not actually countries but moments of time in the party systems within countries; to the extent that we can compare party systems over time within the same country, we have in effect many cases.

## SUMMARY OF REMAINING CHAPTERS

In the next chapter we focus on district-level elections. We summarize the research around Duverger's Law and evaluate the formal theoretical models in this tradition. We then present electoral data from our four countries that are broadly consistent with the law, at least as it applies to district elections. There are enough exceptions within districts, however, to warrant a closer analysis, and so we examine these exceptions with an eye toward confirming or challenging the fundamental premises behind the law. The results are consistent with the notion that voters most of the time adopt some weak version of strategic voting at the district level.

Chapter 3 presents the main theoretical arguments of the book. We discuss the incentives for voters and candidates to link across districts and to aggregate their votes into regional or national party vote totals. Federalism and the degree of fiscal and political centralization play a large role in party aggregation. The fourth chapter focuses on the establishment of party formation and partisan voting in district elections in all four countries and discusses the gradual disappearance of independent candidates. Parties in all four countries were formed by politicians who sought to influence public policy. As control of policy by a group of legislators grew in importance, independent candidates lost their raison d'etre for the voters. Several trends are identified and discussed, including the changes in the number of independent candidates running for office and winning substantial numbers of votes.

In the fifth, sixth, and seventh chapters we examine economic data and electoral data to link centralization and party system change. We categorize periods of centralization and provincialization in our four countries in chapter 5, and then in chapters 6 and 7 we show that periods of change in party systems correspond as we predict for these periods.[12] Evidence strongly supports the idea that centralization leads to national party systems, an effect that is especially pronounced in federal systems. We also devote considerable attention to the degree of regionalization of the party system and of parties themselves. How well regional parties survive depends on the nature and the degree of the centralization.

In chapter 8 we discuss alternative explanations for the patterns in our data, addressing whether party systems can account for patterns of centralization and provincialization. We conclude with an analysis of cross-national data from more than forty countries, discussing the implications of these results for extending this research program to countries with a variety of electoral systems.

---

[12]We opted to use the term provincialization rather than decentralization or noncentralization.

# Chapter 2

# ELECTORAL COMPETITION
# AT THE CONSTITUENCY LEVEL

OUR MAIN ARGUMENT in this book is that the relative authority of national and subnational governments in a country helps determine the success or failure of regional and minor parties and, therefore, the formation of national party systems; however, we also concur with prevailing research that says electoral rules shape party systems. The literature on the effects of electoral rules on politics in single-member, simple-plurality systems has devoted considerable attention to testing Duverger's Law—whether or not these rules lead to two-partism. We assert that, although electoral rules directly affect district-level elections, they do not necessarily influence the formation of national party systems, and also that party aggregation at the national level is a function of the relative powers of national or state (provincial) governments. If a country is highly centralized and if the electoral rules reduce the number of district-level candidates or parties to a low number (near 2), then the number of national parties should be low (near 2) and similar to the number of district-level parties. If, however, a state or provincial government has greater authority over large areas of policy, then, even if the electoral rules reduce the number of local competitors, the country's party system could remain highly fragmented and regionalized. Different parties can coexist in different districts and different regions of the country.

Although the effects of electoral rules and centralization have resulted in two-partism in the United States, it does not follow that all countries that are characterized by centralized decision making and single-member districts with plurality rule would have only two parties competing nationally. A fully national party system, where national-level party competition is similar to local-level party competition, could settle on three parties, or more, at different levels of vote aggregation. What is important for our argument is the degree of similarity across these levels. If three parties were to win votes consistently at the district level, that could challenge Duverger's Law, but would not necessarily be an issue for our overall argument. If, however, two-partism dominates at the district level in these systems, then we should expect a Duvergerian two-partism nationally when authority is centralized.

This chapter takes the first step in our argument and explores district-level elections in detail to determine how well voting patterns correspond to properties identified in models of Duverger's Law.

## ELECTORAL INSTITUTIONS

Canada, Great Britain, India, and the United States have single-member districts and simple-plurality election rules to award seats to lower houses of parliament—the Houses of Commons in Canada and in Great Britain, the Lok Sabha in India, and the House of Representatives in the United States. Under the electoral rules for each of these countries, there are no runoff elections, and the candidate with the most votes in a district is the sole representative from that geographic area. For consistency, we use the word *district* when referring generically to the geographic area from which representatives are elected, although the word used is different across the four countries—ridings in Canada, constituencies in Great Britain and India, and electoral districts in the United States.

There have indeed been a few double-member and even multimember (more than two representatives) districts in these countries. In Canada, which has had the most exceptions among our four countries, as many as 10 percent of the seats in the Commons were chosen in double riding elections in the nineteenth century. By 1935 only 2 percent of seats were from double-member ridings, and these were then eliminated in the 1960s. All in all, never more than 5 percent of the ridings in Canada were double member, and the proportion in the twentieth century was about 1 percent in 1965 when it fell to 0 percent. Great Britain had between 2 percent and 5 percent of its constituencies for the Commons as multimember until 1950, when these were made into single-member constituencies. Even the United States has had multimember districts throughout its history, especially in the early years of the republic, and individual states have had at-large state elections with multiple representatives during some eras, including our own. India had several multimember constituencies in the 1952 election. Nevertheless, the four countries have single-member district systems for the most part, as pure as one will find among long-standing democracies.

Three of the four are also federal countries, meaning that there is a *constitutionally* mandated allocation of authority dividing sovereignty over policy between national governments and state or provincial governments.[1] The powers granted to states and provinces are protected by

---

[1] This understanding of federalism is distinct from that of Weingast (1995), who classifies Britain as federal largely because local governments have some autonomy in decision making. We classify Canada, India, and the United States as federal not because there is a

law and enforced by independent judiciaries. Since 1997 Britain has become more federal, with some devolution and the election of assemblies in Wales and Scotland. Our analysis focuses on the elections in Britain prior to 1993.

While the systems for election to the lower houses are virtually identical in these countries, there are marked differences in other institutional features across the countries. As discussed in chapter 1, the most glaring difference is the fact that the United States has a presidential system with separation of powers, while Canada, Great Britain, and India are parliamentary governments. Presidentialism is indeed an important difference between the United States and the other three countries. The argument sometimes made is that, when there are presidential elections, candidates for the lower house often want to link with national-party candidates, and in the absence of presidential elections, such incentives do not exist. Thus, minor parties have more opportunities to gain representation to the lower house when there are no presidential elections (see Lijphart 1994; Samuels 2002; Jones 1994; Mainwaring and Shugart 1997; Cox 1997; Shugart and Carey 1992; Taagepera and Shugart 1989). As we observed in chapter 1, however, the United States did not have a stable, national two-party system in congressional elections until the twentieth century. In fact, there were often important minor parties involved in elections throughout the nineteenth and early twentieth centuries despite the existence of presidential elections (see Figure 1.4). The fluctuation itself in the success of minor parties in the United States implies that presidentialism, which has remained constant, cannot by itself account for the variation over time in the nature of the party system in the United States.

Another major difference between these four countries is that the United States has a strong bicameral system, in which the House of Representatives cannot pass laws without Senate approval (and a presidential signature). Senators are elected to the upper house, although direct elections to the Senate only became standard in the early twentieth century, finally being mandated in 1913.[2] In the other three countries, upper houses are indirectly elected or appointed and are relatively weak compared with the U.S. Senate. The Canadian governor-general, a largely ceremonial position nominally representing the queen of England, appoints members to the Senate on the advice of the prime minister. Al-

---

division of functions between national and subnational governments (in all nations there are local governments that perform some function) but because there is a constitutionally mandated division of authority between the national and state or provincial governments.
[2]Technically, senators in the United States are elected in districts (states) of size two, with staggered terms, and this can be important in some instances in explaining the dynamics of senatorial elections.

though it must formally sign onto legislation passed by the House of Commons, the Canadian Senate has little power, legal or de facto. It does have a geographic basis, however, with seats filled by persons from provinces or territories in rough proportion to population size. In Britain, membership to the upper house is not geographically determined. The House of Lords was until recently a hereditary chamber, nomination to which was determined through appointment to the peerage. With the adoption of the House of Lords Act of 1999 only 92 hereditary peers (about 10 percent of the total) could retain a seat in the House of Lords. The Labour government in 2001 issued a white paper that called for an elected House of Lords with 120 members. A commission is currently examining the matter. In India, as in the United States, membership to the upper house has a geographic basis, but unlike the modern United States each state legislature elects members (using a transferable vote) to the Rajya Sabha and each state has seats proportional to its population allocated to it in the Rajya Sabha. Although the Rajya Sabha does have some say over the legislation passed by the Lok Sabha, it does not share powers with the lower house as equally as the U.S. Senate does with the House of Representatives. Only rarely do the actions of the Rajya Sabha substantially influence government policy, yet on those rare occasions the policies under consideration are salient and broadly important.[3]

Yet even with the different electoral systems for membership to the upper houses and the different powers of upper houses, the implications for the aggregation of party systems are not immediately clear. Cox (1997, chap. 2) compares the number of effective parties (measured with seats, not votes) in lower houses against upper houses in sixteen countries with direct elections to the upper house. He finds that in fourteen of the sixteen cases, the house within each country with the larger district size, or with the more proportional voting system, has more parties. This finding bolsters his case for the importance of electoral rules in

[3] In 1989 the Congress Party of India had an overwhelming majority in the Lok Sabha, the lower house of Parliament, and introduced the sixty-fourth Amendment to the Constitution as Bill No. 50 in Parliament. The purpose of the bill was to reorganize local government in India. Article 243a would have made it obligatory for all states to establish a three-tier system of local governments—known as Panchayats—and for each State Legislature to devolve powers and responsibilities to the Panchayats. The amendment sought to secure authorization from State Legislatures for grants-in-aid from the Consolidated Fund of the State; provide for the constitution of a Finance Commission to review local government finances every five years; and for the Comptroller and Auditor-General of India to audit these accounts. In other words, the central government wished to remake the nature of federalism in India. The bill got more than two-thirds of the votes in the Lok Sabha, but failed in the upper house Rajya Sabha—the council of states—on 15 October 1989 by two votes.

determining the number of parties, controlling for social cleavages, because he compares two chambers of parliament within the same country in each case.

The presence of an upper house and the manner in which it is elected could affect party aggregation of the kind we study here, although to our knowledge there has been no systematic research on this question. The mode of election to the upper house may very well influence party systems in important ways, but in the absence of systematic research on the subject we can only speculate, based on our intuition on these four countries.[4] We leave systematic examination of the topic for future research.

Despite differences in the more formal institutions in these four countries, political scientists beginning with Duverger ([1954] 1963) have emphasized the important effects of single-member districts in reducing the number of parties, with some even asserting that two-partism should be the norm, and that exceptions only arise from peculiarities in voter preferences or political culture (Riker 1982; for a dissent, see Wildavsky 1959). Critics of Duverger's Law have noted that most countries with such electoral systems, including Canada, Great Britain, and India, have more than two parties, and have concluded that the law is not a very good predictor or explanation for the number of parties. As others have pointed out, however, the power of Duverger's Law, at least as it has been formalized and extended beyond Duverger's original formulation, applies at the district level and not at the national level (Sartori 1986; Cox 1997; Gaines 1997a, 1999; Chhibber and Kollman 1998).

Properly understood in its modern form, the law predicts that (and explains why) two parties will capture all the votes in district-level elections in countries with single-member, simple-plurality rules. While dis-

---

[4] If the upper house is elected indirectly (as in the United States in the nineteenth century and India today) and on the basis of geographic representation, and has important legislative powers, it could affect lower-house elections substantially. Regional alliances could dominate both the upper and lower houses. If state governments appoint members to the upper house, then perhaps we should observe a close correspondence between parties at three levels, the state governments, the national lower and upper houses. In such circumstances there could be a problem of party aggregation as regional parties could have a substantial presence in the national legislature. If, on the other hand, the upper house is nominated and has meager legislative powers, as in Canada, then we could see lower-house elections that could offer voters a chance to counterbalance the Senate's potential veto power. This veto is virtually never used in Canada. Whether this would lead to national or regional parties getting votes in lower-house elections remains unclear and much depends on the configuration of the Senate. If the upper house is nominated and has virtually no power, as in Britain, it should probably have little, if any, effect on which party gets votes in lower-house elections. If the upper house is directly elected, has a geographic basis of representation, and has important legislative powers—like the U.S. Senate—then elections to it should conform closely to the dynamics of lower-house elections.

trict-level elections certainly influence national parties, two parties winning most of the votes in each district would not necessarily lead to two-parties nationally. In fact, it takes significant coordination and aggregation on the part of politicians and voters to make district-level party systems line up neatly into two party systems nationally. As shown in chapter 1, "lining up" is quite rare. Further discussion of national parties and party aggregation takes place in the next chapter.

In the remainder of this chapter we discuss the reasons why political theorists expect two candidates to win most of the votes in single-member district elections. We then examine whether this prediction holds up in Canada, Great Britain, India, and the United States. Data show that, on balance, the prediction works reasonably well, even when districts have extremely diverse populations. There are enough exceptions, however, to raise questions about the current models of electoral competition and the number of parties.

## THEORIES OF ELECTORAL COMPETITION IN SINGLE-MEMBER DISTRICTS

At its heart Duverger's Law relies on the assumption that there exists a nontrivial amount of strategic voting in district elections. Following a standard definition of "strategic voting"—that voters prefer not to waste their votes if meaningful and potentially consequential votes can be cast—the implication of such an assumption in single-member, simple-plurality elections is that voters prefer to vote for a candidate who has a chance of winning the election, all else being equal. A voter may prefer party A over party B and party B over party C, but she still may vote for party B if party A has virtually no chance of winning. Voting is thus "strategic" or "fully rational" in the sense that voters do not base their decisions solely on their preference rankings among candidates or parties but choose based on a combination of their preference rankings and their assessments of how their behavior will best affect the election outcome and thus their well-being. If voters are rational, then they will take into account the likelihood that their votes will help decide election outcomes and will thus pay attention to how other voters are behaving.

Evidence in favor of the notion that voters behave in such a manner, at least evidence of a limited kind, is plentiful in the political science literature. It has been difficult to discover definitive evidence from surveys that voters comprehend their full range of choices in manipulating elections results (Abramowitz 1995), and no one can reasonably say that many voters accurately calculate the optimal strategies given the institutional and informational constraints. Many scholars, however, have found evidence from surveys and from aggregate election results, especially from Germany, Great Britain, and Canada, that voters often split their votes. This shows that voters give some thought to policy outcomes as opposed to merely following deep partisan attachments, refrain from supporting sure winners in order to improve representation of minor parties, and jump on the bandwagon of winners rather than vote for sure losers (Cain 1978; Tsebelis 1986; Galbraith and Rae 1989; Niemi, Whitten, and Franklin 1993; Alvarez and Nagler 2000; Kim and Fording 2001; Blais and Nadeau 1993; Laver 1987; Fisher 1973; Bawn 1993; Johnston and Pattie 1991).

Cox (1997) summarizes this literature extensively and adds to it by examining data from Britain indicating that voters tend to throw their support behind candidates who were involved in close elections previously but do not do so as much or as often for candidates involved in one-sided elections previously (85–89). Kedar (2003) demonstrates that because in most democracies policy outcomes are a product of power sharing (e.g., among parties in the parliament or the governing coalition, between local and federal governments, or between executives and legislatures), many voters compensate for the dilution of their vote by supporting parties whose positions are more extreme than their own issue positions instead of supporting parties with positions that are most similar to the voters' own positions. In addition, the more power sharing allowed by the institutional environment and the more sophisticated the voter, the more likely the voter will engage in such instrumental behavior. Finally, the closeness of elections, as anticipated by voters following poll results, may affect turnout in the United States (Cox and Munger 1989; Shachar and Nalebuff 1999), suggesting that voters are paying some attention to the possibility that their votes will matter.

From our point of view, the precise mechanism that leads to a reduction in the number of competitors for seats or for majorities in legislators does not matter much, and we do not need to know whether voters actually make decisions based on the strict assumptions of some of the models of Duverger's Law. Voters may simply follow cues from their friends and families. They may think very carefully about their chances of changing election outcomes. They may adapt their voting behavior over time based on heuristics or may vote for people or parties they know something about. Some voters do all or some of these at various points in time. Our interpretation of the literature and of our own data is that voters often exhibit "herdlike" behavior. All else being equal, citizens prefer to vote for candidates and parties that have a chance of winning, that other like-minded citizens are voting for, and that have familiar names or party labels. The upshot is that, as we shall show, Duverger's Law aptly accounts for many electoral results at the district level. Without some notion of rational voting, even in a very limited sense, it is hard to make the law seem anything more than an empirical assertion. In other words, for the law to have any theoretical content consistent with the data, one needs to posit that some form of strategic voting must take place, even of a primitive kind.

While strategic voting may have the consequence of discouraging voting for hopeless causes (or for sure winners) in any electoral system, the exercise of such logic is perhaps easiest to see in single-member, simple-plurality systems. These systems, in Duverger's ([1954] 1963) and Riker's (1982) formulation, have two interrelated effects that reduce the number of parties to two. First, the mechanical effect refers to the fact that a party can win up to 49.99 percent of the vote in a district (or in all districts across the country) and still fail to win a single seat. If districts are of unequal size by population, then a party can win a majority of votes nationwide and yet win a very small number of seats in the parliament. For a simple example, consider a country with four districts, one very large district of a million voters, and three districts of 100,000 voters. If party A wins all 1 million votes in the large district but loses all the votes in the three other districts to party B, then party A will have taken 77 percent of the national vote but only have received 25 percent of the seats, and party B will have taken 33 percent of the national vote but will have received 75 percent of the seats. More common, however, are situations where a party has tepid support across the country, wins a respectable portion of the national vote (say 10 percent) yet gains a small number of seats (or perhaps none at all) in parliament because its vote is diluted across districts. For example, the right-wing party in India, the Bharatiya Janata Party (BJP), received approximately 10 percent of the national vote for almost two decades, though on occasion the number of seats it won for the Lok Sabha did not even cross the 1 percent mark. In 1992, to take a typical recent election in Britain, the Liberal Democrats received a little over 18 percent of the national vote, but only 3 percent of the seats in the House of Commons.

This distinction between the proportion of the popular vote won by a party and the party's quantitative representation in parliament—often called the seat-to-vote ratio—has been extensively studied by scholars using a wide variety of data. Lijphart (1994), for example, in comparing the seat-to-vote ratio across many electoral systems, shows that the ratio is largest for large parties in single-member, simple-plurality systems and smallest for small parties in single-member, simple-plurality systems. In other words, single-member, simple-plurality systems reward larger parties more than other electoral systems and punish smaller parties more than other electoral systems. Note, however, that although the research on seat-to-vote ratios has more to do with the allocation of seats at the national level, it begins at the district level. Simply put, since single-member, simple-plurality systems give the entire district prize to the plurality winner, when this is repeated and aggregated across many districts, the results can be hugely disproportionate nationally, as our aforementioned examples demonstrate.

The discussion of the mechanical effect, such as the study of seat-to-vote ratios, takes as a starting point the votes cast and asks how procedures aggregate those votes into representation. Missing from these discussions is an accounting of how voters' knowledge of the procedures affects their choices. Undoubtedly there is some feedback, and the mechanics of voting systems affect how voters make strategic decisions. Thus, as Duverger and Riker continue their discussions, a psychological effect follows from the mechanical effect. Enough voters understand the punishment that single-member, simple-plurality districts dole out to lesser candidates, and they choose not to waste their votes for minor parties. At the same time, strong candidates, political leaders, and financiers of campaigns understand the same logic and tend to gravitate toward running under the label of or supporting one of the major parties. As recent theoretical treatments of Duverger's Law have focused on the psychological effect, it is worth examining its application in some detail.

How exactly does the psychological effect in Duverger's Law work at the district level? Various formal theoretical models that share common features have been proposed. We discuss three here, although there are more (see, e.g., Myerson and Weber 1993). In all three models, the key insight is that the logic of strategic voting, when carried out to its extreme form, virtually eliminates parties or candidates who are not expected to finish among the top two vote getters in district elections.

Feddersen (1992), for one, describes a kind of political "state of nature" in his model. There are no parties and no restrictions on citizens' voting choice. There are only citizens who have policy preferences and who live under a plurality-rule electoral system in a single district. Voting is costly in the model. Citizens can vote for the policy position of any citizen they care to. In other words, they are not restricted to vote for any citizens identified as candidates in advance since all citizens are candidates.[5] Feddersen studies the equilibrium properties of voting in a single-shot election, and the coordination of votes for particular citizens emerges endogenously. He proves that under his assumptions only two citizens will receive votes in equilibrium and that the election will end

---

[5]In fact, this may not be an unrealistic assumption since for nearly all elections in the United States, citizens can vote for any write-in candidate they want, and the vote counts as long as the person is eligible to hold the office and the ballot is not spoiled.

in a tie. Any other outcome means that some voters are behaving irrationally. The keys to Feddersen's result are twofold: in the model the world of elections is a full-information environment where all citizens conjecture correctly what other citizens will do; and citizens would prefer to abstain from voting (because it is costly) rather than waste their votes on persons who do not have a chance of winning. Because there is full information and voting is costly, a citizen only votes if his or her behavior is pivotal (i.e., the election outcome literally depends on how he or she votes). And someone's vote is pivotal under two kinds of circumstances: either the citizen breaks a tie or creates a tie. Feddersen proves that three-way ties and nontie outcomes are not in equilibrium.

Feddersen's model is more general and more abstract than one proposed by Palfrey (1989). In the Palfrey model, there are three parties in a district election, A, B, and C, and each citizen has a strict preference ranking among them. There is no abstention in the model, and voters form accurate expectations over how the parties will fare in the election (perhaps from polls or gossip), with a level of accuracy up to the ranking among the parties. Because these expectations are accurate, all voters know, for example, that party B is expected to finish first, C second, and A third. Every voter has the same expectations. Further, what Palfrey defines as an equilibrium, consistent with the notion of Bayesian equilibrium from the game theory literature, is when these expectations are fulfilled at the ballot box. If this is not the case, then either the expectations were wrong for everyone or the citizens were not behaving according to the expectations, and neither can be true if all citizens are behaving rationally.

For convenience, let us consider an AB-voter as a citizen who prefers A over B and B over C. Palfrey proves that in equilibrium, if A is expected to finish third, it receives no votes, even from AB-voters. AB-voters, if the expectations are as specified above (BCA in descending order of finish), will vote for B except in extremely rare circumstances. Palfrey claims (but does not prove) that the outcome where one party wins and the other two parties tie for second is an extremely fragile equilibrium. Thus votes for A should almost always be zero if A is not expected to finish first or second. As in the Feddersen model, so-called pivot probabilities play a large role in Palfrey's model. Rational citizens do not vote for parties when their votes do not have a chance of swinging election outcomes. Palfrey's proof relies on showing that the pivot probability for voting for the party expected to finish third goes to zero in the limit (i.e., in equilibrium as the number of rational voters becomes large).

Cox (1994) proposes a model that generalizes Palfrey in two ways. First, there can be more than three parties or candidates seeking votes;

and, second, while the district operates according to plurality rule, there can be more than one candidate chosen from the district. If the district sends three representatives to parliament, then the top three vote getters win the seats. Cox also changes several technical assumptions regarding how citizens calculate pivot probabilities, and these changes turn out to have an important effect. Otherwise the Palfrey and Cox models are similar in structure.

In outcomes, too, the models are similar with one crucial exception resulting from Cox's different technical setup. Cox proves that under one equilibrium scenario, which he names a "Duvergerian" outcome, for $n$ seats chosen from the district, $n + 1$ parties will receive votes and the remainder of the candidates will receive zero votes. For this equilibrium, the logic is virtually the same as Palfrey's. Candidates expected to finish below Cox's "first loser" will not receive any votes from rational citizens. There is another equilibrium, however, where $n + 2$ candidates receive votes, and where the first and second losers tie in votes.[6] Unlike in Palfrey's model, this kind of outcome is not exceedingly rare (at least theoretically). It can happen that voters preferring the first and second loser fail to coordinate to defeat the winner with the lowest vote total among the winners. The reasons for this difference between the Palfrey and Cox models are not important to our argument, and we refer readers to the specific articles for details. Cox's non-Duvergerian equilibrium, where the first- and second-place losers tie, is discussed later in this chapter as it suggests the possibility within a strategic voting framework of having more than two parties winning substantial votes in a single-member, simple-plurality district election.

Other game-theoretic models have also led to Duvergerian conclusions for district-level elections. Myerson and Weber (1993) provide a very general version of the Cox model, with similar results. Fey (1997) shows how opinion polls and sequential elections (e.g., in presidential primaries in the United States) tend to reduce competition down to two candidates in single-winner, simple-plurality systems. Morelli (2001) presents a model of district-level Duvergerian results with non-Duvergerian national-level results.

The conclusion we draw from these models is that Duverger's Law, which was once an empirical assertion and a loose theoretical argument, holds up under rigorous theoretical scrutiny if the realm of analysis is the single electoral district, and if one adopts a game-theoretic mode of analysis. There has yet to be a convincing theoretical demonstration that contradicts the claim that strategic voting leads to two parties or candi-

---

[6]Actually, in the Cox model, more than two candidates can tie in this kind of equilibrium, but he focuses attention on the case where two candidates tie.

dates winning the votes in single-member districts, with the exception of Cox's non-Duvergerian equilibrium. The question then becomes, does the prediction of two district-level parties hold up in the real world?

## EVIDENCE ON THE NUMBER OF PARTIES IN DISTRICT ELECTIONS

The theoretical literature on Duverger's Law, in toto, makes a point prediction that two parties will get all the votes in these districts. The one caveat is Cox's idea that three or more parties can get votes if losing parties tie. When examining election data in any single-member, simple-plurality system, there obviously will be few cases that match the point prediction exactly. Indeed, most district-level elections in our four countries do not have exactly two parties getting all the votes, and testing the predictions systematically involves choosing a standard to determine whether the data conform. As it turns out, focusing on means and modes in the data leads to the conclusion that Duverger's Law works quite well in the district elections in our countries, whereas focusing on the deviations around those means and modes leads to the conclusion that there are notable and systematic exceptions to the law.

We calculated the effective number of parties using Laakso and Taagapera's (1979) measure N for each of 58,534 district elections in our data set. Recall from the previous chapter that N weights parties by the proportion of votes they receive, thus reducing the influence on the measure of parties or candidates that receive few votes. We also repeated most of the analyses from this entire book with other measures from the literature, and our results hold up.[7] The measure N is the most standard and, in our opinion, represents our concept of interest best among the possible alternatives. N is calculated for n parties receiving votes, and for $p_i$ representing the proportion of popular votes received by party $i$, by

$$N = \frac{1}{\sum_{i=1}^{n} p_i^2}$$

or, one divided by the sum of the squared proportions of the votes. For other purposes, the element $p_i$ could be the proportion of seats in the legislature controlled by party $i$, although throughout this book we use the proportion of popular votes.

[7]Other measures from the literature, such as NP (Molinar 1991) and I (Kesselman 1966) lead to somewhat different quantititative results for both this analysis in chapter 2 and the analysis of national-level measures. The overall trends in the data are the same regardless of the measure we use, and our substantive conclusions about the dynamics of party systems are the same as well.

In districts in which elections are held according to single-member, simple-plurality rules, two candidates or parties get nearly all the vote. The overall mean effective number of parties across all our cases is 2.08, as shown in Table 2.1. There are notable differences across the countries, however, and because nearly half of the cases are from the United States, which historically has had a low number of parties, the overall average may be misleading. For the three remaining countries the mean effective number of parties is 2.28. Thus, in the typical district, more than 2 parties are getting votes, but 2 parties get most of the votes. What kind of distribution of votes can lead to 2.28 effective number of parties? If there are 3 parties receiving votes, then the following percentages can lead to close to a measure of 2.28: [.47, .46, .07], [.60, .22, .18]. These are typical of the distributions found in the data from Canada, Great Britain, and India. Both example distributions are consistent with strategic voting, especially with Cox's extension of Duverger's Law. In the first case 2 parties get almost all the votes, whereas in the second the ratio of the first and second losers is close to one.

Figure 2.1 summarizes the data in another way. The bars show the total number of cases, and then categories of cases according to their district-level N. The middle three bars show that more than four-fifths of district elections resulted in fewer than 2.5 effective parties, three-quarters fell within the range of 1.5–2.5, and more than half fell within the range of 1.75–2.25. Perhaps most striking, only a very small proportion of districts had more than 3 effective number of parties (last bar). Given that in these countries the number of effective parties at the national level is occasionally upward of 5 or 6 political parties (for India especially), it is notable that so few district elections resulted in more than 3 parties receiving a large proportion of the vote.

The histogram graphs in Figures 2.2 and 2.3 show the distributions of N across all cases and then by country. Focusing first on the mode of these data, we can see that by far it is most common in all of the coun-

TABLE 2.1
Average Effective Number of Parties in District Elections

| Country | Mean | Standard Deviation | Number of Cases |
|---|---|---|---|
| Canada | 2.27 | 0.54 | 8544 |
| Great Britain | 2.21 | 0.40 | 15932 |
| India | 2.52 | 0.71 | 5348 |
| United States | 1.87 | 0.43 | 28710 |
| Total | 2.08 | 0.52 | 58534 |

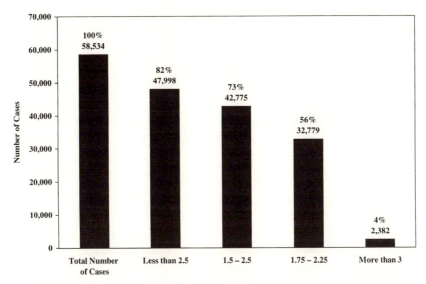

Figure 2.1. Distribution of the Effective Number of Parties in District Elections in Canada, Great Britain, India, and the United States

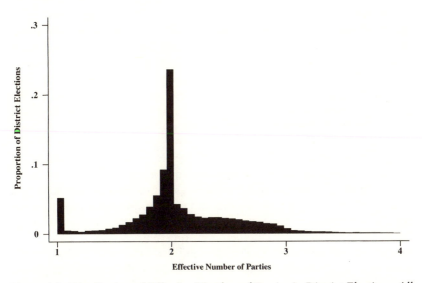

Figure 2.2. Distribution of Effective Number of Parties in District Elections, All Four Countries

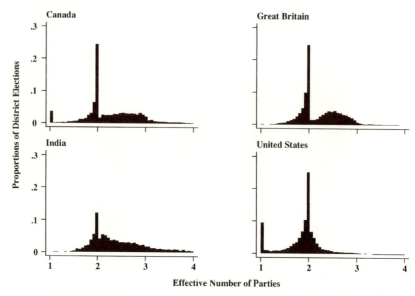

Figure 2.3. Distribution of Effective Number of Parties in District Elections, All Four Countries

tries to have an effective number of parties very close to 2, and that the deviations from 2 tail off toward higher values. The countries tail off to the right, however, in different ways, as we shall discuss in more detail shortly. For now, just note that Canada and Great Britain have smaller modes near 2.5 and that for all three countries other than the United States there are significant numbers of cases between 2.5 and 3. Note also the large number of cases with 1 party receiving all the votes. We prefer to keep these cases in the data set, as we do not feel there is a good theoretical justification for excluding them. For the record, however, excluding cases with an N of 1, mostly uncontested races in Canada and the United States, the mean N for the entire data set is 2.12.

These results cast doubts on explanations for party systems that imply the axiomatic translation of social cleavages into the number of parties. There are many, many more groups and interests present in these district populations than there are parties or candidates receiving most of the votes. In India, for example, there are sometimes dozens of castes, languages, and religions within districts, and yet voters and candidates are coordinating effectively enough to whittle down the number of parties to 2.5 or less most of the time. Consider Table 2.2. In a national survey conducted in 1971, respondents in India were asked to list their caste and religion (two factors deemed as the most important "ethnic charac-

TABLE 2.2
Effective Number of Groups and Parties
in the Large Indian States, 1971

| State | Effective Number of | |
|---|---|---|
| | Groups | Parties |
| Andhra Pradesh | 17.80 | 2.01 |
| Assam | 3.86 | 2.42 |
| Bihar | 12.88 | 2.92 |
| Gujarat | 8.38 | 2.13 |
| Haryana | 9.11 | 2.25 |
| Karnataka | 10.37 | 1.71 |
| Kerala | 7.11 | 2.12 |
| Madhya Pradesh | 18.65 | 2.28 |
| Maharashtra | 6.48 | 1.97 |
| Orissa | 8.34 | 3.14 |
| Punjab | 4.23 | 2.39 |
| Rajasthan | 8.04 | 2.16 |
| Tamil Nadu | 17.80 | 2.07 |
| Uttar Pradesh | 17.60 | 2.51 |
| West Bengal | 8.81 | 3.25 |

teristics" driving the vote in India). From the respondents' self-identification, we calculated the effective number of groups in each Indian state in which the survey was conducted and for which there was a large enough sample. As is apparent, the effective number of groups in each state is far larger than the effective number of parties in each state as measured by the votes from the national parliamentary elections in 1971. The effective number of parties hovers around 2 in most states. Clearly, there are dynamics at work in India that appear consistent with Duverger's Law at both the district level and the state level.

One might ask if districts with size larger than 2 (more than two representatives elected from the district) lead to higher numbers of effective parties. Figure 2.4 shows the time series of the mean values for the district level N in all four countries, and then Figure 2.5 includes the mean effective number of parties across the districts from Britain's double and multimember districts. The mean number of effective parties for these districts is significantly different (using a standard t-test) from the numbers of effective parties for the single-member districts for each election year in the data. For the same party system nationwide, district-level election results are sensitive to the size of the electoral district. Greater district size means a higher number of effective parties.

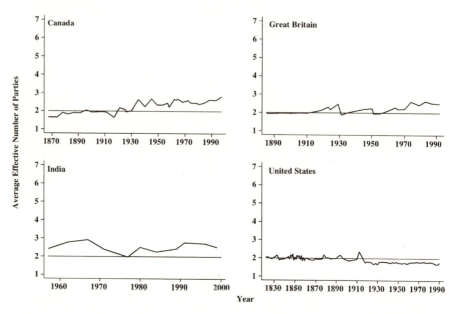

Figure 2.4. Average Effective Number of Parties in the Districts over Time, All Four Countries

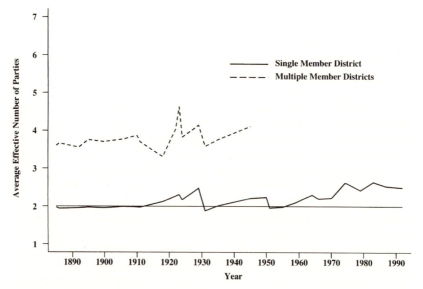

Figure 2.5. Effective Number of Parties in Single-Member and Multiple-Member Districts in Great Britain

While we measure the number of parties using N, we acknowledge that there is some question in the literature on voting and elections whether this measure is appropriate (see, e.g., Niemi and Hsieh 2002). Two general criticisms stand out. First, N measures the fractionalization of the vote but says little about the number of *competitive* parties or candidates (Niemi and Hsieh 2002), which is often what people claim to be measuring, especially in cross-national studies that include a measure of the effective number of parties in regression analyses. We agree with this criticism more generally, but for our study the fractionalization of the vote is exactly what we care to measure. We are primarily interested in this chapter in the degree to which most voters support two parties or candidates only, or whether they distribute their votes among larger numbers of competitors. In later chapters, we devote attention to the degree to which voters choose to support national parties as opposed to local, state, provincial, or regional parties, and N is only one measure among several others. In both instances, the district-level and the national-level analyses, N is an appropriate measure of our concepts.

A second and related criticism involves the basic problem that multiple distributions of votes can lead to each level of the measure N. The measure N leaves it unclear whether the residual vote, the vote not awarded to the top two candidates, is allocated solely to one candidate or to many small candidates. For instance, the following distributions of votes both give N = 2.46: [.444, .444, .112]; [.45, .45, .01, .01, .01, .01, .01, .01, .01, .01, .01, .01]. In the first distribution, the third-place candidate (receiving .112 of the vote) does reasonably well and might be encouraged to run again in future elections. In the second distribution, each of ten candidates receives a minuscule portion of the vote, and perhaps all will be discouraged and drop out of electoral politics. Moreover, we are inclined to say that the second distribution conforms to Duverger's Law more than the first distribution, although they both lead to the same N. Relying solely on N to make a determination of the validity of Duverger's Law in district elections could lead to mistakes in our evaluations; we would want to find that the second distribution conforms to the law, yet our measure, N, suggests that the district has nearly 2.5 effective parties.

How many district-level elections in our four countries have instances of the second kind of distribution? How often are we misled by our using N to test Duverger's Law? Figure 2.6 indicates few instances of the second kind of distribution and suggests that we are not misled by using N. The figure first shows the average share of the vote for third parties or candidates at each range of the value of N for our data. The typical district in our data with N = 2.5 has, for example, a third candidate receiving approximately 10 percent of the vote. A district with N =

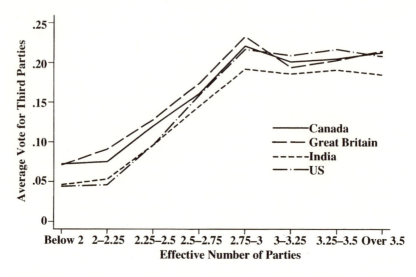

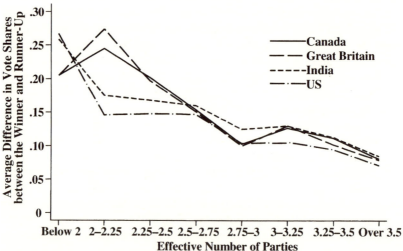

Figure 2.6. Typical Vote Distributions in District Elections, All Four Countries

3 has, on average, a third candidate receiving approximately 20 percent of the vote. In other words, it is not the case that N = 2.5 in our data means that many small parties are splitting the residual vote. The second part of the figure shows that the average difference in the proportion of the vote between the top two parties is below .05 until N reaches 2.75 or higher. This means, in combination with the other part of the figure, that for the typical district, with N in the range of 2 to 3, the election

races are reasonably close between the top two parties or candidates, and if N is greater than 2.5, a third candidate receives approximately 15 percent of the vote—greater than the average vote difference between the first- and second-place party.

To summarize, while N can be a flawed measure in theory, in practice it effectively captures our concept of interest, the degree of electoral support for major and minor candidates or parties in the districts. When a district election measures N = 2.25, for example, on average the distribution of votes in that district looks like the following: [.49, .45, .06].

## Systematic Variations

As evident in the previous figures, there are, nevertheless, many district elections that stray from the point prediction of Duverger's Law. Are these deviations randomly distributed across countries and time? Is it the case that having 2 effective parties is an average outcome everywhere and at all times, with deviations occurring because of district-level phenomena uncorrelated with time and space? To put the question another way, when a district has more than 2 parties or candidates receiving votes, is it just as likely to be in the United States as in India, or is it just as likely to be in 1999 in India as in 1977 in India or as in 1935 in Canada? We find that deviations from two-partism in the districts are not random but are systematic; systematic factors outside of the individual districts push the number of parties above 2 for particular election years within the countries.

Although in all four countries the modal effective number of parties is 2, the countries vary in the degree to which the point prediction of 2 parties in the district matches the data, as was shown in Table 2.1. India has the most parties and the United States has the least parties in the districts, and the differences across the countries are statistically significant by any standard test assuming any reasonable, "true" distribution of the data. It is not appropriate, strictly speaking, to conduct a simple t-test for the data across these four countries, because we cannot comfortably assume normal distributions of the data. But as the measure of the effective number of parties uses squared proportions, data entered into the formula using squared proportions should come close to approximating a chi-square distribution. A distribution of errors around a chi-squared distribution approximates a normal distribution in the limit, so a t-test is not altogether inappropriate. Therefore, if we regress the effective number of parties on country-election dummies in the districts, we get t-statistics that give us a good idea of how randomly distributed the variations from 2 parties are across countries and across time. We did this (the data are not shown but are available from the authors), and for virtually all country-elections, the t-statistics are large in absolute value and statistically significant. Thus we can comfortably reject the claim that departures from Duvergerian predictions are random and can say confidently that there are systematic factors in the countries and within election years that push the number of parties higher in the districts. Context outside of the districts matters, even in the effects of electoral laws on district elections.

Any criteria we use to determine that a particular district does not conform to the predictions of Duverger's Law, other than a standard that says only 2 parties or candidates will get votes and all others (if they exist) will get 0 percent, will be arbitrary. For our purposes, we settle on an effective number of parties of 2.5. If a district has more than 2.5 effective number of parties, we will say for present purposes that it violates Duverger's Law. There are good reasons for using such a cutoff. Cox (1997) argues persuasively that Duvergerian logic *reduces* the number of serious competitors in plurality elections but that the logic does not lead to any conclusions about whether plurality elections increase the number of competitors above 1. For example, having fewer than 2 parties in a single-member, simple-plurality district does not necessarily contradict the predictions from modern versions of Duverger's Law, whereas having 4 parties does. Thus, it makes sense to divide districts into categories, not by whether they conform to Duverger's Law within a range around 2 (say, between 1.75 and 2.25 as in Figure 2.1), but whether they fit below a particular value. In Figure 2.1, we see that 82 percent of all of our cases had less than 2.5 effective number of parties. How are the remaining 18 percent of cases in the whole sample distributed among the countries and over time? A relatively liberal criteria such as a 2.5 cutoff enables us to present a strong case that deviations from Duverger's Law are not random. Using strict criteria—for example, any deviation from 2—would lead us to reject the value of the Law too hastily (a type II error, loosely speaking). Further, as Figure 2.6 reveals, only at an N of 2.5 could the vote share of the third party in the average district have influenced the outcome of the typical election, as it is only then that the vote share of the third party becomes larger than the difference in the vote shares of the first- and second-place parties.

If the 2.5 number of parties is used as a cutoff, one test to determine the validity of Duverger's Law is to divide the data into two categories, those cases conforming to the law and those cases that do not, and then to measure the variance from the population distribution within specific countries and in particular elections. We can calculate several statistics to measure these variances in such bifurcated data. A chi-square statistic offers a confidence interval, while a Cramer's V offers a more straightforward interpretation. These two tests give essentially the same information, which is the same as the regression and the t-statistics summarized earlier.

Beginning with the country differences, Table 2.3 indicates that the countries differ greatly in the proportion of districts with more than 2.5 effective parties. In the three countries other than the United States, approximately one-third of the districts violated Duverger's Law by our criteria. Moreover, given the high chi-square values for the differences in variances across the four countries' data, it is extremely unlikely that the district-level election results are drawn from the same underlying distribution. Simply put, it is not random whether these district elections conform to Duverger's Law. While we wish to stress once again that it is still altogether remarkable that countries like India have 60 percent of districts conforming to Duverger's Law (by our criteria using the 2.5 cutoff), it is certainly misleading to assert unqualified support for the predictions of the theory with these data.

To analyze election-specific differences, we calculated a chi-square statistic for each election in each country, using as a base-line distribution not the overall four-country distribution (82 and 18 percent) but the country-specific distribution as shown in Table 2.3. Table 2.4 shows an example for how we calculated the chi-square statistic for the United States in 1990. We do not show the complete chi-square data for all the election years, although it is easy to summarize the results. Most of the specific elections within the countries have chi-square statistics that are significantly different than zero, and many of them have very large chi-squares. Our interpretation of this result is that election-specific factors influenced the number of political parties in the districts in nearly every

TABLE 2.3
Distribution of Districts with Number of Parties below and above 2.5

| Country | Districts below 2.5 | Districts over 2.5 | Total |
|---------|---------------------|--------------------|-------|
| Canada | 5,745 | 2,799 | 8,544 |
| | (67.24%) | (32.76%) | (100%) |
| Great Britain | 11,759 | 4,173 | 15,932 |
| | (73.81%) | (26.19%) | (100%) |
| India | 3,206 | 2,142 | 5,348 |
| | (59.95%) | (40.05%) | (100%) |
| United States | 27,278 | 1,432 | 28,710 |
| | (95.01%) | (4.99%) | (100%) |
| Total | 47,988 | 10,546 | 58,534 |
| | (81.98%) | (18.02%) | (100%) |

TABLE 2.4
Comparing the U.S. 1990 Election against
U.S. Elections Overall: An Example

|  | Below 2.5 | Over 2.5 | Total |
|---|---|---|---|
| U.S. 1990 Election | 409 | 8 | 417 |
|  | (98.08%) | (1.92%) | (100%) |
| Rest of U.S. Elections | 26,869 | 1,424 | 28,293 |
|  | (94.97%) | (5.03%) | (100%) |
| Total | 27,278 | 1,432 | 28,710 |
|  | (95.01%) | (4.99%) | (100%) |

Related statistics
Pearson $\chi^2_{(1)}$ : 8.4119 (Pr = 0.004)
Cramer's $V$ : −0.0171

case and that deviations from two-partism were not random across elections within the countries.

A graphical representation of Cramer's V, in contrast to the chi-square statistics, can take on positive and negative values and offers a more intuitive interpretation of deviations from the country-specific distribution. Cramer's V correlates very highly (r = .88) with t-statistics from a regression with country-election dummies (as described earlier). Figure 2.7 shows Cramer's V for each election in each country, using the 2.5 cutoff rule. Note that, as with the chi-square statistic, the data in Figure 2.7 compare each election distribution to the distribution for the particular country, not for the overall sample across all four countries.

Figure 2.7, in combination with the chi-square statistics and their confidence intervals, shows conclusively that the deviations from two-partism in the districts are not random and that they clump together disproportionately in some countries during some periods in time. More specifically, a large proportion of cases with more than 2.5 effective number of parties occurred in Canada and Great Britain in recent decades. There are also many deviating cases in India, although the major deviations are actually for those years when the effective number of parties in the districts was *lower* than the average for the country and, therefore, strictly speaking are not disconfirmations of the theory.

Rejection of the null hypothesis that deviations from Duverger's Law are random can be demonstrated even further by comparing the data in Figure 2.7 with those in Figure 2.4. The data tend to trend over the course of decades, not from election to election. Close scrutiny reveals that in Canada the average district N rose beginning in the 1930s and

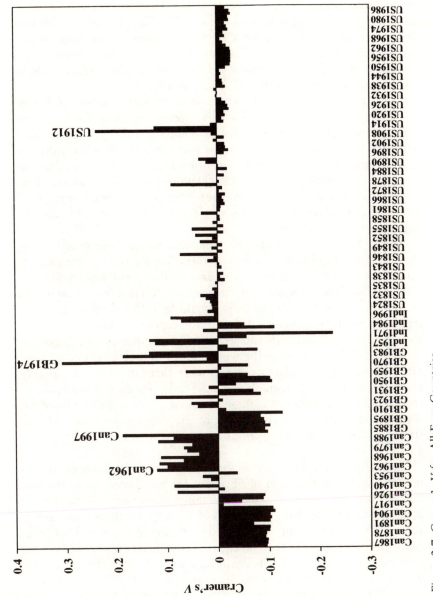

Figure 2.7. Cramer's *V* for All Four Countries

rose in Great Britain beginning in the 1960s. Further, the effective number of parties fell in India starting in the 1970s. Finally, the United States
data, after fluctuating somewhat randomly around 2 for most of the
country's history, dip below 2 slightly in recent decades owing to an
increase in the number of uncontested elections. We shall return to these
patterns and country-specific differences shortly.

One potential explanation for these relatively high numbers of parties
in the districts is consistent with Duvergerian logic and follows from
Cox's model, which illustrates the possibility of a tie between the sec-
ond- and third-place parties. If voters and candidates within a district
dislike the front-runner party and want to defeat it but cannot come to
a workable agreement on which candidate or party should be the chal-
lenger, then it is possible for those voters to act as derived in the Cox
model and to end up dividing their vote evenly. Voters can fail to coordinate on specific candidates.

To test for evidence of this phenomenon, we can calculate in each
election what is called by Cox an "SF ratio," or the ratio of the proportion of votes for the third-place candidate, or the second loser, and those
of the second-place candidate, or the first loser. If Duverger's Law works
as ordinarily expected, the SF ratio should be 0 (the third-place candidate gets no votes), whereas if the Cox exception occurs, the SF ratio
should be near 1 (the third- and second-place candidates tie). Ratios toward the middle of the range between 0 and 1 indicate that many voters
are choosing the third-place candidate when that candidate has virtually
no chance of winning. A graph of the SF ratios for each election, therefore, should have modes at 1, 0, or both, but not near the middle of the
distribution. Ratios near the middle of the distribution would violate
strategic voting in district elections with a district magnitude of 1 (Cox
1997).

Figure 2.8 shows the SF ratios for three of the four countries. We do
not present the distribution of SF ratios for the United States because
they are not very revealing and can be summarized briefly. In the United
States nearly all cases have an SF ratio of 0, except for those from several
years in the 1870s and in 1912. The distribution in Figure 2.8 for India
confirms the presence of the Duvergerian equilibrium proposed by Cox,
with many cases bunched at 1. Figures 2.9 and 2.10 then show examples
of distributions of SF ratios for Canada and Great Britain in specific
years. We present specific yearly data from only these two countries
because there is over-time variation in the nature of these SF ratio
graphs, whereas the same cannot be said about the U.S. and Indian data.
The country-elections in Figures 2.9 and 2.10 are chosen to demonstrate
some extreme versions of the SF ratio distributions and to indicate some
representative years from recognizable eras in party politics in Canada

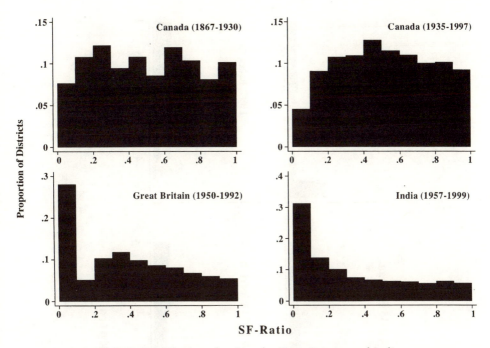

Figure 2.8. SF-Ratio Distributions for Canada, Great Britain, and India

and Great Britain. For these two countries in specific election years, the SF ratios work as expected, with most elections having modes at 1 or 0, or both. In other election years, the SF ratios are quite different.

Before discussing the temporal patterns in the SF ratios in Canada and Britain, a general comment on Cox's exception is appropriate. In taking account of all of the distributions of SF ratios across our four countries, we are led to reject the idea that when two-partism is violated at the district level it is because the second- and third-place candidates or parties are virtually tied. There are very few cases where the SF ratio is near 1, and vastly more cases where the SF ratio is between .3 and .7, especially in Canada and Britain. In fact, the SF ratios bunch near the midrange even more so in recent decades when the flow of information about election outcomes was presumably more rapid and accurate than in earlier periods. We shall have to look elsewhere, other than Cox's exception, to find explanations for why Duverger's Law does not work in nearly one-fifth of our cases, especially in Britain and Canada.

It is difficult to characterize succinctly the districts that do not conform to Duverger's Law, as they are diverse in how they do not conform.

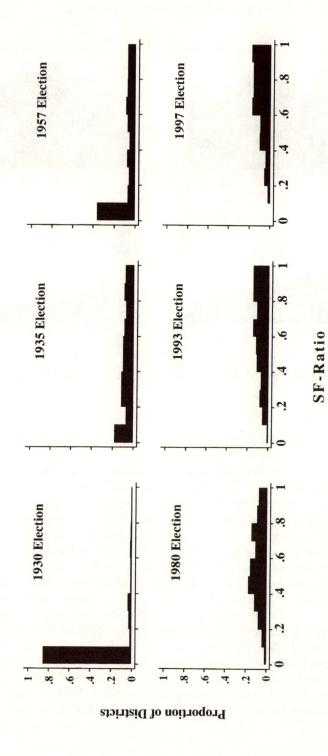

Figure 2.9. Six Distributions of SF Ratios for Canada

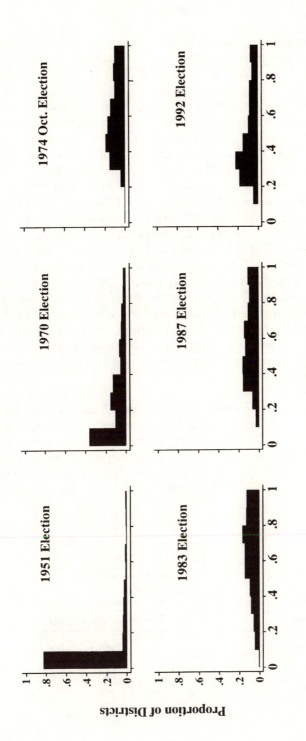

Figure 2.10. Six Distributions of SF Ratios for Great Britain

We can draw some general conclusions by comparing across countries. In Canada the vast majority of district elections that had more than 2 parties occurred after 1935, when the NDP burst on the Canadian political scene. It was a common occurrence after 1935, for example, for the NDP to receive 10–15 percent of the district vote, and the Conservatives and Liberals to split the remainder. So, as seen in Figure 2.4, there was a general upturn in the effective number of parties in the districts in Canada starting in 1935, and continuing upward. In later decades, the fragmentation of the vote in the districts became quite dramatic, when the NDP was still getting votes, and the right in Canada was split between the Conservatives and Reform parties. Take the Yukon, which is itself an electoral district. In 1997 the proportion of the vote in the Yukon was that shown in Table 2.5, revealing a highly fragmented district party system. This is by no means typical—after all, most districts in Canada in 1997 saw Conservatives and Liberals together getting more than 65 percent of the vote—but it is also not highly unusual.

Note also, in Canada, that the distribution of SF ratios in later years looks almost uniform across values from 0 to 1 (see Figure 2.9 for 1993, where only the lowest value, the Duvergerian two-party prediction, is unrepresented!). This means that many Canadians in recent decades were voting for candidates or parties in the districts that had little chance of winning.

The situation in British districts after the 1960s is similar. As seen in Figure 2.10, third parties in the districts get substantial votes starting when the left splits and the Social Democrats and Liberals revive. The distributions of the SF ratios tell the story. Whichever party ends up third in the district—it could be one of the two major parties, Labour or Conservatives, or the centrist party, the Liberals or Social Democrats—receives between 10–15 percent of the vote. The dynamics of

TABLE 2.5
Distribution of Votes in the Yukon, 1997
(one electoral district)

| Party | Proportion of the Vote |
|-------|------------------------|
| Conservatives | .14 |
| Liberals | .22 |
| NDP | .29 |
| Reform | .26 |
| An independent | .09 |

Duverger's Law, as formulated in its modern versions, do not seem to apply.[8]

India has a different pattern than that found in these two countries. In India it is not the case that the number of parties in the districts increased monotonically over time in recent decades. Rather, the effective number of parties in the districts decreased in the 1970s and then increased again. As we show in later chapters, this trend is part of a broader national pattern, where the state-level parties aggregated effectively in the 1970s. Moreover, the distribution of N across the Indian districts has a much longer tail than in the other three countries. Some districts, though a small proportion relative to the whole number, had upward of 6 and 7 parties, a phenomena much rarer in the other countries. These districts inflate the average district N in India considerably. It may, in fact, be easier to understand within a Duverger or Cox framework how a district might have 6 or 7 effective parties. At some point in the process of voters and candidates trying to coordinate, it could be that no one can coordinate, the electoral process descends into recrimination, and all candidates running gain votes.

Finally, in the most important contrast to the themes of this book, when there are more than 2 effective parties in Indian districts, the losing parties are a mixture of various state parties and the Communists and are not solely the national minor parties, as in Canada and Great Britain. When the effective number of parties in the districts in India dropped in the 1970s, it was not because these parties went away, but rather they agreed to consolidate to oppose the Congress Party, abandoning individual party labels (temporarily, it turned out).

## WHY VOTE FOR HOPELESS CANDIDATES?

We should pause to summarize the differences just described. In Canada and Great Britain the rise in the number of parties in the districts in recent decades is because of an increase in voting for nationally or regionally competitive third parties, such as the NDP, Reform, or the Social Democrats or Liberals. National political forces influenced those district elections. In India the rise in the number of parties in the districts

[8]One of Cox's (and Palfrey's) most important assumptions is that voters all have the same expectations about how the candidates will finish. Without that assumption, there is no way to tie down the beliefs and behavior of the voters in the models into an equilibrium. This one assumption may not describe what really occurs, of course. It is intriguing, nevertheless, that voters are choosing hopeless candidates or parties and doing so persistently and increasingly over a span of time when information about election results and candidates is widely available.

was due to an increase in voting for state-level parties. State-level political forces seemed to encourage Indian voters to abandon the national
parties. In all three countries, voting for those parties, often in proportions less than 15 percent, clearly violates the spirit of the theoretical
research on Duverger's Law. These parties have virtually no chance of
winning the district elections, yet a reasonable proportion of voters are
supporting them from election to election over decades.

The persistence of voting for hopeless parties in the districts (hopeless
in terms of winning the district election) is something of a puzzle for
political scientists. Of course, apart from the abstract theories of Duverger's Law, it is highly misleading to expect that each district offers a
pristine laboratory to test the law, where national and regional influences do not intrude. There are clear historical trends at work that are
influencing district-level election results in these countries. The SF ratios,
the time-series trends, the differences across the countries, and the distributions of N for each election year offer striking evidence that Duverger's Law works often enough to remain an important regularity in the
social sciences, but not often enough to ascribe deviations as merely
random disturbances from the norm.

So, which assumptions from the models of Duverger's Law are not
tenable? We have mentioned one, namely that voters do not have identical expectations of how the candidates or parties will fare in upcoming
district elections. Without convergent expectations, voters cannot coordinate effectively. There are other possibilities.

The literature on voting for minor parties in the United States, Canada, Great Britain, and a few other countries usually asks the question
the other way around. Virtually all studies focus on why people do *not*
vote for small parties, which is the traditional idea behind strategic (or
"tactical" in the British literature) voting. It is not easy to find systematic
studies on why people actually vote for small parties. Most common is
the explanation that voters are simply voting their preferences or, in a
spatial voting framework, they are voting for the party "closest" to them
in ideological or issue space. Using a different terminology, one might
claim that many people vote expressively. For example, it could be said
that supporters of the Social Democrats or Liberals in Britain in the
1980s were moderates who found the two major parties too extreme. If
voters are *not* voting for their most preferred party, that is seen as evidence of strategic voting (Niemi, Whitten, and Franklin 1993). The most
recent research controls for demographic factors and the proximity between the voters' expressed preferences and the parties or candidates,
and looks for partial correlations between the competitiveness of the
election and voting for competitive parties (Alvarez and Nagler 2000;
Fieldhouse and Russell 2001). Rohrschneider (1993) argues that more

sincere voting for minor parties will occur when there is a new issue dimension being openly debated and contested, such as environmentalism.

As we noted at the beginning of this chapter, we are convinced by the idea that some kind of strategic voting must be taking place to observe the small number of parties in the districts that we observe. Perhaps it is the case, however, that voters are not so myopic as to consider only the results from the election at hand but that they are also considering the effects of their vote on future elections. Substantial support for parties or candidates (e.g., 15 percent of the vote) that will certainly not win the current district elections can occur for a variety of reasons, even if we want to maintain some semblance of the rational-choice assumption that behavior is instrumental. It can occur because voters want to send a message to the major contenders, or because voters want to keep alive a fledgling party that may come back strong in the next election or in some future election, or even because voters are completely indifferent between the two major contenders and could not rank-order the utility differences between the parties if either one were elected. Naturally, if we wish to depart from rationality in the narrow sense of instrumental action, then we can say that voters are just expressing their true preferences in the voting booths. The only problem with this reason is that support for the hopeless parties comes in waves, and it appears that voters are responding to some evidence of hope for a future election victory on a better day.

It could be argued that if there were one clear winner (all voters knew who the winner was going to be), then voters could vote more sincerely when one party is sure to win. At that point many other parties, ones that had no chance of winning, could get votes. Voting for those parties would not be a wasted vote in that the vote would not have had a bearing on the identity of the eventual winner. We examined the possibility that support for the hopeless parties increased as the winning parties increased their vote shares in the districts. There is no evidence in our data from Canada, Great Britain, India, and the United States that this is the case.[9]

We end this chapter with a question: why do *some* voters in Canada and Great Britain in recent decades vote for parties that have no chance

[9]Searching for this kind of pattern within particular countries or within elections is an interesting topic for future research, and some of this idea flavors the research of Alvarez and Nagler (2000). Incidentally, we did find a relationship in Quebec in some years, of all places. As the winning party's vote increased, voting for the third-place party increased. This was the only systematic pattern of this type we could find, and we have little choice but to mark it up to a topic for future research. It could very well be a random disturbance from the norm.

of winning the district elections to the national parliament? We hope that future research can help to answer this question because we cannot offer a satisfactory explanation, given our evidence.

That being said, we should not lose sight of the main result here. There is little doubt that having single-member, simple-plurality systems in districts drives down the number of parties or candidates receiving votes, and that most of the time two candidates or parties get nearly all the vote. Whether national party systems will resemble the predictions in Duverger's Law is entirely another matter. In the next chapter, we discuss the process of party aggregation, the pooling of votes across the districts.

# Chapter 3

# PARTY AGGREGATION

THE FUNDAMENTAL BUILDING BLOCKS of political parties are candidates running for election in electoral districts. In the previous chapter we showed that the most common outcome in single-member, simple-plurality district elections in Canada, Great Britain, India, and the United States is for two candidates to garner a very large proportion of the vote in a district. Even in highly diverse districts, such as those in India, with many identifiable groups of voters differentiated by language, class, religion, and caste, it is typically the case that only two candidates compete seriously for election. These outcomes indicate that, more often than not, voters are coordinating on specific candidates, even if the mechanisms for that coordination are not easy to detect or describe. Somehow, candidates who are not expected to finish first or second in the balloting lose votes in droves or drop out, at least in most districts most of the time.

Theoretical models of Duverger's Law for district elections draw conclusions that are consistent with these findings. The models, summarized in chapter 2, conclude that in nearly every circumstance two candidates should receive all the votes. To reach this conclusion, the models rely to a certain extent on the notion of strategic, or fully rational, voting. In fact, coordination of voters on candidates essentially requires some form of strategic voting, because it means that some voters are implicitly agreeing to rally behind a candidate who may not be their first choice in the hopes of avoiding a bad outcome. According to Cox (1997, 72):

> Strategic voting in a simple plurality election means voting for a lower-ranked candidate that one believes is stronger, rather than for higher-ranked candidate that one believes is weaker. . . . [If] voter beliefs about which candidates are stronger and weaker will be generally correct, [then] strategic voting will generally transfer votes from objectively weaker (vote-poorer) to objectively stronger (vote-richer) candidates.

Many district elections among the cases discussed in chapter 2, however, do not conform to the expectations of Duverger's Law. The exceptions may require some reevaluation of models of Duverger's Law, but their existence does not have a bearing on our argument. Our interest lies in the formation of national party systems and whether the same parties compete across the nation in all provinces or states. Whereas candidates who finish first or second within the electoral district become contenders because of district-level voter coordination, political parties become viable only because of the coordination of voters and candidates across districts. Except in the case of a degenerate party that consists of a single person (a true independent or someone who runs under a label not shared by anyone else), electoral parties are made up of candidates in multiple districts running under the same label. Coordination also means that voters cue on party labels, recognizing that voters in other districts will be cuing on those same labels. We term this coordination *party aggregation*, because the process of assessing party strength nationally or regionally entails adding up votes of party candidates across multiple districts. Cox refers to this process as "linkage," emphasizing the linking together of like-minded candidates into parties. Whichever term is used, the goal of electoral political parties is for candidates to link, to aggregate votes, or to coordinate party labels for a policy purpose (we provide more evidence for this claim in chapter 4).

To understand the aggregation of candidates' votes into party vote totals, we bring together a variety of ideas from different sources in this chapter. From our perspective, explaining the variation in party aggregation across time and across countries requires another approach. We need to think carefully about what parties do and how they form to assess these over-time and cross-national differences. Our argument on the formation of national party systems blends some of the concepts discussed in the previous chapter with concepts from the literature on legislative parties and in public economics.

The focus on the role of federalism and the centralization of government policies distinguishes our argument from previous research on the formation of party systems. We claim that only by considering the relative authority that national (federal) and provincial (state) governments exercise can we begin to understand why some parties have distinctively geographic bases and other parties are national in scope, why two-partism survives in the United States, and why it is that in some countries minor parties are national whereas in others they are limited to particular regions.

## DEFINITIONS AND MEASUREMENT

A word is in order about definitions and measurement of what constitutes a political party. First, our definition of a political party, as stated in chapter 1, is a group of candidates running for public office under the same label. The definition focuses attention on the electoral side of political parties as opposed to the legislative side. Of course, these two sides are intimately related, as we discuss later in this chapter. Our definition, focusing on the electoral side, leaves out some important aspects of party activity, most noticeably the organization of elected officials once they are in office; moreover, it also does not include party organizations devoted to mobilizing voters and raising money.

Second, on the related issue of measurement, it would be possible in principle to supplement our electoral data with other data on legislative parties and on party organizational strength, such as seat totals in legislatures, roll-call voting data measuring party discipline, or measurements of organizational strength of local party offices. This would undoubtedly add to our knowledge about the mechanisms used to build and maintain regional and national parties. The main reason we focus on the vote totals of party candidates is simply that it tracks best the coordination of politicians and voters across districts. These other measures of party behavior and strength can be misleading.

Suppose, for example, that we were to measure the distribution of seats captured by the various political parties as a measure of the number of parties in a system. The vote totals of candidates who captured reasonable numbers of votes but did not win office would be completely submerged if we adopted seat totals to build our measures. Likewise, politicians sometimes switch party labels once in office, a common practice in select eras in our four subject countries. Once again, analyzing seat totals alone obscures the coordination that politicians seek with other candidates in the process of seeking elected office. Finally, there are studies of parties comparing the organizational strength of local party offices, which measure fund-raising capacity, the number of staff members, and the stability of leadership (see, e.g., Cotter et al. 1984; Frendreis, Gibson, and Vertz 1990; and Eldersveld 1982). So, what is the best measure of party strength to employ, given the research question at hand? We take the position that using the votes of party candidates measures the ability of voters and candidates to coordinate, and that other measures of party organizational strength more accurately indicate the means by which this coordination occurs. We essentially measure the ends of those means of coordination.

To clarify, consider in turn the United States in 1878, Canada in 1979, and India today. There were several electoral parties that received significant votes in the 1878 congressional elections in the United States, including the Republicans, the Liberal Republicans, the Democrats, the Greenbacks, and the Prohibitionists. The number of effective parties using vote totals in 1878 is 2.95. From the records of the Office of the Clerk of the House of Representatives, however, only 2 parties were represented in Congress in 1878, Democrats and Republicans. Some

winning candidates switched to major-party labels, affecting congressional representation. Using the seat totals from Congress thus obscures
this fact as well as interesting regional variation in party labels on ballots, and it buries the vote totals of candidates, such as those from the
Prohibition Party, which won votes but not seats. In 1979 in Canada,
at least 5 parties recorded a reasonable number of votes in the election,
including the Rhinoceros Party, but only 3 parties won seats, the Conservatives, Liberals, and the New Democrats. Using the vote totals from
the election, the effective number of parties in Canada in 1979 was 3.01.
Using seat totals the effective number of parties was 2.45. Finally, in
India there have been quite a few instances of candidates being elected
on the label of a minor party and then switching to the majority party
once elected to the legislature. These defections even prompted the adoption of an antidefection law in 1985 to prevent individual legislators
from switching parties.

## WHY PARTIES? (REVISITED)

Three questions have motivated research on party formation and party
systems in recent decades. First, there is the question of how new parties
form in electoral democracies. Most studies of new parties have examined the processes by which such parties emerge from the discontents of
mass publics. This prominent tradition, as we discussed in detail in chapter 1, derives from the seminal research of Lipset and Rokkan (1967),
who portrayed the political parties in Europe as derivations of important
social cleavages that arose out of massive societal shifts like the Refor-
mation and the industrial revolution. More specifically, nearly all countries in Europe with lengthy histories of democracy have parties that
represent Christian Democratic values (main-line Protestant and Catholic voters); labor unions; free-market business groups; and, more recently
environmental conservation. The parties have endured not because of
electoral rules, Lipset and Rokkan argue (while they also seek to refute
Duverger), but because of social cleavages that have persisted for decades. The origins of parties, they argue, lie in these social cleavages.
Key (1949) set the tone earlier in *Southern Politics*, when he argued that
the American South was one-party because Southern political elites were
united in their opposition to intrusion from the national government on
matters of race. This research tradition, one that emphasizes group interests and voting, is related conceptually to the pluralist research of Truman (1954) and others, who observed that new interest groups form

when new social disruptions cause people to become dissatisfied with government actions in a new domain.

To explain when and in what fashion new parties emerge, one might then examine the influence of economic disruption, prosperity, or changes in political culture. Inglehart (1997) and Dalton (1984), for example, trace the origins of minor parties in recent decades in many Western democracies, especially environmental and reformist parties, to the rise of postmaterialist values. Likewise, Kitschelt (1999) finds that new parties arise from a combination of the demands made by citizens dissatisfied with the existing parties and the ambitions of politicians shut out or demoted by those parties. In order to become viable and sustain itself for the long term, a new party needs some members committed to an ideological program, some members willing to sacrifice elements of the ideology to win office, and some members who navigate between these two types of members. Without the first group, whose ideologies form out of a sense that government policies need to change in directions not proposed by the mainstream parties, these new parties cannot even get off the ground. They pursue policies that none of the major parties can address in a coherent or consistent manner, such as environmental or nuclear freeze policies in the 1960s and 1970s in Europe, or the antislavery policies in the 1850s in the United States. Caramani (2004) argues that a major transformation in European party systems occurred in the early twentieth century, when politics became less geographically based and more economic, ideological, or religious based, thus allowing for the formation of truly national parties centering on ideas and not geography. The transformation occurred mostly because of the changing priorities of voters and politicians.

The subject of chapter 2 reflects a second question in the literature, which asks how many parties should we expect to see in a given party system. It is important here to point out how this question relates to the research on party formation. The link is most clearly seen in Cox's *Making Votes Count* (1997). In studying party systems, researchers have found it useful to consider parties as solutions to coordination problems among voters, and Cox's book has taken the logic of this approach to its furthest point so far. In district elections, when n + 1 candidates win most of the vote, where n is the size of the district, voters coordinate to improve their chances of electing the candidates with policies they favor. For example, if the left in a single-member district fails to coordinate on a candidate, then the votes of leftists will be diluted among multiple candidates and those candidates may lose to the right, especially if the rightist voters coordinate on a candidate. Under the assumption that like-minded voters will eventually figure out how to coordinate, which candidates and how many of them will emerge depends on the electoral system and on the configuration of voters' preferences.

A similar process occurs in the formation of political parties across districts. Candidates and voters have to coordinate on party labels across districts, and failure to coordinate among like-minded candidates and voters means that those who successfully coordinate can win. Mass elections and representative democracy, the argument goes, inevitably lead to coordination among like-minded folks, typically on party labels, and it is in this process of coordination that parties form. In short, to understand party formation, one needs to understand the need for voters and candidates to coordinate and organize to accomplish policy goals.

What many scholars of strategic voting (e.g., Farquharson 1969; Cox 1997; Miller 1980; McKelvey and Neimi 1978) have been at pains to make clear is that voters have two kinds of preferences: policy preferences, and candidate or party preferences. Candidate and party preferences are induced from policy preferences. In other words, the preferences over candidates and parties follow from decisions over how to achieve certain policy outcomes. Sometimes citizens have to vote against their most preferred candidates or parties to achieve their policy goals. They may have to coordinate on someone else's favorite candidate. The nature of that coordination (which parties will likely emerge and how many of them will survive) depends not only on the electoral system in the districts but also on the configuration of the parliament and parliamentary rules (Taagepera and Shugart 1989), the rules for executive governance (Shugart and Carey 1992), the options listed on the ballots (Kedar 2003), and the degree of fiscal and political centralization (Chhibber and Kollman 1998).

The third question motivating scholars to study party formation is the most fundamental. Some social scientists have asked, Why have parties at all? Instead of studying how and when new parties form to challenge existing parties, these scholars seek to understand how parties come about in the first place (Aldrich 1995; Morelli 1999, 2001; Jackson and Moselle 2002). In some respects, this may seem like a strange question. Because parties exist pretty much wherever there are free and fair parliamentary elections, their formation and endurance have been taken for granted in many cases. To start fundamentally, at the very origins of parties, is to imagine democratic politics without parties and then to argue for their necessity or sufficiency, to consider what purposes parties serve, and to ask who benefits most from their existence. As part of the research tradition on institutional origin and design that has been sweeping political science and economics in recent decades, much of the previous research on party origins combines history, rational-choice theorizing, and, where possible, data analysis.

Theorists have focused on three types of actors in abstract models of parties: voters, candidates, and legislators. In research on the number of parties expected under different electoral systems, the focus has been on the role of voters and candidates. Recent research on the origins of parties has stressed the role of legislators. It is argued that, to understand the origins of parties, especially in the United States and England, where the first mass parties were formed, one has to begin with legislative groupings.

Theories of party formation by Aldrich (1995), Cox and McCubbins (1993), and Jackson and Moselle (2002) all propose that parties solve collective dilemmas for legislators. Aldrich, for example, considers parties to be a sufficient means by which legislators can enforce collective agreements to vote for each other's bills. Without parties or some other institution, policy outcomes in a legislature may cycle indefinitely among possible policy proposals. Without parties, implicit agreements or deals among legislators to support each other's pork barrel bills could be reneged upon.

Cox and McCubbins (1993) provide a somewhat different interpretation about the stability of parties in the United States Congress. Following Kiewit and McCubbins (1991), they include an important role for party entrepreneurs and for elections. Party entrepreneurs and leaders in the legislature offer to provide public goods to their party members in the legislature in exchange for party loyalty displayed by those members. In return the party leaders get special privileges, like extra pork for their districts, more campaign financing, or more influence in policy formation. What public goods are provided by the leadership? This is where elections come in. Cox and McCubbins argue that the party's reputation in the electorate is the major public good—that is, public good to the party rank and file in the legislature—produced by the collective action of the legislators. Sometimes the party members have to pay a small penalty for voting with the party as opposed to voting for their district interests, so the party leaders have to enforce party discipline in some way. They can reward loyal party legislators by granting choice committee assignments and agreeing to pork barrel legislation, and these benefits can be enough to keep alive the party coalition and preserve the party's reputation as a public good.

Likewise, Jackson and Moselle (2002) model a legislature deciding among distributive and ideological issues. In their stylized model, following on the models of Baron and Ferejohn (1989) and Harrington (1990), over sequential time periods legislators are randomly chosen to propose a policy, and all legislators vote on each proposal. They find that the set of legislators supporting a majority-preferred policy does not have to include the ideologically median legislator, which means that, because of the distributive aspects of the policies, coalitions can form among ideologically unconnected legislators. As a result, strange bedfellows may enter into policy coalitions. More important, Jackson and Moselle show that parties, which are defined as subsets of legislators who agree in advance of any policy proposals to cooperate and vote together, can be beneficial for the legislators and can lead to Pareto-improving policies over those policies chosen in the absence of parties. Under specific distributions of preferences, forming a party makes enough of the party members better off that the agreement to vote together will not become unglued. In short, parties can both improve the lot of the entire legislature and can be equilibrium institutions (they do not unravel due to free-riding). The conclusion from their model is similar to that of Aldrich, indicating how parties can make legislators better off collectively. Jackson and Moselle not only model how parties benefit legislators but also demonstrate how parties can be stable coalitions.[1]

Among these formal theories of party formation in legislatures, only Cox and McCubbins incorporate a role for elections, but they nevertheless do not model explicitly decision making among voters. Morelli (2001), in an innovative paper, offers a model of parties where politicians decide whether to become candidates, candidates decide whether to link across districts under a common party label, and winning candidates commit to vote with party comrades in the legislature to pass policies. Voters are then offered a menu of parties within their districts. The Morelli model, interestingly enough, leads to the Duvergerian conclusion that single-member, simple-plurality electoral systems result in only two parties forming, not because of strategic voting but because of strategic politicians deciding whether to become candidates. Because only two parties end up forming, voters do not have any incentives to vote strategically since sincere voting is a dominant strategy in two-party elections.

These formal models highlight abstract but general features of legislative politics that lead lawmakers to form parties. There are also historical studies of party formation that trace behavioral patterns of legislators over time. Aldrich (1995) supplements his formal model with a study of partisan voting in the U.S. First, Second, and Third Congresses. He demonstrates with roll-call data that members of the Third Congress exhibited much greater partisanship in voting on major bills than members of the First Congress. "[I]t is reasonable to conclude," Aldrich writes, "that parties arose out of the step-by-step strengthening of fac-

---

[1] Levy (n.d.) provides a related model of party formation that stresses the importance of bargaining among legislative factions over multiple policy dimensions. Stable legislative coalitions (i.e., parties) can form, she argues, only when the factions can trade off utility losses in the various dimensions when they take bargaining positions. Single-dimensional conflict will not lead to stable legislative coalitions.

tions into political parties as a means of avoiding the consequences of voting disequilibrium and, in particular, setting a clear pattern of precedents on the revealed power and energy of the new national government" (91). (The last clause of this quotation is perfectly consistent with the arguments in this book.)

Cox, meanwhile, explores a similar lever for partisanship. In an influential historical study of the emergence of party discipline in the British House of Commons, Cox (1987a) emphasizes the increasing powers of the Commons to set national policy standards. Members of the Commons mostly looked after their narrow constituency interests in the eighteenth and early nineteenth centuries. Increasing industrialization of the British economy and greater trade across regions of Britain brought demands to the crown for policy standards set by a national authority. As the national government became responsible to the majority in the Commons, meaning that the government was elected by a majority in the Parliament and a majority in the Parliament had the power to dismiss the government at will, members of the Commons in the mid-nineteenth century began to band into like-minded groups (with party labels) around policy ideas. These groups had a tendency to fray and unravel when constituency interests came into conflict within the groups. Gradually, citizens in the districts began to adopt policy preferences that correlated with party labels and candidates began to use party labels on ballots. With the formation of citizen preferences over parties in the mid-nineteenth century, British party democracy had become complete, with voters and legislators voting almost strictly along party lines and the government being responsible to the majority party in the Commons.

According to Cox, Conservative and Liberal labels in Britain became national in scope and meant similar things to legislators, voters, and candidates during this period. In determining the causes of this change, Cox focuses attention on the "efficient secret," the fact that the cabinet was responsible to the majority in the Commons. What is noteworthy is that Cox establishes that party formation happened in a relatively short period of time. The processes of producing strict party discipline in the Commons, party voting in the constituencies, and the mass use of party ballots all took place over the course of several decades. It is hard to discern from the historical data, however, the precise mechanism by which the party labels among candidates, and party voting by constituents and by legislators, aggregated perfectly. Cox's discussion concerns party discipline in the Commons, rather than party systems or the number of parties.

According to Caramani (2004) European national parties formed when class, religious, and ideological rivalries supplanted geographic rivalries among voters and politicians. There was a rapid transition prior to World War I, when partisan loyalties among voters and politicians became more consolidated across vast stretches of the countries—in other words, the parties aggregated effectively—as opposed to being fragmented among smaller regions or cities. (The timing he identifies is consistent with our claim that the increasing role of the national state causes voters to choose national parties in lieu of more regional or state-based parties.)

We can summarize the research on national party formation as follows. The first question addressed—When do new parties form?—focuses attention on the changing preferences of voters and activists and how these changes lead parties to form around new issues not confronted or exploited by the existing parties. This research obviously has its strength in explaining and describing changes to established party systems.

The second question on the number of parties compares electoral systems and other institutional differences across countries. If electoral institutions change, then new parties can form because the incentives of voters and candidates to coordinate have changed—for example, when systems move from plurality rule to proportional representation, or vice versa. If preferences among voters or candidates change, then the resulting changes in the party system can take various forms, although more than likely it will result in a new party replacing an existing party. This is because the electoral system typically places constraints on the system and provides an upper bound on the number of expected parties. (This conclusion we believe needs to be amended given the results presented in the remainder of this book.)

Research on the third question—Why have parties at all?—could properly be considered a close cousin of the research on the second question. Both research traditions emphasize coordination of actors to accomplish policy goals. In fact, some formal models seek to explain both the emergence of parties and the number of parties under certain electoral systems (Morelli 2001). Scholars who address this third question focus mostly on legislative parties, and these researchers often have the advantage of being able to compare data on a legislative world without parties (e.g., the first few United States Congresses, or early British House of Commons) with data on a legislative world with parties (beginning in the Third U.S. Congress, or following mid-nineteenth-century Britain).

Limited research compares periods of time when voters or candidates, for whatever reason, do not coordinate effectively in the district or across districts with periods of time when they do. Party systems, as we showed in Figures 1.1–1.4, slip in and out of periods where national parties aggregate effectively. Morelli's model provides one explanation for how the number of parties in a plurality system can fluctuate between two parties and multiple parties (more than two). In his model, to have more than two parties, there needs to be significant preference heterogeneity across electoral districts so that cross-district coalitions are virtually impossible to form, a situation he ascribes to modern India. Riker (1982) offers a similar explanation for India. Both scholars are in agreement that as ideological preferences among voters become more or less correlated by the district location of the voters, party systems can change under plurality voting from national party systems to more fragmented, localized party systems, or vice versa. In the next section, we argue that it is important to focus on how trends in the authority of different levels of government can shape voters' and candidates' induced preferences over parties.

## The Process of Party Aggregation

Political systems are, of course, more complicated than any theoretical model of party formation or aggregation can manage to capture. So, for example, Canada, Great Britain, India, and the United States have various levels of government, two houses of parliament, and the United States has separation of powers and a strong presidency. In all four countries, voters, candidates, and legislators operate in multitiered, variegated systems where they may have to pay attention to many layers of party competition at once. For the purposes of building an argument about party aggregation we discuss an abstract version of a parliamentary political system, where the national lower house alone decides policies that voters care about.

As in the literature reviewed here, we focus on the interactions of three sets of actors: voters, candidates, and legislators. Each set plays an important role, but under our definition of electoral parties, ultimately it is the role of the candidates across many districts that completes the process of party aggregation. They are able to link together under common party labels on election ballots.

Citizens in our abstract system have a single instrument, the vote in a district election, to choose a candidate for parliament and to influence government policy at the national level. To understand the district-level dynamics, we borrow ideas and conclusions from the models summarized in chapter 2 on Duverger's Law in district elections. In these models, when marking a ballot for a candidate or party in the district, voters make decisions based on how their votes will affect their well-being, and they are rational in the sense that they maximize their utility given that information. Voters can be rational in these situations by making rough estimates of the probability that their votes will be decisive (that their votes will change the election outcome). They take into account how other voters will behave in the election and cast ballots accordingly. In general this means that voters try to avoid wasting their votes on uncompetitive candidates. Typically (though certainly not always in practice, as shown in chapter 2), single-member, simple-plurality rules lead to two candidates receiving most of the votes in a district election.

We can assume that candidates are office-seeking, and they will drop out of races where they do not have any chance of winning. Moreover, they adopt party labels to win and maintain office. Thus, consistent with theories of political ambition by Schlesinger (1991), Aldrich (1995), and others, party labels and parties themselves act as the means for politicians to gain and hold office and to secure the benefits of that office.

If voters cared only about the district-level outcomes and national politics were irrelevant, then the party labels of the candidates in the districts might very well be suited only to local conditions. In Great Britain, for example, candidates could call themselves Conservative or Labour, if these labels communicate to voters something relevant to the district election. Or, they could just call themselves Blues and Yellows, if these labels were better suited to local conditions. If only local results matter, then party labels may differ in surrounding districts. One district has a Green and Red running against each other, and the next district has a Blue and a Yellow running against each other. In principle, with D districts in the country there could be as many as 2D parties. At such an extreme, candidates might as well not use party labels, or they might as well all run as independents.

More realistically, voters care about national politics because the parliament makes important decisions on taxation, the allocation of resources to various government programs, the drafting of soldiers, the location of public projects, and whether to wage war in international crises. Voters also recognize that individual legislators do not make policy. Groups of legislators make policy. Voters know that enough members of parliament have to act in unison to achieve some collective goal. Public goods are decided upon by groups of legislators.

Members of the parliament, meanwhile, have the typical collective action and voter coordination problems endemic to legislatures. Legislators solve these collective dilemmas by developing what has been called "long" coalitions in the literature (Schwarz 1989; Aldrich 1995). It is rational for legislators to create partylike organizations, independent of elections to the legislature, to accomplish collective and individual goals. If legislators do not need to communicate to voters at election time, then party labels are not that important. One can imagine that legislators would have an arcane system of recognition so that belonging to a particular party within the legislature might entail wearing a specific colored shirt, or specific type of hat. Because legislators are also candidates running for election on ballots in districts, however, it is efficient to have widely recognized party labels. And along with party voting come party labels, party discipline, and party whips.

Among incumbent legislators who are subject to the approval of the electorate in the next election, party labels communicate policy positions both to voters and to fellow candidates and legislators. The label on the ballot may add status to the candidate among voters and help that candidate in the election. A label could tie the candidate to a specific policy program, either the incumbent government's policies or an opposing party's proposed policies. The party label of the incumbent legislator and candidate may also endear him or her to colleagues in the parliament or elsewhere in the government, enabling the candidate to secure perks, pork barrel benefits, status, fame, riches, or whatever is desired once in office. These benefits may or may not have anything to do with reelection chances in the district. As Cox and McCubbins (1993) argue, party leaders promise both public goods for party members (party reputation) and private goods (committee assignments, pork, campaign funds) in return for loyalty in the legislature.

Party aggregation up to the national level occurs with the mutual reinforcement of these two functions. Candidates want to coordinate across districts to influence national policies, and they want to adopt recognizable national-party labels because voters understand the need for coordination to accomplish policy goals. Consistent with Cox's discussion of changes in party discipline in the British Parliament 150 years ago, *national* parties require these necessary conditions: national policy-making power by the parliament, and voters' having a stake in which policies are adopted. Party loyalties by both candidates and voters reinforce each other and line up neatly.

This line of reasoning describes how durable national parties might form, but it says little about national party systems. We first consider party aggregation in the simple case of only district-level elections to a national parliament and then, in the next section, reconsider the issue after introducing the role of states or provinces in federal systems.

Party aggregation in any system, federal or not, is more difficult to achieve when voters' preferences are mostly locally based and candidates do not have to coordinate with politicians in other districts. Both voters and candidates are inclined to focus on local matters and local labels. In India, for example, many voters choose regional parties that are ideologically similar to parties in neighboring regions but with distinctive labels and organizations. The Samajwadi Party in Uttar Pradesh and the Rashtriya Janata Dal in Bihar both represent similarly situated castes, and the parties are ideologically similar. Yet each prefers to retain its own organization, and when they sought to cooperate at the national level in 1996, relations were very strained. In Canada in recent years, provincial parties are very strong, and conservative voters across different regions and provinces with similar views on economic policies have been unable to coordinate effectively in advancing Reform or Alliance candidates.

As the national government centralizes authority and voters develop clear national policy preferences, and candidates associate themselves with certain national policy positions, voters may become more inclined to vote for nationally competitive parties, even if those parties are not the most preferred on local matters. Cox and Monroe (1995), in an innovative working paper, discuss voting equilibria in which voters have preferences over the composition of the national legislature and have well-defined expectations about how parties will fare in the elections nationally. They conjecture that, in equilibrium, voters will often vote for less preferred parties. For single-member, simple-plurality systems, this means they will usually abandon nationally noncompetitive parties, even though these may be locally competitive. Furthermore, in such a system, two nationally competitive parties will tend to emerge. As Cox and Monroe summarize their argument, "the net impact of national parliamentary considerations on local Duvergerian dynamics should be clear. . . . There are multiple dynamics that serve to (1) drive down the number of parties, and (2) reinforce the national party system at the district level. . . . These dynamics . . . are particularly strong in single-member district systems" (14–5).

Thus, for single-member, simple-plurality electoral systems, the formal rules for awarding seats have their direct effect at the district level. Voters, by and large, abandon noncompetitive parties or candidates for Duvergerian reasons. At the national level, Duvergerian effects, where the number of parties is reduced due to strategic voting, are found when national policies matter a lot to voters. Therefore, as national governments become more important to voters, we should see a reduction in the number of parties because party aggregation becomes more valuable to both voters and candidates, and local parties, uncompetitive at the national level, lose votes to more competitive parties at the national level.

## FEDERALISM AND PARTY AGGREGATION

If policy preferences influence voting strategies by citizens as we have assumed, then modeling district-level voting behavior by assuming district-level policy preferences, as satisfying as this is theoretically for those who analyze the game-theoretic properties of Duverger's Law, does not capture the mechanisms of party formation. Very few policies are made that only affect a single district, and policies are not made at the district level. Nor, for that matter, is policy made only at the national level in many countries. In Canada, India, and the United States, as in countries around the world, most policies that voters care about are made either at the national level or, one level down, at the state or provincial level. In Britain, many policies are implemented by the localities. Thus, voters naturally are going to pay attention to the policy positions of candidates as those positions relate to policy making at more than one level of government.

We focus here on state or provincial policy making. Of course, city and local governments matter too. Yet, in all four of our countries, city and local governments are creatures of states, provinces, or nations. Although some major cities in the United States, such as Chicago and New York, have city governments that wield substantial power, those powers are granted to the cities directly by state governments (Burns and Gamm 1997). London also has a powerful city council, but, as Margaret Thatcher demonstrated, it could be stripped of its powers by the national government without judicial objections.

The same cannot be said of state governments in India and the United States and provincial governments in Canada. Their existence and sovereignty are guaranteed by constitutions and protected by judicial review. This is not the same as saying that state or provincial policy cannot be overridden by national policy. Rather, the states or provinces cannot be completely stripped of their powers or eliminated altogether without constitutional amendments in Canada, India, and the United States. For our purposes, we will use this kind of constitutional status for states or provinces as our definition of federalism. Therefore, Canada, India, and the United States are federal, and Great Britain (for the period we study until 1993) is not.

Under most federal arrangements localities depend on state governments for their resources. In Ontario, Canada, for example, external funds for local governments come mainly from the provincial government with a few federal transfers amounting to less than 1 percent of total revenues of local governments (Islam 1998, 70). Not only are resources to local governments allocated by state governments rather than national governments, but local governments often exist at the behest of state governments. In the United States, local governments are creatures of state governments (Banfield and Wilson 1963; Frug 1980, 1109; Schultz 1989). Burns and Gamm (1997, 61) note that local politics have been tied to state politics and that "local policy outcomes often occur in

state legislatures." In India, state governments can change the boundaries of local governments, dismiss local governments, and play a key
role in their administration (Bagchi 1991).

In three of our four countries, during the periods under study, states
or provinces had authority over policies that voters cared about deeply,
such as those related to public safety, education, health care, welfare,
infrastructure, taxation, liquor, and agriculture. Thus, it is not surprising that oftentimes party aggregation occurs at the level of states and
provinces.

To extend this logic, it should not be common to observe aggregation
across a few districts within a state, because voters and candidates will
at least aggregate up to the first level at which serious policy is made.
We examined this empirically for three of our four countries[2] and found
that, with one exception, there are no instances of substate or subprov-
ince parties winning elections over time.[3] We used the following thresholds, and found only one example: a party that won more than 15 percent of the vote in each of three or more districts in a single state or
province over three consecutive national elections but won votes in only
that state or province. Furthermore, the party had to win those votes in
no more than one-third of the states' or provinces' districts. In Canada
and Great Britain, there has never been such a substate party. The exception occurred in India, where the Peasants and Workers Party (PWP)
formed in Maharashtra and gathered considerable strength in the 1960s
and 1970s in about one-quarter of the constituencies in the state. It won
seats for the national parliament in many of those constituencies.[4]

Because federalism means that state or provincial politics matters, voters and candidates will have incentives to link across districts within
their own states or provinces. These linkages become the basis for state
or provincial party organizations. And in our three federal systems in
Canada, India, and the United States, state or provincial parties have
been extremely important in the politics and national elections dating
back to the beginning of party politics. In fact, in these three federal

[2]We did not examine the U.S. data for technical reasons having to do with the organization
of the data set. There are undoubtedly few, if any, examples of substate parties that competed for congressional seats in American history.

[3]What are typically called regions (England, Scotland, Wales) in Great Britain are officially
called countries. We searched for subcountry parties for Great Britain.

[4]While it does not qualify under our criteria (it won votes in more than one state), the
Jharkhand Mukti Morcha (JMM) in India comes close. It represented the interests of a
region within the state of Bihar in the 1990s. The party agitated for the creation of a new
state of Jharkhand to be carved out of a few districts in Bihar. The party managed to win
a few seats to Parliament in the 1990s, and the new state was created by Parliament in
2000. Parties like the JMM can promote the interests of geographically concentrated ethnic groups at the state level.

systems, there are state and provincial legislatures (not to mention elected executives in the United States) that somewhat mirror the national government in institutional design. Thus, not surprisingly, the states or provinces develop rich party systems and state party loyalties among voters.

The nature of a country's party system therefore depends on whether state or provincial parties will link together to form regional or national parties. In some periods in some countries, they aggregate to the national level effectively, and in other periods in these same countries, they do not. In an even more complicated variation, during the same periods in some countries, select states or provinces have party systems that mirror the national party systems, and other states or provinces do not. Contemporary Canada and India are two examples of this variation (more on this in chapter 7).

Typically, national governments in federal systems negotiate and share authority with states and provinces (Filippov, Ordeshook, and Shvetsova 2004). Voters and candidates may, therefore, wish to have a voice in state or provincial policy and national policy. Voters in federations who are tempted to vote for representatives from parties that are strong only in their states or provinces may realize quickly that their representative has little voice in national policy making, unless the representative's party joins in an alliance with a major national party. If authority is centralized to the point where the national government dominates the states or provinces, then it is likely that candidates will bypass the state or provincial parties and simply adopt national-party labels. Moreover, to the extent that states or provinces retain some authority, voters may not want to vote for national parties that have little state or provincial power.

Likewise, it will often be advantageous for voters to have state or provincial governments controlled by parties that have national representation, and advantageous to have national representatives who have party affiliations with state or provincial parties. One way to ensure that a local representative has links to the national government and to the state or province is to have him or her affiliated with a state party that shares a common label (and a common ideology) with a national party. Thus, the "lining up" discussed earlier emerges not just from the party loyalties of the voters in the district to the partisanship of the national legislators. It can also emanate from the party loyalties of the voters in the districts to the partisanship of the state-level policy makers to the partisanship of the national legislators. A complete lining up of the three levels roughly describes the situation in the United States since the 1930s. As will become apparent in later chapters, it does not describe our other countries of interest except for short periods of time long ago.

Filippov, Ordeshook, and Shvetsova (2004) highlight the importance of national parties in creating the conditions for stability in federations. In their view, if constitutional designs encourage specific institutional features, such as presidentialism and linked elections across levels of government, that would facilitate the formation of national parties. To allow for completely separate party systems at the provincial or state levels is to invite secessionist troubles and even the complete breakup of the federation. Their focus is on the basic institutional design of federations, such as whether systems are presidential, parliamentary, or bicameral or have linked state and federal elections. Our claim takes the basic institutional features as given and focuses on the potential for changing authority across levels of government over time. Regardless, we largely agree with their argument that having national parties can be an important glue that holds federations together. However, our data show that having regional or state-based parties does not necessarily lead to dangerous movements for secession or breakup (witness India today), and in our four countries, national party systems without regional, state, or provincial parties are the exceptions, not the norm.

## CENTRALIZATION OF AUTHORITY

Our main theoretical argument, stated in perhaps the most abstract form possible, is that as governments centralize authority, taking powers away from or imposing new conditions on lower levels of government, voters will naturally have more incentives to try to influence politics at higher levels. And candidates will become more inclined to take positions on policy issues being dealt with at the higher levels of government and make those positions centerpieces of their campaigns for office. Candidates will thus find it more valuable to take on party labels that are meaningful at higher levels of government. Party aggregation should be easier under conditions of centralization.

Because our primary concern in this book is with the formation of national party systems, centralization to the national level features most prominently. (As we discussed, provincialization, or the gathering of authority at the state or provincial level, also influences party aggregation. It opens the door to regional, state, or provincial parties to gain votes at the expense of national parties.) Centralization of authority itself is a complicated concept, and it is very difficult to measure consistently across countries and over time (we discuss this in detail in chapter 5).

At the conceptual level, we are primarily interested in centralization as it affects the policy-making authority of different levels of government over social and economic policies that are of highest concern to voters.

Also, the focus tends to be on decision making, not implementation, although admittedly the differences between these two are often hard to pin down, and they may work in opposite directions over time. It may be possible, for example, to centralize decision-making authority and to keep policy implementation local, or occasionally vice versa. Likewise, the degree of centralization certainly varies across different policy realms in any country: military policies have been centralized virtually everywhere, whereas streets and sanitation policies remain decentralized everywhere, and schools and broad economic policies (licensing, most redistributive taxation, business regulation, and health care systems and other social welfare systems) can be either. Finally, while specific areas of policy may buck the trend—for example, by becoming devolved during an era of centralization—we shall naturally focus on broad trends and patterns of centralization and decentralization or provincialization over time and across many social and economic policy areas. For example, the New Deal centralized political and economic authority in the United States across many areas of policy, and there is no denying that it was a centralization of the broadest kind. Yet, even during the New Deal, state governments continued to play a role (Patterson 1967).

The relative permanence of the centralization or provincialization that occurs is important. Centralization that is relevant for party formation can be political and economic. Political centralization is indeed important but it is rarely long-lasting in the absence of economic centralization. There were certainly periods of political centralization in the United States, Canada, and India that did not last. During and shortly after the Civil War in the United States, the national government centralized political authority for the purposes of making war and then subjugating and reconstructing the South. During World War II there was political centralization in Canada. In neither case was there a sustained effort by the governments to centralize economic policy-making authority, and thus politics in both countries reverted to regional bases quickly. When coupled with efforts to centralize the economic policy making, such political centralization tends to have enduring and pronounced effects on party systems, as we show in later chapters.

## CONCLUSION

Our theory of party aggregation has been stated abstractly for a pure parliamentary system, but it is meant to apply to all four of our cases. Our hypothesis is that as national governments increase their authority over policies that voters care about, voters and candidates will become increasingly concerned with having a voice in national legislatures. This concern will create strong incentives for voters and candidates to seek to link not only to others in neighboring districts within a state or province but also to others in states and provinces across the nation. Linking across the nation means adopting national-party labels that have common meanings in disparate states, provinces, and regions. In general, this means that centralizing authority at the national level will create more national party systems because voters will be less inclined to vote for regional, state- or province-level, or local parties. The opposite trend, decentralization or provincialization, makes it more likely that there will be an increase in voting for parties with regional, state, or provincial labels.

In the remainder of this book, we provide empirical evidence to support these claims. Chapter 4 provides evidence in support of one of our key claims—that political parties are formed to influence state policy. The next four chapters move to a categorization of centralized and provincialized periods (chapter 5), to correlating party system dynamics and changes in centralization (chapters 6 and 7), and finally to a broader, cross-national analysis of electoral systems other than single-member, simple-plurality systems (chapter 8). At the risk of ruining the suspense, data from elections in our four countries support our claims.

In chapter 8, we also discuss the claim that party system changes cause centralization and decentralization (or provincialization). We show that the process of centralization in all four countries occurred for reasons that were not linked to party politics but were the result of large economic dislocations, technological changes, and war. At the same time, provincialization—in the two countries that have witnessed it in recent years, Canada and India—occurred for reasons not linked to party politics. Changes in the party systems followed changes in patterns of which levels of government had more authority.

*Chapter 4*

---

# FROM LOCAL NOTABLES TO PARTY COMPETITION

IN THE 1790s the world's first modern, national political party system was born in the United States. It began with a set of linked state and local Federalist committees loyal to the cause of Alexander Hamilton and continued with a concerted effort by the so-called Republicans (Jeffersonians) to counter the Federalists. The Republicans formed county- and state-level organizations to coordinate and mobilize electors. By the 1800 elections the Republicans were much better organized than the Federalists and consequently had stunning election triumphs. The Federalists were not yet buried. By 1808 both parties had formal caucuses managing nominations for state and federal offices everywhere in the country (Fischer 1974). For another five years the Republicans and the Federalists competed for control of the national government, not unlike contemporary political parties, as teams of politicians pursuing policy goals. This first party system was, however, short-lived. In the few years after the War of 1812, largely because of their opposition to the war, the Federalists faded away, and the Republicans (increasingly called the Democratic-Republicans, and then just the Democrats) dominated American politics until the 1830s, when the Whigs emerged as a major opposition party and occasionally won power over the next several decades.

Elections for the colonial legislatures in America had been held for a long time prior to the 1790s, and popular election to the Continental Congress and national Congress were in their third decade by then. There were partylike organizations both in the colonial legislatures and among the localities organizing candidates in the 1770s and 1780s (Main 1973; Dinkin 1977). Politicians, before the advent of the national parties, relied on the state-level caucuses or their own personal machinery to campaign and turn out electors, and often nominated themselves or had friends nominate them (Fischer 1974). By the late 1780s in some places and by the late 1790s in all states, however, American political life had changed. Attachment to a national cause, manifest by identification as either a Federalist or a Republican, became an important marker in the relationship between candidates for the Congress and their constituents. Affiliation with one or the other party also became vital to a candidate's prospects for winning. As Dinkin (1982) argues, state-level factions began to link across states into national party organizations in the late 1780s because of the rise of national issues addressed by the Continental Congress. Cox (1987a) records a similar transformation in Great Britain after the second Reform Act in 1867. Campaigns for parliamentary seats became partisan, and it mattered less and less to British voters in the late nineteenth century who was filling the seats from the particular districts as long as the candidates had the right party label.

Today, it is taken for granted in Canada, Great Britain, India, and the United States that serious candidates for the lower houses of parliament, with few exceptions, adopt party labels. Indeed, they have done so for most of the history of popular election to the lower houses. It appears that once party systems define the nature of political competition in a country, party aggregation in one form or another occurs as an apparently irreversible process.

The importance of individual candidates (as opposed to party labels) in voting decisions varies across countries and across time; at one extreme individual candidates hardly matter at all in comparison with the party label, as in Britain in most districts during the twentieth century. Of course, the development of the widespread use of party labels in the four countries did not put an end to the existence of politicians who win and maintain office because they successfully develop personal loyalty among constituents. In any era, including our own, many politicians in these countries have achieved fame independent and distinct from any party affiliation. Yet true political independence, where candidates avoid any party label at all, becomes extremely rare, especially among candidates who have a chance of winning office.

In this chapter we devote attention to several basic questions: how parties begin, why candidates adopt party labels, and why they link across districts with other candidates under common party labels. We argue that party labels are adopted and spread across geographic regions by politicians who are motivated by policy goals. While political parties are, as various scholars have defined them (Downs 1957; Schlesinger 1991; Aldrich 1995), organizational vehicles for ambitious politicians, the drivers of those vehicles are nearly always small groups of politicians who wish to ensure that the government adopts certain policies.

Establishing that policy goals drive the formation of parties is a crucial component in our overall argument. We address in chapters 5–7 the question of which levels of government come to the primary attention of voters and politicians, and the question of how changes in political authority across those levels affect party systems. Before we can demonstrate the links between federal relations and party systems, we must first establish that policy-making power is at the core of the spread of party labels. To achieve their goals, however, national politicians had to win over *local notables*. They needed to attract enough local notables to spread the party label across large geographic areas. For the most part these notables lost their independent status fairly quickly to political parties.

## NATIONAL POLICY GOALS AND PARTY BUILDING

Weber (1946) made the distinction between a party of notables and a party of professionals. Notables have goals separate from politics, but because of their status, economic interests, or personal ambitions, they participate in politics. In a party of notables, according to Weber, the parties are simply means to an economic or political end. Within the category of notables, there are so-called *local* notables (Weber 1946, 101–5), the ones who remain active in the local areas. They often determine the nomination of candidates or end up being the candidates themselves. In a party of local notables, a close relationship exists between the local economic elite and the political leadership of that area.

Professionals, in contrast, are activists whose livelihoods depend on politics. They work mainly for the political parties, and their work in politics is ongoing. Their loyalty is to the party as an organization and they strive to keep it alive. These professionals are not necessarily elites, in the common use of the term, but rather are paid average wages by parties to maintain the local or national organizations between elections. In a party of professionals, there is an organizational machinery in place to manage the business of politics, and its candidates are often people whose lifetime profession is running for and maintaining public office as a member of the party. Duverger ([1954] 1963), and Wilson (1973) also made similar distinctions among party activists and among activists in political organizations more broadly. Distinctions between parties of notables and parties of professionals are not hard and fast, and contemporary parties typically have both types of activists and candidates (Eldersveld 1964; 1982).

It would be nice to represent the formation process of national party systems as following a trajectory of increasing size and scope of party aggregation, from local notables winning office without party labels, to making links across a few districts on local-party labels, to linking to state or provincial labels, and eventually to linking across states or provinces to forge national parties under national labels. Such a gradual, "bottom-up" story, however, would be misleading as a description of the historical process behind the formation of national party systems. In all four countries, the first political parties with influence on national government policy had top-down organizational structures centered in the national capitals.

The party system in Canada began to form in 1854 after the achievement of a responsible government. A coalition called the Liberal-Conservatives under the leadership of John Macdonald slowly consolidated itself from a coalition into a party (Underhill 1935, 369).[1] The initial opposition to the Liberal-Conservatives came from the Clear Grits of Upper Canada and the Rouge from Lower Canada (Underhill 1935, 375–77). Once Confederation was achieved, "these party divisions of Liberal-Conservatives and Reformers were gradually extended *from the central area to the outlying sections of the dominion*" (emphasis added; Underhill 1935, 378). This was made possible because the Liberal-Conservatives believed in a strong national government to carry through the drive for a westward economic expansion. To ensure success, Macdonald had to rein in the local notables. He did so with strong central (and some would say completely personal) control over the dispensation of patronage. Macdonald built the party using the patronage that came with gaining control of the Confederation government (G. Stewart 1986, 66–67). The role of the leadership in creating the party organization and engendering party discipline is described further by Eggleston (1993).

What distinguished Macdonald's dispensation of patronage from the earlier Tory version was that patronage was no longer bestowed based on social and personal connections. Macdonald rewarded those who worked for the party and made his position clear that if an office was vacant it belonged to the party in government (G. Stewart 1986, 67). Macdonald controlled this patronage dispensation almost to the last detail, and this clarity of the implicit exchanges helped form the party and create its distinction from local notables (G. Stewart 1986, 68).[2]

Patronage played a cementing role in the creation of political parties in the years following Confederation because of the government's rapid expansion. Government expansion was necessary, and the continued "growth of government was sustained by three factors—the need to overcome Canada's difficult geographic setting, which meant large-scale government involvement in railways and canals; the need to incorporate the new western territories; the need to build up the other infrastructures of Confederation by the expansion of new federal departments, by es-

---

[1]Initially, the Liberal-Conservatives consisted of four groups. The numerically strongest were the French Canadian Roman Catholics whose leader Cartier was also the solicitor of the Grand Trunk Railway Company. Montreal big business allied with interests in Lower Canada as the latter felt that trade to the West would flow through Lower Canada. The two other groups in the Liberal Conservatives were smaller, urban, and linked to the railroads (Hincksite reformers), and the Upper-Canadian Tory party (Underhill 1935, 375).

[2]Another notable effort to build a party from the top down was by Mowatt, who used patronage to help cement the Liberal Party in Ontario (G. Stewart 1986, 72).

tablishing post offices, custom houses, court systems, as well as associated bureaucracies" (G. Stewart 1986, 82). The Royal Commission on Federal-Provincial Relations (1940) also noted the importance of the dominion government for the Canadian citizens in this period, especially when compared with the provincial governments. Other parties emerged in response to the Liberal-Conservative alliance. As Underhill (1935, 369) notes, "over against the Liberal-Conservatives, the various groups and individuals . . . coalesced into a new Reform or Liberal party" and achieved party cohesion more slowly as "they seldom enjoyed the sweets of national office."

In Britain parties were also built from the top down. Parliamentary parties predated partisan electoral organizations in local areas, and extraparliamentary party organizations were sporadic and typically short-lived until the 1870s (Cox 1987a, 119). What turned the tide? As Cox (1987a) argues, it was the confluence of several events, including the expansion of the electorate, the increasing complexity of policy matters facing the Parliament, and the development of cabinet government. The efforts of national leaders to coordinate constituency-level associations on nominations, however, was the major component that made British electoral politics fundamentally partisan at the constituency level. Conservative leaders greatly feared the consequences of Liberal government and needed to spread Conservative associations to all the local constituencies to defeat Liberal candidates.

In the 1830s the Conservatives (Tories), for example, hired F. R. Bonham to start local electoral organizations. These initial efforts sputtered, but in the 1850s Disraeli, as Conservative leader, hired Philip Rose to develop and coordinate local associations. Finally, in 1870, the Conservatives had a national political office to promote the development and coordinate the actions of local organizations. By 1885 the "professional party agent began to displace the solicitor" (Pugh 1993, 16). The agent's responsibility was to ensure that his party's supporters appeared on the voter list. After 1867 the party began to spend considerable resources on forming local party-sponsored clubs (16), and to support the "sponsored benefit societies, friendly societies, sick and burial societies and even building societies" (17). Formal constituency associations were also created by the national parties after 1867 (17).

In India the first major party was also formed from the center. When it was a nationalist movement, the Congress Party tried to work through a unified national elite—W. C. Bonnerjee stated in the presidential address in the very first session of the Congress that the founders wanted to eliminate "all possible race, creed, or provincial prejudices among lovers of the country" (cited in McLane 1989, 47). Even though the Congress Party purported to have a federal structure with provincial parties in 1937, the central Congress Party exercised control over state governments (Weiner 1967, 45). After independence, the Congress Party built its dominance by its control over the nation-state, which was the agent for economic and social change. "When the British withdrew in 1947, Congress quickly and smoothly took control of the machinery of the state at all levels. Congress then became India's central political institution, more important than Parliament or the civil service or any other formal institution of the state . . . [and] the party's operatives soon came to dominate the civil service so that the formal machinery of the state was subordinated to the needs and demands of the party" (Manor 1990, 26).

Control by the Congress Party of the nation-state helped the leadership of the national party assert control of the party in the state and localities. The central party office, either through the Congress High Command or the prime minister, nominated candidates for election to the Lok Sabha and even for the state assemblies (Kochanek 1968). The party also gradually eliminated from its ranks of organized groups those whose policy preferences differed from the leadership of the party. The two major defections from the Congress in the years following independence were over the adoption of national policy. The socialists formed their party in 1948 when a number of Congress politicians became dissatisfied with the economic policies of the Congress Party. Socialist-leaning politicians wanted a more leftward policy tilt by the Congress. The Jan Sangh (the precursor to the BJP) was founded by politicians from the Congress Party who favored the adoption of a more conservative social policy (Graham 1990). The relevance of state policy for party formation was also felt at the local level. For most of the local political elites, affiliation with the Congress was more a matter of expediency than anything else. Seventy percent of *sarpanchs* (village heads) interviewed after the 1967 election said that most Congress *sarpanchs* would change their support to a new ruling party if there were a change in government at the state level. A *sarpanch* who was willing to change his political loyalties explained it this way: "I want development of my area and this is only possible if I join the ruling party" (Papachristou 1968, 154).

As for the United States, the earliest party caucuses by Hamilton and Jefferson in the 1790s were created to organize the House of Representatives into policy-making blocs. These caucuses were then used to choose presidential candidates. A few years later, the electoral side of the Federalist and Republican parties came into existence. As Chambers (1974, 216–17) recounts, four patterns became evident. First, there arose "linkages of association" and coordinated nominations, extending into states, counties, and towns. Second, from the national leaders came an increasingly standardized set of procedures for nomination, mobilization of voters, and managing officers in different branches of government. Third, the leaders sought to coordinate diverse interest groups to work on behalf of party goals. Fourth, there was a concerted effort to develop "a distinctive set of attitudes and loyalties . . . the beginnings of a partisan ideology."

Members of Congress and the national administrations hell-bent on keeping the others out of power because of deep fears about opposition policies were the motivating forces behind all of these efforts. Their fears of the opposition were not held secret. One Federalist leader publicly summarized a view held widely among his comrades, that the survival of the Republic depended upon the formation of a federal party to check the Jeffersonians. Fisher James wrote, "One of two things will, I confess, take place. Either the advances of the [Jeffersonian] faction will create a federal party, or their unobstructed progress will embolden them to use their power, as all such gentry will if they dare, in acts of violence on property" (quoted in Fischer 1974, 234–35).

The Republicans organized much more effectively than the Federalists in the early years, and it showed in the 1800 elections. "In some districts no Federalists competed in elections that it was thought any Federalist might have won. In others there was a plethora of candidates. 'Nearly a dozen' men competed for Vermont's eastern Congressional seat in 1800. In Essex County, Massachusetts, there were seven Federalist candidates for one place in Congress. In 1798 . . . a Republican Albert Gallatin owed his election to the fact that his opposition was split between two candidates" (Fischer 1974, 233).

Control of nominations was key in the early development of the national parties in the United States. It could not have been clearer to the Federalist leaders, for example, that to have Federalist policies pass and remain in place they needed to control nominations in local areas to keep up with and perhaps surpass the Republicans. Controlling nominations was the only way party leaders could compel local notables to adopt the party label, participate cooperatively in the Congress, defeat the other party, and ensure the survival of the party until the next round of elections. Policy-motivated leaders in the nation's capital made it a priority to establish party committees in the states, cities, and towns throughout the new nation to defeat the Republicans, their policies, and their organizational machinery. The Republicans adopted a similar strategy in order to defeat the Federalists.

In all four of our countries, therefore, political parties were seen as the makers of the policies that were adopted by governments. Political parties gained control over the policy-making process. The demise of the local notable can be tied to the replacement of a local, unregulated political economy controlled by local notables to a political economy that was deeply influenced by the actions of the nation-state or the state or province. As a result local notables found it in their interest to join these parties. And, as political parties became ever more important vehicles for representing policy positions and those policies began to have a bearing on people's lives, local notables who did not join a party quickly lost their relevance.

## PARTIES OF LOCAL NOTABLES AND PROFESSIONALS

Local notables are important in elections and important to parties when the focus of attention is less on the policy positions of the national or regional parties to which the candidates belong and more on the candidates' personal standing in local communities. This may include situations where the candidates are well known as representing specific local factions, clans, or interest groups. Thus, we can think about an electoral politics among local notables for lower-house seats as occurring when district-level competition does not take on the flavor of competition between candidates around ideas associated with state-level or national-level parties, but rather becomes competitive between local elites around local issues and local factions.

Parties of local notables tend to have less programmatic campaign messages across districts and regions and engage in less partisan electoral contests than parties of professionals. It is harder to coordinate candidates on both party labels and ideologies with local notables because they tend to have agendas related to the political economy of the local areas. And, as long as the political economy remains local, there is little sense of urgency about aggregating party votes across districts and regions to take control of government for implementing particular policy.

It is possible to identify periods of history for all four of our countries when local notables dominated party politics in some regions or in the nation as a whole. Several characteristics mark such a period, not all of which are present at any one time and which can vary from country to country. At the extreme, local notables dominate elections, and parties do not exist or are very weak. The United States prior to 1792 is a good example; historians typically call what the country had prior to the 1790s as politics among "personalistic factions" (Main 1973).

In Britain, as Cox (1987a) documents, the period prior to the advent of the efficient secret (cabinet government) in the 1870s and 1880s saw low levels of party discipline in the House of Commons, large proportions of so-called private bills (specific pieces of legislation about per-

sons, companies, or localities) among the total number of pieces of legislation, and low levels of partisanship in the electorate. Members of
Parliament established reputations among constituents largely based on
service to local areas and not based primarily on party labels or contri-
butions to large-scale public policies. To be elected in the mid-nineteenth
century to Parliament a "candidate nearly always needed some money
of his own and the backing of influential men in the constituency. He
was not, as the modern candidate is, *primarily,* the representative of a
potential government" (Hawkins 1998, 24). One reason for this was
that the "the purpose of parties in the constituencies was to win local
elections; no more and no less than this" (24).

Data from early elections in Canada indicate a period when the national parties did not contest elections everywhere, and candidates generally did not feel the need to contest elections in a partisan manner.
Many candidates took on party labels, and there was a modicum of
national-party competition. Within regions, nevertheless, one or the other
national party was dominant, and there was little party competition at
the constituency level. Figure 4.1 shows the proportion of districts
within provinces that the two dominant parties contested. Conservatives
and Liberals contested in less than two-thirds of the districts on average
in the early years of the Dominion.

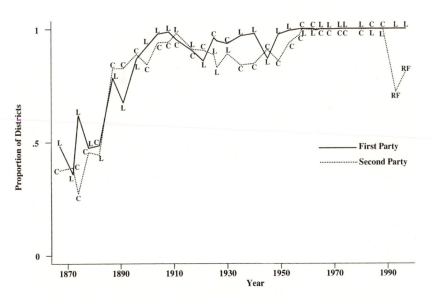

Figure 4.1. The Yearly Average Proportions of Districts within Provinces That
the First and Second Party Contested in Canada

Much of the politics in the decade before and after independence in India occurred among local notables. The Congress Party clearly dominated national politics in the 1950s and 1960s, and while it faced competition from local parties and some local versions of the Socialists, Communists, and the right wing, its position was assured by its ability to control resources at the national level and distribute them strategically. As a nomination by the Congress Party was almost a certain path to election to the Lok Sabha, major competition in this period was among notables for a Congress Party nomination. In the initial period of Congress dominance, the most significant opposition came from within the party itself, especially from disaffected politicians who failed to be nominated by the party as a Congress candidate for the next elections. A Congress Party report in 1953–54 noted, "narrow party reasons and internal factions have in many cases been the cause of the Congress defeats. From almost all the constituencies where the Congress suffered defeats, representations have been received from local Congressmen to the effect that reverses have been due to the bad selection of candidates" (Indian National Congress 1954, 110).[3] A sense of party loyalty was minimal among Congress Party politicians. A substantial number of them, upon failing to receive party nominations, contested elections as representatives of other parties or as independents against the official candidates of the Congress Party.

## AMBITIOUS POLITICIANS

Downs (1957), Schlesinger (1991), and Aldrich (1995) argue persuasively that political parties are first and foremost a means for ambitious politicians to achieve goals. Politicians join parties and run for office under party labels because it would be hard for them to accomplish their goals otherwise. What goals are politicians interested in fulfilling? Winning election and reelection are certainly primary goals for candidates, and it is hard to accomplish much else without meeting those objectives (Mayhew 1974). Contributing to the development of particu-

[3]In the first general elections in Madras "dissatisfaction with the method of selection of Congress candidates for the general elections led to the resignations from the Congress organisation of a few important party members" and the "Tamil Nad Toilers Party may be described as a hotch potch of dissidents from the Congress and the Vaniya Kula Kshatriya Sangha which is essentially a caste association of the Vaniyakula Kshatriyas together with some anti-Congress elements." In Bihar also the rejected candidates offered themselves as independents (Majumdar et al. 1956) while the formation of the KMPP (Kisan Mazdoor Praja Parishad) was largely due to the efforts of Congress dissidents (Kochanek 1968).

lar public policies and bringing back to the electoral constituency some of the pork barrel benefits available to cooperating members of a majority coalition are two other goals. Finally, there are the intrinsic personal benefits of being in public office, including the material perks, the prestige, the fame, and the possibilities for even higher office.

In our view, the histories in our four countries show that it was the second category, policy-related goals, that drove the formation of parties. Political leaders, in pursuit of policy outcomes, used the first and third category of goals to form parties, keep them alive, and create more enduring, extra-electoral organizations. Policy-driven politicians harnessed the more mundane ambitions of local politicians to create political parties.

Duverger ([1954] 1963, xxiv–xxix) suggests there is a common pattern in the genesis of parties. Parliamentary groups and electoral committees come into being somewhat independently of one another. They eventually establish connections, and once those connections become more permanent, there exists a true political party. Chambers (1974, 214) takes issue with this account and says that Duverger's explanation relies solely on an interpretation of the British case. In the United States, parties arose out of a more conscious attempt by the parliamentary groups to establish electoral committees, and the electoral committees hardly emerged independently of the parliamentary groups (Chambers 1974).

Our interpretation of the histories of all four of our countries, including the British case, is more consistent with Chambers. Political leaders sought to link together and coordinate politicians and candidates across vast regions of the country for the purpose of affecting public policy at the national level or at the state or provincial level. Party systems formed and developed under the pressures of competition, as rival teams of leaders reacted to each others' efforts and saw the need to create ever larger organizations. Their efforts to make parties were largely fueled by their fears of the policies that would be adopted by other groups of leaders. In all four countries, however, the attempts by political leaders to form political parties necessitated an incorporation of local notables into political parties.

The point is illustrated in what follows with evidence from the formation of national parties, although state-level and provincial-level parties emerged for the same reasons and by the same means. For example, Quebecois leaders joined together various provincial parties to create the Bloc Quebecois in the late twentieth century to run in national elections, linking together local party leaders to create a broader, province-wide party. The leaders' motivations were to pressure the national government to grant Quebec more autonomy, if not independence, and to provide Quebec with more services and economic benefits. Once again, policy goals were at the center of the party aggregation process.

## NOTABLES AS BUILDING BLOCKS FOR PARTIES

In the early days of party formation local notables held considerable sway in all four countries, although there were significant differences in the role that these notables had in Canada, Great Britain, India, and the United States. In Canada, the power of local notables was at its peak in the elections that were held in pre-Confederation Canada. "Between the 1790s and the 1840s, the ruling elites in Upper and Lower Canada consisted of a series of local notables connected by patronage and influence" (G. Stewart 1986, 97). The most important of these local notables, or patrons as they were known, were often large landlords (Noel 1990, 63). These patrons retained their power through an electoral system that "required open voting at designated polling places, thereby allowing patrons who were so inclined to monitor the votes of their clients" (66). In the 1830s, elections in Upper Canada were "still largely parochial affairs that were beyond the reach of anyone's centralized control. Much depended on how active the mid-level and local patrons were and whether in a given district they were united or squabbling among themselves" (89). There were no clear provincewide issues or ideological conflicts among sets of legislators (90–91).

Attempts at forming national parties by leaders such as John A. Macdonald of the Liberal-Conservative Party "had first to make it [the party] acceptable to a broad constellation of more or less independent local interests . . . even the most sympathetic local patron rarely bestowed his favor without some form of reciprocity" (Noel 1990, 215). In elections in Canada preceding Confederation "Local patrons were still the key to electoral success" (215). Not surprisingly, in the last decade of the Union of the Canadas, the legislature was not composed of political parties as we understand them. Rather, "members of Parliament were typically local magnates, or the nominees of local magnates with their own independent bases of support" and in the "constituencies the old pattern of clientele-based politics, with its intensely local activities, still flourished" (218). As G. Stewart (1986, 62) notes, "within the constituencies, there would often be several party members competing for the same seat in the legislature." Macdonald complained throughout the 1850s that there was a multiplicity of candidates on their side, diluting their strength.

Once Confederation arrived in 1867, elections were still dominated by these local notables who owed little allegiance to a party. Over time, however, the salience and influence of these nonparty politicians declined. One indicator is the mean vote granted to independent candidates across all elections in which an independent candidate contested. This number declines generally, from between .3 to .5 in the nineteenth century, to below .05 by the 1960s (Figure 4.2). The average vote received by independent candidates does not decline monotonically, but over the years it has gradually settled to a very low value. The typical independent candidate becomes less and less relevant to district election outcomes. After the 1960s, serious independent candidates virtually disappear. Another indicator of the decline of independents, shown in the bottom panel of Figure 4.2, is the decline in the total vote granted to independent candidates, as a proportion of the total vote for all candidates. Other than two sharp increases during World War I and during the 1940s, the total number of votes received by independents has declined to a very small value by the late 1950s. Independents gradually lose out to partisan candidates (March 1974, 15).

On top of this, there was the decline of the ministerialists, members of Parliament who supported any government. The last ministerialist was elected in 1921 (March 1974, 16). Finally, the number of elections that have been won uncontested or by acclamation (which suggests the electoral dominance of a local notable in a district) dropped off dramatically in the early twentieth century. The number of members of Parliament who were elected by acclamation dropped from around fifty in the first three elections (1867, 1872, and 1874) to twelve in 1878 and by the 1891 election the number of MPs elected by acclamation was in the single digits and dropped to zero except for 1921 when thirty-two were elected by acclamation.

The power of the local notables in Canada's early period was felt quite keenly in the legislature. Because "many members had been selected on their own merits, or because they were notables" (March 1974, 57), there were "many members of the House of Commons who promised their electors that they would exercise an 'independent' judgment on *all* legislation" (56). The Macdonald government, despite a majority in Parliament, was defeated five times on government bills and some of those who voted against the government "even joined the cabinet later" (56). Initially, then, given the importance of local notables, differences between the parties were never as clear-cut. "[I]n fact, in their early days they never quite became parties at all in the modern sense. There were too many individuals whose allegiance was uncertain—'loose fish,' 'shaky fellows,' 'waiters on Providence'"; members of the legislature passed "with remarkable ease from one political camp to another" (Underhill 1935, 369). In 1867, only 27.5 percent of MPs

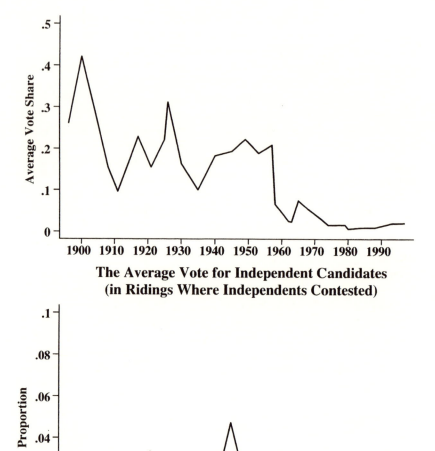

Figure 4.2. Independent Candidates in Canada

never voted against their party. The rest voted at least once against the party with more than 50 percent voting more than twice against the party. In 1963, in contrast, 78 percent voted with party (March 1974).[4]

A similar decline of local notables occurred in Britain. In the early eighteenth century, "in the constituencies the degree of organization remained dependent for the most part upon the individual initiatives of the parliamentary candidates and their local supporters" (Hill 1976, 24). Until the tide turned in the 1870s toward elections as contests between national parties, where candidates mattered much less than the party label on the ballot, British politics was essentially that of local notables. While "there is much evidence to confirm the hypothesis that party in the ideological sense did make a difference in election results [during the reign of Queen Anne beginning in 1702] . . . the vast majority of Englishmen would have been offended by the proclamation of interests and connections as the basis for party distinctions or for choosing MP's (significant though these efforts were in coordinating election efforts)" (Richards 1972, 18).

The power of notables was most apparent in the voting patterns in the House of Commons in the mid-nineteenth century. The governments of the 1850s regularly suffered ten to fifteen defeats a year. Voting along party lines was as little as 37 percent for Liberals and 45 percent for Conservatives in 1850; by 1903 the party voting was far more common, when 88 percent of the Liberals and 83 percent of the Conservatives voted along party lines in the House of Commons (Berrington 1968, 342). Local notables, especially the hereditary political elite, also had dominated the House of Commons in the eighteenth century. In 1774, 82 percent of all members of the House of Commons came from parliamentary families (Wasson 1991, 643). "By 1865 only 165 MPs were the sons, or near relations, of peers; in 1880 the number was still 155" (644). After 1875, however, there is a monotonic decline in the number of parliamentary families as a percentage of all MPs and by the middle of the twentieth century the number had become very small (647).

Concomitant with the waning influence of local notables was a decline in the number of uncontested seats. "Before the Second Reform Act about half the seats were uncontested" (Lloyd 1965, 260). In England in 1859 "of the 136 uncontested constituencies returning 249 members, 43 were divided between the parties, returning 44 Liberals and 49 Conservatives. This practices had almost disappeared before the 1885 redis-

---

[4]This view of Canadian party politics as constituted by "loose fish" is contested by Eggleston (1993). Eggleston observes that there was more cohesion in the legislature than either Underhill or March would acknowledge and that this cohesion appeared quite quickly (Eggleston 1993, 314).

tribution reduced the opportunities for compromise so sharply" (261). In 1906 only 20 seats were uncontested in England—the number for the United Kingdom is higher because of the large number of seats that went uncontested in Ireland (74 seats). As in Canada, there is a sharp decline in the number of independent candidates (data not shown). One reason for this decline in the number of independent candidates was that "an eighteenth-century candidate would not have run in a constituency where he had no hope; he himself could do no good, and he might do harm to his social position by pushing in where he was not wanted. By 1910 contesting a hopeless seat was accepted as a way for a politician to earn the gratitude of his party" (265).

In India the role of local notables in party formation is different largely because the Congress Party was formed in 1885 as an organization to represent the nationalist aspirations of Indians.[5] As the Congress Party geared itself to contest elections for limited self-government under British rule in the 1930s, the party suddenly found a need to build local organizations to contest these elections. The party's ability to reach across the country was limited by the self-interest of those joining the party. Local notables captured the party at the local level to further their own interests (Gallagher, Johnson, and Seal 1973). C. A. Bayly notes that the Congress was essentially a secondary organization that facilitated the persistence of "circumscribed local and sectional aims that derived from lower levels of politics"; the local notables used the Congress Party to pursue their interests just as the Congress Party "employed the backing of the notables to forward their careers in provincial and later in electoral politics" (1975, 4, 66). David Washbrook (1973, 209) also observes that the Congress Party was trying to construct politics on a base of local institutions and that the nationalist movement formed a political system over the district structures that were often independent and could continue to exist without the party. Local notables often kept

---

[5] The Congress Party led the fight for India's independence, and in its role as the organizer of the independence movement it limited the role of local notables. After independence the party undertook quite consciously an effort to transform India economically and socially. The Congress Party was identified with the independence movement until 1947 and an attempt at large-scale transformation of the Indian nation. The early formation of the Congress was, therefore, not similar to the parties that were formed in the early periods of democratic elections in United States, Canada, or Britain because the Congress governed a state that had a much larger role (and greater ambitions of social and economic transformation) in the economy than the governments of Canada in 1867, Britain in the 1880s, and the United States in the 1790s. Despite these differences, once Congress entered the electoral arena it demonstrated some characteristics found in the other cases. The party initially relied on local notables to mobilize support. The party was, as with the parties in other nations, formed from the top down by leaders with policy goals, and other parties in India largely formed in reaction to the national policy adopted by the Congress.

their lines of contact open with several groups of political leaders (Wash-brook 1976, 316). Tomlinson (1976) also points to the critical role of local elites in the creation of the Congress Party during the independence movement. In addition, he notes how the Congress was beholden to the provincial elites for mobilizing support for the party during elections held under British rule.

The role of local notables in the Congress organization persisted after independence. Alliances led by local notables were important to the electoral success of the Congress Party (Kothari 1964; Sisson 1972). Factional struggles (with factions being associated with particular local notables) within the local units of the Congress Party were prevalent in many parts of India. These factions were known as "support[ers of] Congress in one election, and an opposition party in the next" (Weiner 1962). In Gujarat a local notable of a particular caste, the *Khadiata*, was denied a Congress nomination in 1957. He then worked against the Congress Party in those general elections. The candidate was later given a ticket to contest elections from another constituency in the same district and was elected as a member of the Legislative Assembly (MLA) of the Congress Party. The candidate and those associated with him then returned to the Congress's fold and worked for the party (Kothari and Shah 1965).[6] The power of local notables was most pronounced in the areas of India that had been ruled indirectly by the British. After independence was gained, the Congress often relied on the aristocracy of those areas to mobilize support, although quite a few contested against the Congress (Richter 1977).

Over time, however, the power of these notables declined and few independent candidates could win elections without a party label. Figure 4.3 shows the declining role of independents in India. In the top panels, we see that the average number of independent candidates per district and the average vote per independent candidate decline over time. It is interesting to note that the average vote per independent candidate increases, however, in the 1980s and 1990s. This is because the number of independent candidates was low in this period, but those who ran did quite well. Only those with the highest chances of winning chose to run. The proportion of the total vote going to independents and the proportion of seats won by independents both decline over time, as show in the lower right panel. In the lower left panel we see the proportion of independent candidates receiving more than 10 percent of the district vote. That number also declines over time.

---

[6]Weiner (1962) also associates factions within Congress to access to state largesse. Brass (1965; 1981) shows how access to the state was influential in creating splits within a political party.

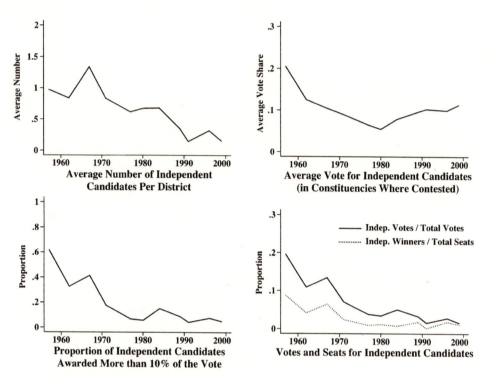

Figure 4.3. Independent Candidates in India

In the United States, local notables were also important before the formation of the national parties. The political bases of these notables were built and maintained on personal loyalties and the established prestige of their breeding or economic stature. "The nationalizing of parties under Washington's Administration marks the beginning of great changes in methods of nomination and campaign. Before this time, politics and office-holding were confined to the 'well-born,' who constituted the enlightened minority." (Luetscher 1903, 1). It is true that established politicians in the United States prior to 1792 were often organized into factions loyal to particular state-level leaders (Chambers 1974), but even into the late 1780s the idea that an enduring partisan organization would control nominations and coordinate policy making in the government would have been incomprehensible. The transition to partisan competition was not easy on politicians, especially the old-timers. Reactions varied; many complained, and some resisted. Thomas Dwight, a veteran Massachusetts Federalist, expressed his disapproval to an invitation to attend a party event, "I shall not be of the party . . . having

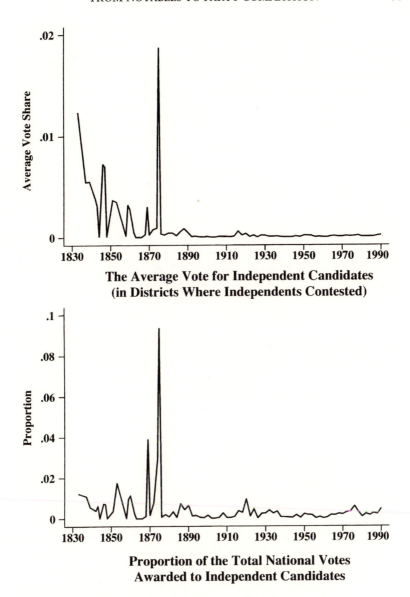

Figure 4.4. Independent Candidates in the United States

inevocably [*sic*] determined to assert and enjoy my own independence"
(Fischer 1974, 237).

With the formation of parties oriented around federal and state policy
these independent notables gradually fell away from the electoral scene,
although some retained prominence in the Democratic and Whig parties.
We see in Figure 4.4 that over the course of the early nineteenth century
the average votes for independent candidates dropped, as did the proportion of total votes for independents. Other than a large increase in
the 1870s, votes for independents come in very low numbers after the
Civil War.

## CONCLUSION

To form political parties in Canada, Great Britain, India, and the United
States, political leaders had to deal with notables who held sway in local
areas. Although these notables were important in the early elections,
political parties gradually came to dominate the electoral politics in all
four countries. Political parties rose to importance because they controlled the policies of the government. As these policies came to be ever
more relevant to voters, the voters turned away from local notables to
political parties. At which level of government these parties were formed
and whether the parties that emerged were national or regional in scope
are the subjects of the next three chapters.

# Chapter 5

# CENTRALIZATION AND PROVINCIALIZATION

IN CHAPTER 3 we developed the argument that the centralization of economic and political power in the national government makes party aggregation easier to accomplish in elections to the national parliament. As policy-making authority migrates toward higher levels of government, voters will be more inclined to choose candidates who adopt party labels at broader levels of aggregation. Candidates will in turn prefer to choose labels that communicate policy positions on issues that are primarily dealt with at the higher levels of government. Smaller, more regionally concentrated parties will be squeezed as voters will increasingly prefer that candidates belong to parties most able to influence policy making at the levels of government that can either regulate economic activity or secure public resources. As a general pattern, we should expect to see the concentration of power at the national level to be accompanied by a nationalization of the party system.

A corollary of this argument suggests that when authority over the issues voters care about is dispersed to lower levels of government or is provincialized (power is dispersed among different governments), regional and state-based or province-based parties can more easily find the political space to form and survive. This is especially true in federal systems where state-based or province-based parties can control state or provincial governments.

In this chapter we examine empirically the first part of this argument, the independent variable, if you will. We categorize eras in Canada, Great Britain, India, and the United States into centralizing and provincializing periods. In the next two chapters we devote attention to the second part of the argument, the dependent variable, which illustrates how the party systems responded during and after these periods.

Federalism is often presented either as an equilibrium solution to the problem of how diverse nations or cultural groups can band together to achieve a common purpose while retaining their individuality (Elazar 1987) or as an "unstable halfway house between unified national government and an alliance among separate sovereign states" (Eskridge and Ferejohn 1994, 1355–56). A surviving federation is regarded by some as an equilibrium in the sense that it stabilizes between two undesirable outcomes; one has it spinning apart with the constituent units going their own ways, and the other has it unifying to such a degree that the constituent units become completely amalgamated into an undifferentiated polity (Bednar 2001; de Figueiredo and Weingast 2002; and Riker 1964). Too much drift in either direction would lead to the end of the federation. The notion of a federal equilibrium is useful, and it makes sense to the extent that it refers to the stability of the component units of the federation. Yet, in federations the relationship between the central government and the constituent units rarely remains still. This relationship is always changing, and the bargaining between the various levels of government never stops, creating dynamic patterns of centralization and provincialization within countries (Riker 1964; Gibson 2003).

In each of our four countries, the relationship between the national government and governments at lower levels has been defined by broad historical trends. These trends, as we demonstrate in the next several chapters, correspond to broad changes in party systems. It would be interesting to examine year-on-year trends, or changes in direction many times over the course of a decade. For example, data on the effective number of parties at the national level from the nineteenth century in the United States, as shown in Figure 1.4, indicate many peaks and valleys, and there is some suggestion in the next chapter that a number of these jumps correspond to brief episodes of centralization and provincialization. We do not, however, seek to explain each twist and turn in the party systems, except to say that provincialization provides a space for subnational parties to survive. This is reflected in more frequent spikes in the number of parties in decentralized periods than in centralized periods. Rather, we focus on trends that happen over many years, which are deep and consequential and have profound effects for the political and economic life of the country. With that in mind, we examine our four countries in turn.

For each country, we can divide time periods into three categories: clearly centralizing, clearly provincializing, and ambiguous. We choose to use the word *provincialization* rather than decentralization because the former is less suggestive of an act on the part of the central government to devolve authority to a lower level. Authority often passes to lower levels of government as an unintended consequence of political and economic changes.

The ambiguity in typing some of the periods stems from several factors. It could be that the country is centralizing in some policy areas and provincializing in others, where the balance is difficult to discern for contemporary commentators during the process and for a historian of the era after the process. It could also be that the movements between centralization and provincialization are fluctuating rapidly so the responses of the political system—such as the rise or fall of regional parties—do not have time to take root and thrive. Finally, it could be that there is truly an equilibrium where neither centralization nor provincialization is occurring. This last pattern seems unlikely to endure in any federation, but it is conceivable, at least in the short term.

While we discuss periods of centralization and provincialization in all four nations, it is important to keep in mind that governments are not spigots that can be turned on or off. In any nation where there are many levels of government, all levels continue to play a role. In periods of centralization, the provincial governments continue assigned activities and in periods of provincialization the national government is not completely irrelevant. Still, the relative importance of each level of government to voters and candidates has varied over time in all four countries.

## THE RELATIVE AUTHORITY OF DIFFERENT LEVELS OF GOVERNMENT

For parties to aggregate, either at the national or the provincial levels, what matters are voters' perceptions of which levels of government make decisions that are salient to the voters. When voters are choosing candidates in lower-house elections, how much does it matter to them that the candidates are affiliated with groups of policy makers who decide issues at the national level? How comfortable are voters if the candidates are affiliated with groups of policy makers deciding issues primarily at the state or province level or local level?

Ideally, data would enable us to draw contrasts between different eras by comparing the degree to which *voters think* the national or provincial governments control policies voters care about. Unfortunately, it is difficult to obtain comparative survey data on voter perceptions of which level of government has more authority over the issues that concern them. Survey data are unavailable over long enough periods—such as for the United States from 1788 to 1990—to test our claims about changes in centralization and provincialization of party systems. There have been a few instances of appropriate questions asked of large populations in Canada and India, but these have been sporadic and are not helpful insofar as the surveys do not correspond to the eras of centralization and provincialization in the nations under study. Two surveys, for example, deal with the relative role of the state and national governments in India, but both were carried out in periods of provincialization—1967 and 2001. In our view, the actual votes cast by citizens in an election are valuable indicators of where voters think authority rests. If voters believe that the government of a state or province has more authority relative to the national government, they are more likely to vote for a party that can control state or provincial government than if the reverse were true. How do we know which level of government has more authority?

The centralization and/or provincialization of political and economic authority is too multifaceted a process to peg it to a few statistics over the range of years in our study. To determine which level of government exercises greater authority in which eras, we rely on four criteria: changes in constitutional-legal authority; threats to the integrity of the nation-state that invite responses by governments; fluctuations in the economic role of the national and/or provincial governments; and alterations in the size of national and provincial governments.

We use three factors to ascertain changes in the constitutional-legal authority that is vested in different levels of government. First, we explore where constitutionally mandated powers rest. Second, we evaluate the frequency of preemption by the central government of decisions by state or provincial governments and/or the tendencies of the central government to use constitutional authority to usurp the power of the state or provincial governments. Third, we analyze historic court decisions that fundamentally altered the legal authority of state or provincial governments to regulate economic activity.

Threats to the integrity of the nation-state, such as war and secession, typically invite responses by the central government that result in centralization. There are, however, cases—such as in Canada in recent decades—where such threats have led to a devolution of authority following interprovincial bargaining. Significant variance exists over time and between the countries on the frequency of such threats. Over long spans of time in some countries, no such threats occurred.

We employ the regulation of economic activity and the role of the government in economic development as the criteria to determine the relative role of the state or provincial and national governments in the economy. In all four countries, the role of the government in the economy has generally increased over time, yet the latitude granted in some of the countries to state or provincial governments to pursue independent economic policy has oscillated.

We track the relative size of state or provincial government to the national government using some quantitative measures—specifically, government spending by and the number of public employees at various levels of government—and by examining the degree of autonomy granted to lower-level governments for social welfare policies and in establishing public corporations. The quantitative data are sparse for earlier periods, but we present these data for later periods from all four countries.

When scholars in the public economics literature analyze quantitative data on centralization and provincialization using time-series, cross-sectional techniques, they typically use data from Organization for Economic Cooperation and Development (OECD) countries since World War II. In these cases, the accounting standards for public spending and taxes are somewhat uniform and the time frames fairly tight (see, e.g., Panizza 1999). Unfortunately, it is extremely difficult, if not impossible, to rely too much on aggregate economic data from our four countries to assess the degree of concentration of power to the national government.

Centralization and its converse, provincialization, of political or economic authority are not easy to measure quantitatively in any systematic manner to compare equivalent trends across our four countries. Such an analysis is hopeless if the goal is to compare patterns of centralization across different countries using the same measure, and it is extremely difficult even if the goal is merely to track a specific measure over time within a country. Let us say, for example, that we wished to compare the ratio of spending by national governments in our four countries with spending by state or provincial or local governments as a measure of centralization and track this ratio over time. There are a host of problems with this approach, most arising from the fact that obtaining comparable cross-national economic data on provincial and federal government spending prior to World War II is virtually impossible.

First, and most generally, it turns out that data on government finances are quite limited over long spans of time, although we can make some use of these. For example, we have not been able to find enough adequate public finance data for Britain during two periods, World War I and World War II. Not only do these two eras comprise a substantial portion of British history in the first part of the twentieth century, they are also precisely the moments when there was much consequential activity in the role and size of government.

Second, for the data that are available, different countries use different accounting standards, keeping certain spending categories off the books or folding them into other categories in ways that are extremely difficult to track. Data on defense spending and broader spending on war efforts, which are not counted as defense spending, are intertwined and present the most difficult challenges. There are others as well. For instance, countries sometimes channel national spending through lower levels of government, but it is not clear always whether the national government granted any authority to the localities to spend the funds as they wished. Thus, the decision to factor in or out transfers from national governments to local governments becomes particularly difficult under the circumstances. Did the transfers come with strings attached? Were they more like block grants to be spent at the discretion of local governments?

Third, not only is there variation in what the data mean across countries, there can also be variation in what the data mean within countries over time. All countries change accounting categories from time to time, and these changes not only are complex to understand and account for but also may correspond to or overlap with eras in party politics. In some cases it is impossible to separate out the accounting changes from the real political and economic changes. Moreover, we are trying to compare centralization over broad time scales stretching back to the nineteenth century, and were we to restrict our analysis to the years after World War II, when accounting standards for three of the four countries (Canada, Britain, and the United States) were more uniform, we would not be able to analyze a good deal of the interesting variation that occurs in party politics in those countries prior to World War II. India reports voluminous public finance data, and these data are generally reliable in comparisons over time within India, but over the course of the decades following independence, India has shifted its accounting categories. For instance, the categories of expenditures that compose state government spending on agriculture have been changed, making direct comparisons on government spending on agriculture difficult between the 1960s and the 1980s.

Because we cannot conduct clean statistical tests with quantitative data to compare our four countries over the appropriate time spans, we piece together facts about centralization and provincialization using whatever data and historical materials are available. We have relied on accounts from historians and some of our own data collections and analysis efforts to categorize specific eras in these countries.

Consistent with our own primary research on data and texts, our survey of the political and economic history of all four countries reveals that there are few qualitative disagreements among scholars about when any particular country in its history was experiencing a trend toward political and economic centralization. For many cases the historians of the period share a consensus on which level of government had more authority even though the official data on public finances are not clear in indicating whether provincial governments retain substantial authority over a policy area. There are also some ambiguous periods, where historians themselves are divided, or historians indicate that the period was neither centralizing nor provincializing.

There is another important point we wish to make on measurement and the discussions in the remainder of this chapter. We are seeking to establish periods of centralization and provincialization in four countries with different histories and somewhat different political systems. The mechanisms for centralization and provincialization can be different across the countries. In some eras in some countries, centralization occurred through the establishment of statutes mandating welfare policies. In others, it occurred through the waging of war or the establishment of emergency powers in the executive, and in still others resulted from court decisions, which enabled central governments to encroach on the authority of states or provinces. We rely on the kinds of events and data that are prevalent in the established, recognized histories of these countries to make our case. The symmetrical application of evidence across countries would be not only impossible because of the limited availability or comparability of data but also misleading due to the different mechanisms for change in intergovernmental relations in each of the four countries.

We now discuss our countries and their eras. We do not proceed chronologically in each country but rather proceed categorically within each era in each country. That is, for each kind of era we discuss the relevant indicators of centralization or provincialization in that country: constitutional and legal authority, threats to national integrity, development policy, and the size of government.

## CANADA

The modern federal state of Canada came into existence with the adoption of the British North American (BNA) Act of 1867. The Dominion government (as the government of Canada was called in the years following the adoption of the act) played a key role in the economic development and territorial expansion of the Confederation, especially the integration of vast areas of western Canada. Consequently, the Dominion government early on played a much larger role in the political and economic life of the nation relative to the provinces. Nevertheless, provincial governments had control over key aspects of their economies, and authority was granted to the provinces under the BNA Act because of the need to protect the rights of French speakers, to manage religious divisions between Protestants and Catholics, and to complete the union of Lower and Upper Canada. As economic conditions changed, provinces used the authority granted to them in the 1867 act to assume a larger role for themselves in the economic life of the nation. Despite brief periods of centralization generated by the two world wars, Canada had entered by the 1960s a phase known as "province building." By the end of the twentieth century, Canada was one of the most decentralized nation-states in the world.

### Centralizing Period, 1867–1921

Two periods in Canadian history are generally regarded as having the greatest degree of central authority over provinces. The first extended from the founding of the Confederation in 1867 to the period immediately after World War I. The second was during the two decades following the onset of World War II, although the centralization that followed World War II was brief and had little impact on the trend toward provincialization that had begun earlier.

"The intention [behind the Confederation, established in 1867] was to form a strong federation in which the central government played the dominant role . . . this was intended to be a centralized federation, with only such powers granted to the provinces as seemed absolutely necessary at the time" (McInnis 2000, 92). From 1867 to the late 1910s the central government in Canada controlled most authority relative to the provincial governments.

The Dominion government exercised more political control over the legislative actions of the provinces during the first fifty years of Confederation than at any other time in Canadian political history. Under the provisions of the BNA Act of 1867, "the Dominion may disallow any provincial Act within one year after its receipt at Ottawa; a lieutenant-governor may reserve any provincial bill for the signification of the governor-general's pleasure, . . . and a lieutenant-governor has a legal right to refuse assent outright" (Forsey 1938, 48). The first premier, John Macdonald, was aware of this right and asserted the authority of his government by stating in 1868 that "under the present constitution of Canada, the general government will be called upon to consider the propriety of allowance or disallowance of provincial Acts much more frequently than Her Majesty's Government has been with respect to colonial enactments" (48). Between 1867 and 1920, the Dominion exercised its power of disallowance ninety-six times, on a great number and variety of grounds. In sharp contrast, between 1920 and 1937, there were four cases of disallowance, all between July 31, 1922, and April 29, 1924 (50). A detailed study of the Dominion-Ontario relationship notes that disallowance (and even the threat of disallowance) largely ceased to be a means by which the federal government could exercise discipline over the provinces after 1910" (Armstrong 1981, 65).

The Dominion government's role was reinforced by the courts in this period, although the courts promoted more provincialization toward the end of the period. F. P. Varcoe divided the eighty years during which the Judicial Committee was the court of last resort in Canadian constitutional cases into three distinct periods: the "Colonial Period," extending from 1874 to 1912; the "Provincial Period," which began in 1912 and stressed the autonomy of the provincial legislatures"; and finally a "National Period," extending from 1932 to 1954, which followed the passage of the Statute of Westminster during which the committee stressed, and to some extent restored, the preeminence of the Parliament of Canada (cited in Hopkins 1968, 207–8).

## DEVELOPMENT POLICIES

The real importance of the Dominion government in this period, however, lay in its role in the development of Canada. The Dominion government was the major force behind the development of railways[1] and provided economic support for the geographic expansion of the state to the west.[2] For approximately the first fifty years of Confederation the policies of the Dominion government "gripped the imagination of the people" and, more concretely, gave employment to labor and capital (Royal Commission on Dominion-Provincial Relations 1940, 134).

It was well understood that the Dominion government was the engine of development policy. If private interests felt that their interests were not being represented adequately in the provinces, they also turned to the Dominion government for protection. For example, in 1900 the Ontario government imposed a tax on all nickel ore exported from Canada and refined outside of the British Empire (Armstrong 1981, 43). This legislation was opposed by the Canadian Copper Company, which lobbied Ottawa for relief (44). The Dominion government did not disallow the legislation but put enough pressure on the provincial government that the legislation was not proclaimed (47). At the beginning of the twentieth century "clashes over company regulation occurred on several fronts." Most of the conflict "was primarily provoked by private interests eager to exploit the profit potential of the new hydroelectric technology in supplying power and transportation services. . . . Faced with a provincial government determined to regulate utility companies, ambitious entrepreneurs sought to escape local control for the more hospitable climate of Ottawa, which seemed less disposed to interfere in their affairs" (86).

---

[1]The expansion of the railroad that created a national economy in Canada was the result of a proactive Dominion policy (Royal Commission on Dominion-Provincial Relations 1940, pp 69–71).

[2]The "settlement of the Prairies took place within the framework of the *national* policies of all-Canadian transportation and protective tariffs" (ibid., 64; emphasis added). As a result of these policies, the "economically loose transcontinental area was transformed into a highly integrated national economy" (68). Support for the development and occupation of the frontier and urbanization in eastern Canada came from the Dominion government, which experienced, consequently, a large increase in government expenditures between 1896 and 1913 (80). Dominion expenditures in this period almost quadrupled whereas provincial expenditures only trebled (80). This rapid growth in government expenditures was made possible by the wheat boom and the general upswing in the Canadian economy between 1896 and 1913.

SIZE OF GOVERNMENTS

The role of the Dominion government relative to that of the provinces was also pronounced in economic policy. Section 91 of the BNA Act established exclusive federal jurisdiction over monetary policy (Campbell 1995, 188). The federal government also had unlimited taxing power over indirect taxes. Provinces were given the authority to levy direct taxes, although it was understood at the time of Confederation that the main source of revenue for the provinces would be the Dominion government and not direct taxes (Royal Commission on Dominion-Provincial Relations 1940, 44).[3]

The Dominion government retained its position of authority because of its control over finances. At the moment of Confederation it was agreed that revenues raised through customs and excise duties were to be transferred to the Dominion government. This left the provincial governments with less than a fifth of their former revenue (Royal Commission on Dominion-Provincial Relations 1940, 44). As a result, the provinces often could not afford to undertake all of the projects that the courts were ruling were their responsibilities, so the Dominion government, therefore, was able to regain much of its lost influence through its "power of the purse and a variety of tax-renting, revenue sharing, and conditional grant schemes" (32–33). The primary reason for this was that since a goal at the time of Confederation was the creation of a national economy this "meant that not only customs but also excise duties had to be given to the federal government; customs for obvious reasons and excise because otherwise provincial governments would be likely to use duties of this kind as an indirect way of protecting their own industries" (32–33) Dominion control over excise taxes was questioned by the provinces. The courts ruled in favor of the Dominion in the case of these duties. In *Severn v. The Queen* (1878), "The Court decided in favor of the Dominion, because it felt that the Dominion excise tax legislation in question was constitutionally permitted, and it ruled, therefore, that Ontario could not affect the Dominion's right to regulate the sale of liquor" (Mahler 1987, 35).[4]

By 1874, therefore, the real basis of Dominion-provincial financial

---

[3]Federal and provincial governments, however, did share some jurisdiction in important areas of expenditure (Campbell 1995, 188–89).

[4]This decision pushed the balance of financial power in the direction of the Dominion for "customs and excise duties yielded over 80 per cent of the revenue of the three provinces that joined the initial confederation, and not even the most enthusiastic advocates of centralization thought that the federal government would become responsible for 80 per cent of their expenditures. After the delegates from the Maritimes had emphasized the virtual impossibility of imposing direct taxes sufficient to bridge the gap, the Quebec Conference

relations had been established for the next half a century. The Dominion government derived the greater part of its revenue from customs and excise duties, which—partly because a policy of protection was adopted in 1879—were to prove an adequate source for the Dominion until the outbreak of World War I. The provinces in 1874 derived 57 percent of their income from federal subsidies (Royal Commission on Dominion-Provincial Relations 1940, 65).

Federal subsidies remained relatively static between 1873 and 1905 (Eggleston and Kraft 1939, 19), despite two provincial conferences and petitions that sought larger subsidies. There was a general upward revision of these subsidies in 1907 following an improvement in Dominion finances, although this system of subsidies remained essentially unchanged until 1938–39 (34). In addition to subsidies, the Dominion government gave conditional grants to the provinces to help the latter meet their responsibilities. These conditional grants were first introduced in 1912–13 by the Dominion government, which instead of increasing the subsidies for provincial governments, offered the provinces conditional grants. The first was a scheme of assistance for agricultural education followed by grants for the employment service of Canada. In all cases, grants were made available only after bilateral arrangements were reached on how the money was to be spent and the conditions that a province had to fulfill to receive federal aid (Gettys 1938, 19). As Gettys (1938) observes, the Dominion government exercised a fair degree of control over the administration of the grant but less control over provincial administration of conditional grants introduced in the 1920s and 1930s, such as those for venereal disease control, old age pensions, and unemployment and farm relief.

## Provincializing Period, 1960–2000

### CONSTITUTIONAL AND LEGAL AUTHORITY

Significant constitutional changes in this period signal the far greater authority that provincial governments now exercise in Canada. The major change was the adoption of the 1982 Constitutional Act that allowed Canada to amend its own constitution (until 1982 the Canadian constitution could only be amended by an act of the British Parliament). After 1982 provinces came to play a more important role in the amendment process than ever before. A constitutional amendment now needs the approval of the legislatures of two-thirds of the provinces, provided

---

had to face the fact that the need for Dominion subsidies to the provincial governments was inherent in the plan for confederation" (Mahler 1987, 52).

those provinces have 50 percent of the population of the country. Further, unanimous consent among provinces was required for changes on matters such as the composition of the Supreme Court. The other major change with the 1982 act was that provinces, for the first time, gained constitutionally guaranteed control over their natural resources. Each province could now determine the export of primary production from its mines, oil wells, and forests to any other part of Canada provided, of course, that it did not discriminate against other parts of Canada in prices or supplies. Further, provinces were also allowed to levy indirect taxes on its products from those natural resources, taxes that were formerly the preserve of the federal government.

In contrast to the period of centralization, the role of courts in adjudicating federal provincial relations was also limited in this period. "The courts, and in particular the Supreme Court of Canada, have not had a decisive impact on Canadian federalism since the Judicial Committee of the Privy Council was displaced as the final appellate tribunal in Canadian constitutional cases in 1949." Moreover, "Ottawa and the provinces have shown a marked preference for intergovernmental negotiation over judicial decision in managing their conflicts with each other and appear to regard the submission of one of their disputes to the courts something like an ultimate weapon when one party or other has failed to come to an acceptable result through intergovernmental bargaining" (Smiley 1988, 93).

### DEVELOPMENT POLICIES

The provinces also expanded their own role in the provincial economy beginning in the 1960s. In all provinces there has been an increase in the number of public corporations. Chandler (1982, 739) attributes this increase in provincial public corporations to the general phenomenon of province building. "Increased resources as well as a heightened consciousness of provincial interests have been the basis of a willingness to use state business as an element of industrial strategy. This has meant not only a continuation of the use of facilitative corporations but also an increase in the more intrusive nationalistic type. Since 1960 both the left and non-left have used public enterprise as an instrument of nationalism. The nationalistic crown corporation reflects the provinces' response to problems of economic development in vastly different economic and political milieux."[5]

In a white paper issued in March 1965, for example, the province of Quebec announced that it would ensure a minimum standard of services

---

[5] By nationalism, Canadians mean the kind present in Quebec, which can be considered regionalism in other contexts.

for all citizens regardless of the locality in which they lived; as a result of this policy declaration, the provincial government assumed control over education, social welfare, health, and all assessment and tax collection (Dyck 1986, 152–53). Starting in the 1960s, moreover, the Quebec government created a number of public-sector corporations, such as Hydro Quebec, Sidbec (the Quebec steel operation), and the Asbestos Corporation. The provincial government also ran an auto insurance corporation, and the government was involved in mineral exploitation, petroleum, and forestry as well. Most important of all was the role played by the Caisse de Depot et Placement du Quebec, which managed funds collected by the Quebec pension plan and had assets worth $20 billion (Canadian). It was "an important instrument of provincial economic policy" (194).

### SIZE OF GOVERNMENTS

Beginning with the early 1960s, there has also been a greater transfer of funds from the federal government to the provinces for a wide variety of social programs. "The federal government, since 1957, more than quadrupled the amount of tax room made available to the provinces in the personal income tax field, partly by means of tax transfers enabling provinces to finance expenditures in areas of social policy" (Leach 1988, 12). This fiscal provincialization, on the expenditure side, began in the late 1950s and extended into the 1960s. The federal government's share as a proportion of total provincial and federal government expenditures dropped by 20 percent in the decade from the 1960 to 1970. Figure 5.1 details the declining fiscal relevance of the federal government. In 1921 the federal government spent eighty-three cents on every dollar spent by the provincial and federal governments. That number had dropped to less than fifty cents per dollar by 2001.

In 1974 provincial government expenditures totaled 39 percent of all government expenditures. By 1993 the proportion of provincial expenditures had grown to 41 percent, and in 2001–2 provinces were responsible for almost half (49.2 percent) of all total government expenditures, a figure that includes municipal governments.[6]

The federal government also gave increasing room to the provincial governments to set tax rates and make social policy. In February 1961 the federal government made an offer to allow "taxing room for the provinces" with each province free to legislate its own rates with the federal government and to collect taxes. This offer recognized provincial autonomy and provincial needs (Martin 1974, 11). Provinces were also

[6]Source: Canadian National Statistics, available at www.statcan.cn, accessed 15 March 2003.

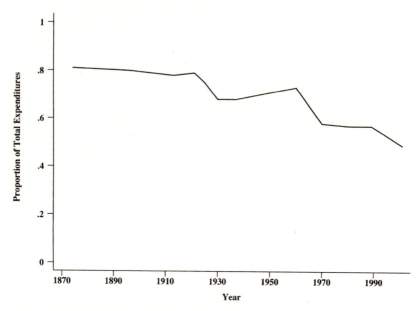

Figure 5.1. Federal Expenditure as a Proportion of Federal and Provincial Expenditures in Canada

allowed to opt out of federal social programs. "In August of 1964 Pearson made good on a Liberal Party platform which had first been announced in the House of Commons in July of the preceding year by writing all Premiers offering them the opportunity to opt out of certain programs. . . . The most important program was hospital insurance, but old age assistance, blind and disabled pension allowances, the welfare portion of unemployment assistance, vocational training, and health grants were also included. If a province opted out of all five programs, it would receive an additional 20 points of equalized personal income tax in lieu of conditional grants. Only Quebec took advantage of the offer" (Martin 1974, 18–19).

Further provincialization occurred with the 1977 Fiscal Arrangements Act. This act, which outlined the arrangements between Ottawa and the provincial governments, made concessions to provincial demands for "tax room, assured federal support of major social programs, such as hospital insurance, medicare, and post-secondary education. Federal expenditures in these areas became tied to the rate of growth in the Canadian economy rather than, as before, to the amount of provincial expenditure therein. Thus, the provinces emerged from the 1977 negotiations with distinct advantages vis-à-vis the federal government. Their revenues were increased, they achieved greater program flexibility, and federal dictation and monitoring of how they spent their money were dramatically reduced. But, even before the 1977 Act went into effect, the provinces had become fiscally much stronger vis-à-vis the federal government" (Martin 1974, 12–13).

Provincialization continued in the 1980s when the federal government began using "enveloping," a process by which, "like the block grant concept in the United States, ... provincial governments [have] more say in expending federal funds than they would have if every project were funded individually by Ottawa" (Leach 1988, 14). By 2000 the bulk of federal transfers to the provinces was unconditional and did not impose significant restrictions on provincial autonomy. "In 1981–1982, for instance, some 81.6 percent of all fiscal transfers from Ottawa to subnational governments were unconditional" (Smiley 1988, 70).

Regarding social policy, Banting (1995) observes the greater importance of the provincial governments during this era. "Fiscal constraint at the center and continued federal-provincial jurisdictional battles together have begun to narrow the federal presence in social policy" (290). "Federal expenditure restraint is in tension with the politics of national integration. As part of the effort to control the deficit, every federal budget after 1986 increased transfers to the provinces for health care and postsecondary education by less than the rate of inflation; the 1991 budget went further and announced that support would be frozen completely until 1994–95, and the 1995 budget shows even sharper cuts over the next couple of years" (290). Fiscal provincialization has weakened "the nationalizing role of the welfare state. At the level of program design, restraint clearly limits federal influence over provincial policies" (290–91). In Banting's opinion, this fiscal provincialization raises "the prospect of growing regional diversity in Canadian social programs, but an even more fundamental outcome stands out: the erosion of federal support for major social programs such as health care, university education, and social welfare reduces the stake that Canadians have in the continued strength of the central government and of the federation itself" (292–93).

Since the 1980s the role of the federal government has declined unilaterally (Banting 1995, 299). Provincial governments gained more authority over social policy when in 1999 the federal government and nine provinces and two territories (but not Quebec) signed a Social Union agreement. Under this agreement, the federal government "is to respect the priorities of provincial and territorial governments for cost-shared or block-funded programs. It is also to consult with other governments about funding changes or social transfers one year in advance of any changes, and the federal government will not introduce changes without getting the consent of a majority of provincial governments. Provincial and territorial governments are allowed to invest program funds in ways that reflect the spirit of the new programs and will receive their share of the funding" (Rice and Prince 2000, 120–21). Similar patterns occurred in housing policy. Carroll and Jones (2000, 279) note that from 1945 to 1968 it was the federal government that took leadership in housing policy, whereas from 1986 onward housing policy was solely the responsibility of the provincial governments.

Another indicator of the increased role of the provincial governments in this period is reflected in the dramatic growth in the number of provincial employees starting in the 1960s, especially when compared with the number federal employees. As Figure 5.2 indicates, there has been a general increase in the number of federal and provincial employees since 1960 with the number of provincial employees increasing most dramatically since 1982. Between 1982 and 1991, the number of provincial employees almost doubled while the number of federal employees only increased by about 16 percent. In 2001 the number of provincial employees was well over a million while the number of federal employees remained almost the same as in 1982.

In this provincializing period, the provinces have clearly grown stronger relative to the national government. Yet, despite the increasing importance of provincial governments, it would be remiss to assert that the

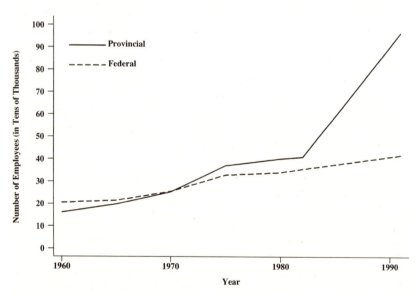

Figure 5.2. Public-Sector Employment in Canada

federal government did not have any role at all to play—especially in social policy. In May 1966 "the federal government announced the program of universal compulsory Medicare to go into effect on July 1, 1967. Ontario, along with all other provinces except Saskatchewan, opposed it" (Martin 1974, 23). The battle over Medicare "was a struggle between a federal government with a very popular political proposal and the provincial governments who knew they could not afford that proposal" (25). "One point became abundantly clear as a result of the federal government's Medicare proposal. In spite of the almost unanimous opposition of the provincial governments to the federal proposal, the fact remained that there was no inter-provincial mechanism which could prevent the proposal from becoming a reality" (26). "Medicare was a major blow to federal-provincial relations, especially at the political level. The provincial premiers could see that Medicare was politically popular and impossible to resist. But they also saw it as being put forward by an irresponsible federal government which would gain political kudos but would not share adequately in the real costs. Furthermore, provincial governments were becoming increasingly concerned about shared-cost programs which, even without Medicare, were 2.5 times larger than unconditional grants to the provinces" (26).

Various programs introduced during the late 1950s and the 1960s also reaffirmed the role of the federal government. These programs were often initiated in response to the special economic needs of particular economic sectors and areas of the country. For example, "the Atlantic Provinces Adjustment Grants above equalization payments were enacted in 1957, as were special federal payments to those provinces for special developmental projects. In 1961 the Agricultural Rehabilitation and Development Act (ARDA), concerned with low income and land utilization of rural area, was introduced; and in 1965 an area development incentives scheme intended to stimulate investment from the private sector was established. Another federal initiative—the Atlantic Development Board, 1962—was designed to improve the industrial infrastructure of the Atlantic region. And still another—Fund for Rural Economic Development (FRED), 1966—attempted to deal with problems associated with chronic rural poverty which could not be covered under the more general ARDA scheme" (Savoie 1981, 15). "Partly to promote a more coordinated approach to economic development and partly because the recently elected Trudeau government wanted to give an even higher priority to federal attempts to reduce regional economic disparities, which would in turn increase the federal visibility in this area, DREE was established in 1969. Senior DREE officials, however, stressed in our interviews that a principal motivation behind its establishment was the desire to elevate planning for economic development from the provincial to the regional level" (15). "In establishing DREE, most federal programs and initiatives concerned with economic development, including ARDA and FRED, were consolidated under one department" (16).

Still, by the 1980s Canada had entered its most provincialized phase. The role of the federal government by 2000 was considerably circumscribed compared with earlier eras. The Constitution Act of 1982 gave the provinces control over energy, a key economic resource that until then had been the preserve of the federal government. Section 92A of the act listed key areas of new provincial legislative jurisdiction that included exploration for nonrenewable natural resources. A second clause also gave provincial legislatures jurisdiction over laws relating to export of primary production from nonrenewable natural resources and forestry resources and in the production of electricity (Mahler 1987, 139). As Smiley (1988, 91) states, "the story of Canadian federalism from the late 1950s onward is that of the relative weakening of the power of the national government and the strengthening of that of the provinces." And, Perry (1997), in a wide-ranging study of the financial arrangements of Canadian Federation, too, regards this period as one in which Ottawa is descendant.

## Ambiguous Period, 1921–1960

We categorize the period from 1921 through the early 1960s as ambiguous. During this period both levels of government continued to play a significant role, but which level had more authority and was more relevant to voters is not immediately apparent.

### CONSTITUTIONAL AND LEGAL AUTHORITY

Court decisions had the effect of encouraging greater provincial authority in this period. Toward the end of the Colonial Period (1912 or so), courts began a process of provincialization. There was a marked tendency on the part of the Judicial Committee to favor provincial autonomy at the expense of parliamentary sovereignty. "The eminent Lord Chancellor, Viscount Haldane, wrote the reasons for judgment in twenty-five cases, most of which disclose a clear and consistent purpose of protecting provincial autonomy from federal encroachment" (Mahler 1987, 213). With the express purpose of protecting the authority of provincial governments, the court in 1935 struck down efforts by the federal government to introduce national social policy. Provincial responsibility for social service, they said, emanated from the BNA. The constitution had thrown "the responsibility of public welfare on the provinces (and municipalities) and within the limits of their resources they tried to meet it. These activities brought the provincial governments into a closer relationship with the people. In their intimate contact with the movements and tendencies of the time, the provincial governments added greatly to their economic and social importance and *thus to their political power and prestige"* (Royal Commission on Dominion-Provincial Relations 1940, 112–13; emphasis added).

### ROLE OF GOVERNMENTS

By the 1920s provincial governments had also gathered substantial authority over a range of issues, including social services. In 1913, 28 percent of all welfare spending in Canada was undertaken by the provincial governments. By 1921 this share had risen to 34 percent, while over this same period the Dominion share dropped from 17 to 13 percent (Royal Commission on Dominion-Provincial Relations 1940, 106). By 1930 provinces were spending more on social services than any other level of government (42 percent as compared with the 18 percent share of the Dominion government).

Provincial governments had also gradually extended the range of their activities. "Beginning with Ontario in 1884, followed by Quebec in 1885, Manitoba in 1900, and the other provinces later, the provinces enacted Factory Acts regulating the working conditions of industry" (Rice and Prince 2000, 39). "Workers' compensation was introduced, initially in Ontario in 1914 and followed soon after by Nova Scotia (1915), British Columbia (1916), Alberta and New Brunswick (1918), and Manitoba (1920). About a decade later Saskatchewan (1929) and Quebec (1931) enacted comparable legislation, and much later Prince Edward Island (1949) and Newfoundland (1950) did the same" (40).

The report of the Royal Commission on Dominion-Provincial Relations (1940) notes that by the mid-1920s provincial governments had "assumed a larger importance in the daily lives of the people. At the Dominion-Provincial conference of 1927 Premier Tascherea pointed out that 'provinces were more in contact with the people, educating them, building them roads, and looking after their health.'" The report goes on to say that "the popular basis of provincial political power was being solidly laid at a time when the Dominion was losing its intimate touch with the people, and when its developmental projects no longer gripped the imagination and no longer gave increasing employment to labour and capital" (134). To meet these increased responsibilities, the provincial governments introduced direct taxes. These ventures into "new fields of taxation date from the 1890s after unsuccessful demands for subsidy revision" (64). British Columbia and Prince Edward Island developed an income tax while the other provinces relied exclusively on taxes on corporations and succession duties that in 1913 yielded 26 percent of the total provincial revenues (87).

SIZE OF GOVERNMENTS

As their activities increased in scope, government expenditures at both levels also increased. In the years before 1914, "the growth of Dominion and provincial expenditures was at about the same rate, and the distribution of functions and fiscal resources between the governments appeared to be in balance" (Maxwell 1936, 374). Since then, however, "the provinces found it expedient to enlarge their welfare expenditures. Mothers' allowances and old age pensions were provided; activities relating to health were extended; educational facilities were improved; the remarkable changes in transportation forced heavy expenditure upon highways. In short, the provincial governments were faced by new responsibilities" (375). Although the increase in government expenditures in the 1930s was not only a response to the Great Depression, "the growth in expenditure on public welfare was, in part, an incident of the depression. When private provision for the poor and aged faltered, the provincial governments felt impelled to assume a larger share. But, in part, it was a continuation and acceleration of tendencies which had begun earlier" (378). This view is supported by Cameron (1985) who also states that, "Since 1913, there has been a very great increase in the cost of government in Canada, both provincial and federal" (31).

This discussion should not lead to the impression that the federal government had, all of a sudden, completely limited its role. The 1930s Depression forced a larger role for the federal government by leading to changes in the delivery of social services. The first dramatic surge in government expenditures came then (Cameron 1985, 32). First, the sponsorship of social care and control began shifting from the private and charitable sectors to the public sector, and public bodies took on responsibility for child welfare, public health, education, and the income needs of injured workers, single mothers, soldiers, and seniors. Second, the levels of government involved in social programs changed from a heavy reliance on municipalities to a reliance on the provinces and on federal initiatives and federal-provincial arrangements. Third, and related, the structures for administering and providing services changed from being local and nonprofessional to being more centralized to the provincial or federal level and professionalized.

It could be argued by those who emphasize the centralization of authority that came with World War II that our characterization of this period as "ambiguous" is not correct. Consistent with Cameron (1986), and with the report of the Mcdonald Commission,[7] however, we see the war not as centralizing authority in the long term, and hence, it belongs more appropriately in the "ambiguous" category. The federal govern-

[7] The Royal Commission on the Economic Union and Development Prospects (1985).

ment did increase its expenditures relative to the provinces during the Second World War, but the war did not have a long-term effect of biasing government expenditures toward the federal government and away from the provinces. The federal government used the relevance it had gained during the war to introduce social programs almost unilaterally, but it made provincial governments partners (some reluctantly, of course) in the implementation of these social programs. Social policy in Canada remained more provincial and less federal than in other countries. This pattern stands in contrast to that in the United States, where the provision of welfare after the New Deal was more centralized.

World War II did have a predictable effect on government spending. The world war and the Korean conflict led to sharp increases in federal spending (Cameron 1985, 33). The big effect of the war was the ability of the federal government to introduce many social programs in the 1950s and 1960s (with the help of two constitutional amendments— Unemployment Insurance in 1940 and Old Age Pensions in 1951). But Cameron goes on to note that, despite the programs, the share of the economic product represented by federal spending remained remarkably similar. This was largely due to the fact that "many of the costs were borne by the provinces and municipalities. . . . Provinces and municipalities provided a disproportionate share of the personnel necessary to deliver those services and a disproportionate share of the increment in personnel and services as well" (35). This finding is echoed by Bird and Clack who also observe that the most rapid growth of spending between late 1940s and middle 1970s occurred in the provinces and not only because of federal social policy but because of "their *own* programmatic innovations" (cited in Cameron, 1985, 35; emphasis in original).

This view of the joint role of the provincial and federal governments during this period is supported by the Mcdonald Commission, which reported increases in the role of the federal government but also observed that the increase in federal expenditures was accompanied by "the development of shared-cost programs in health, welfare" (Royal Commission on the Economic Union and Development Prospects 1985, 144). While the federal government did establish its predominant role in the Canadian social security system, "the provinces have also been principal actors in many areas of vital importance for economic management, such as education, health, social services, occupational health and safety and labor/management relations"; hence, in the postwar period it would be safe to say that governments at both levels grew (144).

In the 1960s, provinces began to acquire greater strength and self-confidence as they bargained successfully for more resources and became more active in economic and social development. This led to the phase known in Canada as province building (Royal Commission on the Economic Union and Development Prospects 1985, 145–46), a period that preceded the formal provincialization of the 1980s. The description of this era as province building, advocated by a number of Canadian scholars—notably Black and Cairns (1966)—was criticized by Young, Faucher, and Blais (1984), who observe that provinces were no more important in the 1960s than they were in prior years. A key element of their critique is based on aggregating the activities of provincial and municipal governments. From the perspective of the voter, if authority is transferred to the province from the municipality, then voters would pay attention to politics at the provincial level (and, according to our story, aggregate at the provincial level).

## GREAT BRITAIN

Unlike the other three countries, Britain has not been federal. It has been, in many respects, the most centralized among our four countries. In recent years, however, some authority has been devolved from Westminster. In the late 1990s Parliament granted taxing and spending authority to some regional parliaments and allowed for those parliaments to be elected directly.

Until recent years the national Parliament was sovereign, and had the power to nullify policies enacted by local governments or to abolish those governments altogether. In contrast to the other three countries, there has never been a lower level of government in Britain, such as states or provinces, that has been granted specific powers guaranteed by a constitution and by interpretations of constitutional law in national courts. Moreover, until the 1990s the regional governments were not directly elected (though many city councils were directly elected). Even today, all powers granted to lower levels of government in Britain accrue from parliamentary legislation in Westminster and can be rescinded by legislation from Westminster. In short, there are no large constitutional issues at stake in whether Britain is more or less decentralized; it all depends on what the national government decides to legislate.

This is not to say that British government and economic policy have been centralized, and there is nothing more to add. In the literature on British government, politics, and public economics, the ups and downs in the importance of regionalism and regional policies have been recurring themes. In British politics, as in other countries even if they are federal, centralization means that the national government plays an increasingly important role in the lives of ordinary citizens, whereas provincialization means that the national government grants to local governments more authority. The difference lies in the fact that in Britain before the 1990s there was no space comparable with state politics in the United States and India or provincial politics in Canada for regional political parties to control lower-level governments. While nationalist parties have formed and survived in Britain, prior to 1998 they could not control regional-level governments. The situation has changed following the restructuring in the late 1990s, although it is unclear so far what the enduring affects of the new (post-1998) British federalism on the national British party system will be.

Although the British government tracks and reports spending by local governments, it is a challenge to categorize periods as centralizing or provincializing based on public spending data. Not only are data in the years surrounding the major wars of the twentieth century either missing or incomplete but the public finance data available for other eras are difficult to interpret in terms of which level of government has the authority to decide how the monies are spent, or how resources are raised. Because our task is to determine the trends in British public authority, public finance data can be misleading when trying to determine the degree of political and economic authority across its various levels of government. In official government statistics, one can find categories for spending by local governments, but that spending often includes money funneled from Westminster to local governments with little discretionary authority vested in local governments. In short, it is simply harder to determine which level has the authority over spending compared with spending in the federal countries. Unless one has intimate knowledge of specific public programs in Britain and tracked down every expenditure, one could not comfortably draw conclusions about some eras based solely on public finance data.

As an example, few doubt that Great Britain had moved authority away from Westminster in the 1990s, even prior to the advent of the regional parliaments. Spending by the national government, however, increased at a faster pace than spending by local governments. In fact, spending by local government decreased as a percentage of GNP in the 1990s, while spending by the national government as a percentage of GNP increased![8] Nevertheless, it would be a stretch to argue that Great

[8]For example, Moore notes that even during the Thatcher administration, when local government spending, including that on economic development, probably declined, "local authorities have also played an active role in supporting inner city economic regeneration and the intensity of economic development initiatives increased sharply in the late 1970s and early 1980s. A survey of local authorities in 1986 revealed that significant resources were devoted to economic development (£145m of capital spending by 161 authorities and £77m of revenue expenditure by 177 councils). By the end of the 1980s over 200 authorities were engaged in economic development (Audit Commission, 1991)" (Moore 1992, 125).

Britain was centralizing in the 1990s, or that Great Britain was more centralized in 1996 than it was in 1970. If we were to rely solely on public finance data provided by the British government to various international organizations like the OECD or the World Bank, or to the public in official reports, we easily could arrive at an unwarranted conclusion.

Public finance and employment data to a certain extent help, and we rely on some of these data in the following sections. Nevertheless, as in the case of Canada, the historical sources provide a fairly straightforward account.

## Centralizing Period, 1940–1970

### DEVELOPMENT POLICIES AND THE SIZE OF GOVERNMENTS

If we had to choose one era since the 1880s that was centralizing in Britain, it would be the middle thirty years of the twentieth century. Centralization in Britain in this period occurred through two interrelated processes. First, development of a generous and comprehensive welfare state began in earnest in the 1940s, which was similar to those developing in other western European countries and in Canada and Australia. Second, by the mid-1940s there was a transfer of many social and economic services from local governments to the national government, which "solved the problem of lack of cooperation between local authorities and met the functional requirements of the services concerned" (Owen 1989, 53).[9] Starting in the 1970s, the period of centralization ended gradually, when bold initiatives to bolster local and regional governments started a process of provincialization that culminated in a major restructuring of British government in the 1990s.

The establishment of the welfare state in Britain raised the stakes that all citizens had in national politics. For one thing, the government increasingly taxed and spent much more of the national income. In 1908 the first old-age pensions were introduced, although government spending (minus defense) was less than 10 percent of the economy even ten years later. Government spending rose steadily through the 1920s and 1930s and climbed dramatically to about one-third of GNP by the 1950s. A national heath insurance program was established in 1946, and by the early 1950s there was a full social security program, including comprehensive unemployment insurance, programs for national schools, public housing, and many other social services. Britain soon

---

[9]See Loughlin (1986, 127) for a discussion of the nature of these changes.

had in place one of the most comprehensive, centralized welfare states in the world at that time.

British citizens and residents interacted with the national state after 1946 in many new ways, and this corresponded with a reduction in the autonomy of local government officials to make and implement public policy. Immediately following World War II, efforts to build a centralized welfare state resulted in the transfer of many areas of social and public welfare from local to central authorities, including responsibilities for health care and education, and for the provision of electricity and gas, which was taken over by public corporations. It is true that local governments expanded in this era as well; between 1950 and 1975 the number of local employees increased three times. Nevertheless, local autonomy became increasingly limited.

The method for health care delivery is a good example of the centralization. Prior to the late 1940s, health care services were for the most part locally operated. However, when discussions took place in Westminster before and just after the end of World War II on the proper design of the national health care system, there were forceful advocates for two different means to achieve universal coverage and access. One set of groups wanted to centralize authority to the national level, whereas other groups wanted to decentralize authority to local hospitals and doctors' groups. Both sides maintained that their plans would keep costs down and maintain quality. These divisions were present both within the governing Labour Party and outside of it among bureaucrats who would administer the policies.

The resulting plans for the health care system on paper were a compromise of national and local control, although later observers have noted that in practice the Britain health care system was remarkably centralized, especially in comparison with similarly ambitious plans in other countries. There were regional and local councils devoted to administering health care provision, but these were constrained and coordinated by national-level bureaucracies (Jones 1991). British citizens in the latter half of the twentieth century could not help but understand that it was the national government, not their local or regional government, that was ultimately responsible for the quality of the health care they received.

For our purposes, an interesting contrast is with Canada. The Canadian health care system was designed and implemented during roughly the same period, although its operation was much more decentralized than the operation of the British system. In Canada provinces played a key role in the delivery of health care to their residents (Moscovitch and Albert 1987, 22). Although in Britain the localities played a role in implementing health care, the post–World War II era saw the central government creating many new mandates and imposing new responsibilities on the localities (see Griffith 1966). Taxation for, and spending on, health care was done by the central government.

The many instances of British government intrusion into the regulation and financial support of companies, including the nationalization of entire industries, were as noticeable to British voters as social service issues. In true Keynesian style, the British national government, which under Labour governments typically pledged to work for full employment, used the national budget to boost employment, and develop infrastructure.

When Conservative governments regained power in the 1950s, they did not dismantle the newly expanded welfare state. They nibbled at the edges and claimed to set in place policies to make the provision of services more efficient. By the mid-1960s, the welfare state and Keynesian policies in Britain had only expanded over the previous decade. Not until the 1970s did growth in the British national budget slow.

Local-government spending as a proportion of total government spending (taking into account the war years) declined from the turn of the century to the 1930s, and then to the 1950s (see Figure 5.3). Local governments were only spending half the proportion (approximately 20 percent) in 1950 compared with that in 1910 (approximately 40 percent).

## Provincializing Period, 1970–

Three changes occurred from 1970 to 2000. The first, and most significant, was the creation of elected regional governments in the 1990s. The second was the change in the balance of finance and services provided by the central governments with the demise of the centralized welfare state in Britain. The third, related change was begun by the Labour government in the late 1970s and then accelerated by the Thatcher administrations: the replacement of central provision of services with programs of marketization and the contracting out of services to private providers. These final two changes, which were associated with reduced local responsibilities for service provision, required the transformation in the role of local bodies from service providers to regulatory agents.[10]

### CONSTITUTIONAL AND LEGAL AUTHORITY

Once the British government decides to devolve authority to local and regional governments, or to centralize authority away from those gov-

---

[10]For a further discussion of the shift in local authorities' responsibilities toward regulation, see Clark (1997).

ernments, it has only to pass legislation in the House of Commons. It does not need to amend a Constitution, as in Canada or India, or rely on a change in judicial interpretation by the Supreme Court, as Roosevelt had to do in the 1930s in the United States. British authority ultimately rests with the Parliament in Westminster. Thus, devolution in Britain after the 1970s came about through a series of parliamentary decisions that granted more authority to regional and local governments. It was not a continuous process, and it was not a major restructuring of authority in the same way that Canada has devolved since the 1980s and India in the 1990s. After several failed attempts to pass measures devolving political authority to the regions, for example, the Scotland and Wales Bill finally passed in 1978, only to be repealed in 1979 before its implementation by the newly elected Conservative government. The bill would have allowed for directly elected parliaments in Scotland and Wales if at least 40 percent of voters in those regions approved such changes in referendums.

Ironically, the provincialization of British politics at times appeared to be a centralization of authority away from local governments because it has granted more authority to regional governments. Moreover, there were periods when it looked as though devolution would stop and even reverse. The early Thatcher period from 1979 to 1984 briefly slowed the process of devolution. Thatcher, in principle, wished to devolve authority and roll back the "nanny state" that was centered in Westminster but administered by local governments.

Thatcher's attacks on local government were part of the Convervatives' broader policies of marketization and a general effort to curb public spending (King 1989, 468). Specifically, her government attacked spending by local governments that were seen as the agents of social welfare extension since World War II and whose inefficiency Conservatives had decried throughout the 1970s. Her stated intentions were to decentralize away from government in general. She substantially dismantled regional aid, for example. In 1984 the Thatcher government abolished the Special Areas for regional assistance, and collapsed other categories for aid covering some 35 percent of Britain's working population, as opposed to the almost 50 percent coverage achieved at the end of the 1970s.[11] By 1985–86, real expenditure on regional policies amounted to only 10 percent of its mid-1970s peak.[12]

When local governments were controlled by leftists who displeased her, or when bureaucratic reform (which often meant eliminating public programs) slowed, the Thatcher government did not hesitate to exert

[11]Martin and Tyler (1992, 144–47).
[12]Martin and Tyler (1992, 148).

central authority.[13] In the mid-1980s her government abolished six local governing councils, including the Greater London Council, and pushed various centralized tax schemes overriding local-government tax policies, including one that created enough dissatisfaction within her own party to lead to her ouster in 1990 in favor in John Major.[14] Finally, her strict deflationary policies in the early 1980s, which led to deep recession and higher unemployment, greatly increased the amount of unemployment benefits paid out by the central government. Thus, if measured by social spending on the part of the central government relative to GDP or to local-government spending, the early 1980s were a time of centralization. For example, unemployment payments by the central government increased more than 300 percent from 1979 to 1982.

Nevertheless, authority devolved in Britain between 1970 and 1993, and then even more noticeably in the mid-1990s. The changes in the mid-1990s put in place concrete political structures to continue a process begun through policy changes starting in the late 1960s.

Bowing to intense electoral pressure from separatist and nationalist parties, Westminster offered some kind of administrative devolution in the 1970s, granting local governments the authority to implement policies but not to make policy decisions. It was as far as Britain would go at that time (Keating 1989, 161). The pressure, and the rhetoric to respond on the part of mainstream politicians, continued for decades. Yet the major parties would not budge from parliamentary sovereignty, and the actual policy responses amounted to joint planning councils consisting of local and regional leaders and national administrators, funding for regional development, and movements toward allowing more local and regional autonomy in implementing policy. True *political* devolution, with directly elected regional parliaments, did not occur until 1998.

DEVELOPMENT POLICIES

The devolution that has occurred since the 1970s was gradual and subtle. On the surface, attempts to devolve failed. So-called regional policy in the 1970s was run from the center, "with no input from local govern-

---

[13]Increased national interest in the fate of cities also centered on concerns with leftists. The transition of cities from manufacturing to service centers, the rise in unemployment, and urban riots prompted Conservative efforts to revive urban centers. The revival process was aided by an effort to find new solutions in the urban areas and the arena of local government where Labour had always had a strong political base. Political resistance to Thatcher's efforts to privatize the public sector and reduce local spending resulted in hostility from local Labour leaders and local officials who saw the new policies as a fundamental attack on the welfare state.

[14]For a discussion of Thatcher and the British state's possible motives in abolishing the Greater London Council and six other metropolitan authorities, see King (1989).

ments" (Keating 1989, 162). The Regional Economic Planning Councils, begun in the 1960s, were controversial in their inception and design, and were the favorite targets of criticism from Tory politicians, who claimed they were irrelevant, corrupt, and/or inefficient. They largely failed in their promotion of economic development autonomous from the dictates of the national government. Funding decisions for a long time emanated from Westminster.

## SIZE OF GOVERNMENTS

Despite the brief tendency toward centralization by the Thatcher government, more government work was being done by the early 1990s at the local and regional level than in the early 1970s. The slow accretion of devolving administrative authority piece by piece made its mark. Figure 5.3 shows data on government spending across levels of government in the United Kingdom, and while these data are somewhat misleading for this era (see the previous discussions), we can see that the proportion of total government spending that was local increased from the mid-1950s to the mid-1970s, declined during the recessions of the late 1970s and early 1980s (which required increased unemployment payments from the central government). It rose again in the 1990s. In the bottom part of the figure we see that data show a jump in local government employment in the 1990s.

Some scholars have interpreted the period after the 1970s as a string of failed efforts to decentralize British government and society (Keating 1989). This is accurate, if the goal was simply to devolve policy-making authority to duly elected regional governments or councils. The evidence is clear, however, that the national government did devolve some authority to regional and local governments, despite the fact that those councils were typically not elected.

## Ambiguous Period, 1890–1930

How centralized was the British state prior to the advent of the welfare state? This is not easy to answer. Britain was centralized politically but was quite decentralized economically. Local issues were extremely important, and most voters almost certainly cared more about their local area than about broad national issues. As one observer writes, "Before 1914, politics was based as much upon locality as it was upon class" (Bogdanor 1999, 166). This is in sharp contrast to the 1950s, when British politics in all regions hinged primarily on class. Prior to 1914, however, what was often at stake in Britain was the question of how particular localities, and their institutions, were going to be accepted and accommodated within the United Kingdom.

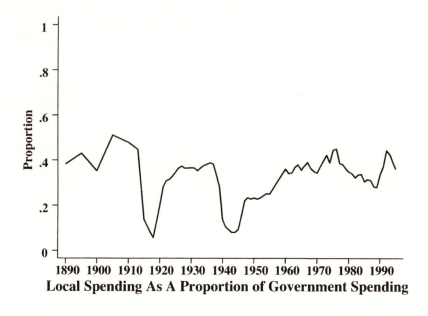

**Local Spending As A Proportion of Government Spending**

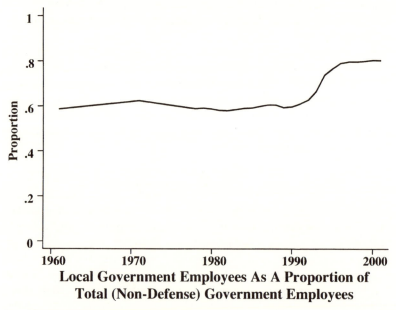

**Local Government Employees As A Proportion of
Total (Non-Defense) Government Employees**

Figure 5.3. Local Government in Great Britain

### THREATS TO NATIONAL INTEGRITY

The national government through this era struggled with one major issue regarding provincialization: Irish home rule. We do not need to go into details here, but it is safe to say that the controversy of how to maintain Ireland within the union, and the ultimate settlement of that issue following bloody conflict in 1920–21, had implications for the relationship of the national state to Wales and Scotland for many years hence. The question of whether the local Welsh church would be disestablished in Wales in favor of the Anglican Church was another example. The issue resonated deeply with Welsh voters in the national election of 1910.

### DEVELOPMENT POLICIES AND THE SIZE OF GOVERNMENTS

To say that local issues were very important is not the same as saying that local governments were more important to voters than the national government, as was the case in the United States in the 1830s and India by the late 1990s. Local governments during this time had very little authority and were often encroached upon by Westminster. But it would also be incorrect to say that British politics and society were highly centralized and that voters paid attention to national political issues when casting votes. Economic activities in Great Britain, including social services, regulation (if it existed), and enforcement of taxes, were not centralized to nearly the same degree as they were after 1930. Local authorities' responsibilities were extended to some degree, with the creation of single-tier country borough authorities in 1889, which became more comprehensive after the abolition of the School Boards in 1902 and the Poor Law Guardians in 1929.

The economic stakes for voters in national election outcomes were not high compared with those in later decades. Beginning in the 1920s the Labour Party advocated a dramatic centralization of authority on economic policies. It was an advocacy that culminated in the welfare state following the Second World War and stemmed from the belief that the existing, noncentralized state was leaving people poor, dependent upon greedy capitalists for their livelihood, and faced with economic uncertainty. Their solution was to centralize a decentralized economy.

Much of the new welfare state began during and soon after the Second World War, and the war itself brought centralization to Britain. Of course, both war periods, 1917–21 and 1939–45, were times of intense centralization of authority. Why don't we include the earlier period in our list of centralizing periods? First, it is not easy to understand the role of the wars in explaining or causing trends in British public authority. Much of the relevant data on government spending during these periods are missing. When data are available, it is difficult to separate war-related expenditures from other kinds of expenditures, even when factoring out defense spending. Nevertheless, public spending, even after factoring out defense spending, dramatically increased in the early 1940s. The same cannot be said for the 1920s.

Second, the period surrounding the First World War was a temporary moment of centralization around the war effort but was not followed by major changes in social and economic policy making to the same degree as in the latter war period.[15] By contrast, the earlier war period did not see the establishment of enduring political institutions and economic policies that centralized decision making to the national level on economic matters. In fact, much of the discussion about the welfare state in Britain, and the appropriate level of devolution to be applied in its implementation, occurred during the latter half of the Second World War, following the publication of the Beveridge Report in 1942.[16] Liberal and Conservative governments during and following the First World War were not much interested in socializing large portions of the economy. If anything, leaders in those governments wanted to avoid such policies.

It is worth mentioning, however, that the period surrounding the first war was a time of extreme upheaval in British politics when, as we shall see in the next chapter, the party system briefly fragmented in dramatic fashion. This runs somewhat contrary to what we would predict, namely that brief centralization brought fragmentation, not consolidation, of the party system. The fragmentation, however, occurred in one election early in the war and was only temporary.

## INDIA

Unlike Canada and the United States, India was not formed as a union of existing political entities or states. At independence in 1947 and even in 1950, the year its constitution was adopted, India faced political challenges to its national integrity and pressure for economic development. These various challenges have reoccurred throughout modern Indian history.

---

[15]Observers mark "the interwar period as a crucial intermediate stage in local-central relations. 'Before 1914 and especially in the nineteenth century there was the Victorian municipality locally determining its own policies and actions. Since 1945, when local government has been stripped of many of its pre-1939 responsibilities, it has increasingly become just an implementer of central policy. The interwar period was then a plateau of municipal power, yet by 1939 major erosion had already taken place.'" Hennock, cited in Ward (1988, 155–56).

[16]The Beveridge Report was a detailed statement proposing a comprehensive welfare state for Britain.

The tendency for constitutional designers, therefore, was to give the central government considerable authority relative to that of state governments as a means to ensure national integrity. Moreover, the central government in the first decade following independence decided to become the policy engine for economic development. The dominant paradigm in Indian politics at independence was that the government would be the engine of economic and social transformation. Most of this change would be carried out by the national government. State governments were made partners in this process, while local governments were not incorporated in the enterprise of nation building and economic and social change. As a result there were always countervailing pressures from state governments that still had constitutional authority over large swaths of policy. Although threats (real or perceived) to national integration have tended to support centralizing tendencies, economic reform initiated in 1991 has severely limited the ability of the national government to continue to influence economic policy in the same way as it did in the first four decades after independence. State governments have now come to play a much larger role in the economic life of the nation than at any time in the history of independent India.

### Centralized and Centralizing Periods, 1952–1957, 1971–1977

Central authority was at its peak following the elections of 1971 during the prime ministership of Indira Gandhi. This period, marked by a great expansion in the economic power that accrued to the central government and a general expansion in the role of the state more broadly, ended with the defeat of the Congress in 1977. The five years from the first elections held in independent India in 1952 to the adoption of the Second Five-Year Plan in 1957 is the other period in which central authority was widely seen as much stronger relative to the provinces.

#### CONSTITUTIONAL AND LEGAL AUTHORITY

Article 1 of the of the Indian Constitution states that "India, that is *Bharat,* shall be a Union of States." The term *union of states* was used because the federation was not the result of an agreement by units, but rather was imposed from above. The component units have no freedom to secede.[17] Moreover, the national Parliament can change a state's boundaries by a simple majority, as for instance when the Indian Parliament adopted the States Reorganization Act of 1956, reducing the number of states from twenty-seven to fourteen. The basic principles govern-

---

[17]The Sixteenth Amendment to the Constitution (adopted in 1963) also made it clear that advocacy of secession did not have protection of freedom of expression.

ing the distribution of power between the center and the states are laid out in Part XI of the Indian Constitution. Part XI is itself divided into two chapters: one governing legislative relations, which establishes the constitutional division of powers over policy areas between the center and the states; and one covering administrative relations. The respective jurisdictions of the center and the states are spelled out in three lists. The union list, consisting of ninety-seven items, is the longest of the three and provides control over issue areas such as defense, foreign affairs, income tax, and even interstate trade and commerce and state high courts to the center. The state list consists of sixty-six entries that deal with issues of more local interest, such as law and order, education, and agriculture. The concurrent list consists of forty-seven items that are under the joint jurisdiction of the center and the states, such as economic and social policies, monopolies, and price control. As far as the concurrent list is concerned, a law passed by the national Parliament takes precedence over a state law in cases where the two are in conflict. Moreover, residual powers (those not specified in the Constitution) are also vested in the central government, unlike in other federal systems such as the United States in which residual powers rest with the states.

Although the division of power appears to give the state governments a measure of autonomy, this does not carry into periods of crisis, when the national Parliament can pass legislation on any matter it deems necessary. The power of the center under these emergency rules therefore covers even those issues which are under the jurisdiction of states. These emergency provisions have given the central government considerable leverage over state politics. A provision that directly affects the states is Article 356 of the Constitution, which stipulates that if the president (actually the prime minister) is satisfied with a governor's report (state governors are not elected but rather are appointed by the central government) that the state cannot be governed according to the provisions of the Constitution, then the president can assume executive power over all facets of the state's administration, and Parliament can legislate on behalf of the state assembly.

From 1951 to 1966 "president's rule" was imposed on states ten times.[7] Political problems caused by the reorganization of states and the inability of parties to form a ruling coalition on two occasions rendered president's rule inevitable. In the eight other instances, the center used its power under the Constitution to influence state politics (Kochanek 1968). From 1967 through 1984, in sharp contrast to the earlier phase, president's rule was imposed seventy-two times.[18]

---

[18]The data from this section are drawn from the Lok Sabha Secretariat, various official documents.

The central government in India has more power constitutionally than the states, especially with regard to the allocation of resources. Constitutionally, the states have limited opportunities to raise resources, especially since most of them are unwilling to tax the one source that could generate revenue for them—income from agriculture. The center often had the final voice in determining the rates and levels of taxation, even if these taxes affect the states in critical ways. For example, the center decides whether and at what rate to levy any of the taxes under Articles 268 and 269 of the Constitution, even though the proceeds the tax revenue generated under these articles go entirely to the states (Lakdawala 1991, 11). The center also levies important taxes, such as personal income tax, corporate income tax, customs duties, and excise duties on most goods. Of these, only income taxes, especially personal income taxes, are shared by the states based on a formula determined by a constitutionally mandated body, the finance commission, which is constituted every five years to examine center-state financial relations. States still retain some important taxes, such as those based on land and agricultural income (taxes that the states have been very reluctant to levy), excise duties on alcohol and certain other goods, sales taxes on all goods but newspapers, taxes on mineral rights, taxes on vehicles, taxes on the sale of electricity, and luxury taxes. Apart from these taxes on the sale of liquor, however, the instruments over which the state governments have control are not very elastic. Consequently, state government revenues are not buoyant.

DEVELOPMENT POLICIES

After the first elections in independent India in 1952, which elected the Congress to power, the central government gradually began to extend its authority over economic development policies. In 1955 an extraconstitutional body—the Planning Commission (which made the economic development plans for India and hence was the major source of funds for the states)—was given national salience when it was made a part of the office of the prime minister. This increased the status and power of the commission (Frankel 1978, 113). The authority of the Planning Commission was further buttressed by the fact that state governments did not have the expertise to produce the necessary data and analysis for planning. The Planning Commission, on the other hand, had all the necessary resources—material and human—to produce plans (115).

The authority of the central government was affirmed in the Second Five-Year Plan—a program produced by the Planning Commission that gave control of the "commanding heights of the economy" to the national state. Economic development was to be secured by a public-sector-led industrialization policy. A draft of the Second Five-Year Plan was available for discussion in 1955 (Frankel 1980, 122), and this signaled to the state governments that the center intended to play a large role in the economic development of the nation.

The role of the central government began to expand in the late 1960s. In February 1970 the government implemented the Permit-License Raj, a policy whereby licenses would be needed from the government to set up industry. This measure, in effect, increased the control of the central bureaucracy over business. The licensing requirements reversed the trends toward decontrol that had started in the mid-1960s (Frankel 1980, 437). The central government also nationalized most banks in March 1970 and the general insurance industry in 1972. Other measures of centralization brought large swaths of bureaucracy under the prime minister's control (450).

Central incursion into policy areas that are explicitly reserved for the states under the Constitution also increased in this period. The center had, according to Mitra (1992), "made "massive inroad[s] . . . into jurisdictions reserved for the States" (xi). One such area was agriculture where the center enlarged its influence. Until 1967 the center's role in agriculture was limited. Provisions for agriculture in central government and centrally sponsored programs fell below 10 percent of the total government expenditure on agriculture (by both central and state governments). In the Fourth Five-Year Plan, initiated in 1970, the proportion of central expenditure on agriculture increased to more than two-fifths of the total government expenditure by both the center and states on agriculture (National Commission on Agriculture 1976, 104). This increased resource allocation by the center is significant given that under the Indian Constitution agriculture is itemized as a state subject; it is a policy area over which states are supposed to have complete jurisdiction, yet there has been marked central government encroachment.

The central government also introduced programs for the development of small farmers: the SFDA (Small Farmers Development Agencies) for Marginal Farmers and Agricultural Laborers in forty districts across India, a Drought Prone Areas Program, and central initiatives to address rural unemployment. The Jawahar Rozgar Yojana (Jawahar Employment Plan), a centrally sponsored scheme that addressed rural unemployment, was to be implemented by state governments, although 80 percent of the funds would come from the central government. Similarly, the Integrated Rural Development Program, which was designed to help small and marginal farmers, agricultural laborers, and rural artisans with low incomes, is today a centrally sponsored scheme with half the resources coming from the central government.

SIZE OF GOVERNMENTS

A number of other developments in this early period also affected the balance between the center and the states. First, the center redefined the income tax to exclude the corporation tax from the tax receipts it had to share with the states. This change is significant because corporate tax became a larger proportion of the direct taxes collected by the central government than personal income tax: whereas in 1950–51 personal income tax composed 77 percent of direct taxes, in 1960–61 it was 60.5 percent; in 1970–71, 56 percent; in 1980–81, 53 percent; and in 1988–89, 49 percent (Chandok 1990). Second, the center began to raise revenues by resorting to administered price increases rather than by raising excise duties. The latter, unlike the former, had to be shared with the state governments. Third, the central government expanded its control over the economy by appropriating revenues from broadcasting.

During the emergency period from 1975 to 1977, when fundamental rights were suspended in India, the central government introduced the Forty-second Amendment to the Indian Constitution. This amendment was a source of much controversy because of the limits it placed on individual liberties. The last item in the long, mostly political amendment gave the center the right to appropriate resources gathered from commercial advertising on government-owned radio and television stations. Within the framework of the unamended Constitution, these monies would have been appropriated by the states. When the political features of the Forty-second Amendment were repealed in 1977, the Janata government—which ostensibly had a larger commitment to federalism in its election manifesto than did the Congress—did not repeal this particular amendment. The states were thereby deprived of an important source of revenue.

## Provincializing Periods, 1964–1969, 1991–

CONSTITUTIONAL AND LEGAL AUTHORITY

The Supreme Court of India's 1994 ruling that curbed the central government's use of Article 356 has struck a serious blow at central authority over state governments. In *SR Bommai v. Union of India* the court ruled that the power under Article 356 should be sparingly used and only when the president is fully satisfied that a situation has arisen where the government of the state cannot be carried on in accordance with the provisions of the Constitution.[19] In the opinion of the court, a frequent

---

[19]The brief facts are as follows. The Janata Dal secured a majority in the legislative Assembly of Karnataka. Due to internal squabbles in the party for power and dissatisfaction over the distribution of ministries, dissidents wrote to the governor that they had with-

use of the power vested to the center under Article 356 would upset the constitutional balance. The court, while acknowledging that not all situations can be foreseen, laid out instances when the use of Article 356 is legitimate and also some circumstances when it cannot be used. The article could be used by the center in the case of a large-scale breakdown of law and order, a gross mismanagement of affairs by a state government, corruption or abuse of its power, or a danger to national integration or security of the nation. The court quite clearly said that Article 356 could not be used when a ministry resigns or is dismissed because it has lost its majority in the state assembly without exploring the possibilities that an alternative government could be formed. Article 356 also could not be used to dismiss an elected state government solely on the grounds that a different political party had obtained a mandate in a national election (as had been done in 1977 and 1980). The Supreme Court said that it retained the right to scrutinize the basis on which the advice was tendered by the governor to declare president's rule in a state.

### DEVELOPMENT POLICIES

The first phase of provincialization began in the early 1960s and lasted for much of the decade. After the death of Nehru in 1964, Prime Minster Shastri made some key changes to reduce central control over the economy. The first casualty was the Planning Commission, which lost a significant amount of its authority when it was separated from the prime minister's office. This allowed states' chief ministers the possibility of circumventing the Planning Commission on questions of economic policy (Frankel 1978, 252). In 1964 in a meeting of the National Development Council (the prime minister, the state chief ministers, and the planning bodies), the prime minister announced a rather radical reduction in the role of the central government. For the formulation of the Fourth Five-Year Plan, the prime minister formed five committees that would have the input of the state chief ministers. These committees were to advise on policy issues related to implementation of the plan. Frankel (1980, 256) notes that, with this move "by one stroke, the chief ministers of the states were accorded a role in the definition of national economic policy."

---

drawn their support of the chief minister. The party at the center, Congress, grabbed the opportunity, dismissed the government in Karnataka, and imposed president's rule. This was challenged in the Supreme Court as unconstitutional. The court examined the subjective satisfaction of the president and held that it was an improper exercise of power and hence unconstitutional. It revived the legislative Assembly for the first time in the history of independent India.

The trend toward provincialization continued even in the first years of the prime ministership of Indira Gandhi through 1969. It was agreed that the center would allocate resources to the states in the "form of bloc loans and grants to be distributed according to local priorities" (Frankel 1980, 305). Further, states would have a say in what programs should be included, even in development schemes sponsored by the central government. The role of the state governments in the development process was highlighted when a central government committee—the Administrative Reforms Committee—in March 1968 published a report that echoed the demands of the states to end the Planning Commission's dominant role. In response, a new vision also emerged from the Planning Commission, which would allow states to generate their own plans. These plans could be made without the center telling them anything about content or the nature of the schemes the states intended to use for economic development (subject, of course, to an overall resource constraint) (Frankel 1980, 312). The political situation in the country in the late 1960s was then "marked by an unprecedented confidence of regional leaders" (Dasgupta 2001, 68).

The most significant provincialization in India has occurred since the adoption of economic reforms in 1991. These reforms were undertaken to address a growing fiscal crisis and under the terms of a negotiated settlement reached with the International Monetary Fund (IMF). A reduction of the role of the national government in the economy was the key element of the reform, and the (in)famous permit-license Raj was abolished. Industrial development has increasingly come under the rubric of the state governments, with some state governments competing for industry and developing incentives to create a more favorable climate for private investment.

The fact that state governments now have a large say in their industrial development is a major shift in Indian federalism. A government commission to investigate center-state relations (the Sarkaria Commission) observed that the major complaint of state governments in the 1980s was that industrial development was determined by the central government. The Sarkaria commission report reveals that state governments felt that the national government played too large a role in their economies, especially in the areas of industrial development. Karnataka, a state not governed by the Congress Party when the commission was making its inquiries, cited instances of industries not being located in Karnataka for political considerations. The most egregious example was the relocation of the Indian Telephone Industries, a public-sector unit factory that manufactures electronic telephone exchanges in Gonda in Uttar Pradesh. This move was pursued by the central government, despite the fact that perhaps the best infrastructural facilities for producing the exchanges were available in Karnataka. The location of public-sector units was not only influenced by political considerations, but the Karnataka government also noted that private-sector corporations, such as Glaxos, the Tata Electric Locomotive Company, and Tractors India, wanted to set up industries in Karnataka and were asked by the Congress-controlled central government to locate their plants elsewhere. The Kerala government generally summed up the position of the states when it observed that no objective criteria had been followed in deciding where investment by the center in the public sector would occur and that locational decisions were largely made arbitrarily, that is to say, politically.

All this has changed since the early 1990s. "Under the licence-permit Raj, business location decisions were effectively taken by central planners in New Delhi. With the abolition of this system, both Indian and foreign capital have been freed to seek locations offering the best returns. This has set up an intense competition among state governments to attract investment"; further, the "curtailment of the central government's vast discretionary powers over industrial licensing means that state governments have become the crucial point of contact for entrepreneurs" (Jenkins 1999, 134, 135). Economic "liberalization has created a more competitive environment," which has resulted in the "increased importance of state action" (Ahluwalia 2002). Not surprisingly, the investment climate has begun to vary across states, and some investor-friendly states such as Maharashtra, Gujarat, Karntaka, Andhra Pradesh, and Tamil Nadu are drawing more investment, especially foreign investment, in comparison with such states as Uttar Pradesh, Bihar, and West Bengal (Stern 2001, cited in Ahluwalia 2002; Sinha 2003).

The central government loosened its control over other facets of the economy as well. In 1992 the petroleum ministry decentralized the process of selecting retailers for petroleum products and cooking gas. State governments could now select these retailers, a function that the center had performed up until then (Jenkins 1999, 126). The liberalization also extended to the commodities market. For example, the system of coffee marketing was also changed, enabling coffee growers to sell more coffee on the open market (132). The mining sector was also decentralized, and Jenkins notes that the BJP chief minister of Rajasthan thanked the Congress prime minister for the measure (129).[20]

[20]Not all attempts at liberalization have been successful. State governments often pursue antireform policies if it suits their political interests. For instance, in its first budget proposals after the 1991 elections, the Congress (I) government proposed to reduce the fertilizer subsidy by raising fertilizer prices. Facing pressures from the agricultural sector and state parties, the government reduced its scheduled price increase of fertilizers from 40 to 30 percent. It also gave "total exemption from the hike in fertiliser prices to small and mar-

## SIZE OF GOVERNMENTS

State governments now play a larger role than the center in the management of their economies. Dasgupta (2001) notes that "while the revenue receipts of state governments from 1992 to 1996, for example, showed a modest increase, the revenue expenditures indicated a rapid rise" (69). As a result, the deficit of state governments on the revenue account has increased from 0.9 percent of GDP in 1990 to 2.79 percent in 1999–2000, while the fiscal deficit jumped from 3.19 percent to 4.68 percent over the same period (India, Ministry of Finance 2002, table 3.6). The reduced role of the center can also be seen in the proportion of development expenditures incurred by the central government relative to the state governments. That proportion—which was almost 65 percent in 1990—has dropped to 54 percent by 1999–2000. Further, central government expenditures (excluding defense spending) as a proportion GDP also dropped by 1.5 percent in the 1990s from almost 14 percent in 1991–92 to 12.5 percent in 1999–2000 (India, Ministry of Finance 2002).

## *Ambiguous periods: 1957–1964, 1978–1991*

### DEVELOPMENT POLICIES

The ability of the central government (led by the Congress Party) to plan for economic development was first questioned by the state governments (also governed by the Congress) in the period following 1957. The reach of the center was curtailed as a financial crisis necessitated that state governments mobilize resources from the agricultural sector to finance development projects (Frankel 1978). As the 1957–58 crisis deepened, the foreign exchange situation deteriorated, and domestic inflationary pressures raised the costs of projects, there was a need to raise more resources from the rural sector to finance national projects. State governments clashed with the Planning Commission attempts to raise resources from the rural sector.

---

ginal farmers [and] offered some relief to big land owners" (*Times of India,* 2 January 1992). Opposition to fertilizer policy reform came from the state governments. The Congress led government in Karnataka, for instance, "decided to . . . sell the stock [of fertiliser] procured prior to the presentation of the Union Budget at the old rates *against* [emphasis added] the centre's direction" (*Times of India,* 14 August 1991). The Karnataka government also continued to provide subsidies to the fertilizer sector. For instance, in its 1993–94 budget the Karnataka government allocated a subsidy of Rs. 260 million to complex fertilizers alone (*Deccan Herald,* 23 February 1993). Opposition to fertilizer pricing was also voiced by the Gujarat, Rajasthan, and Uttar Pradesh state governments on the grounds that it would be difficult for them to monitor these policies (*Times of India,* 14 August 1991).

In 1958 Nehru told the National Development Council that states needed to raise money from agriculture. To accomplish this, the national government proposed two measures, promoting the cooperative movement and agricultural commodities trading by the states. State governments opposed both measures (Frankel 1978, 161) and Nehru met resistance from within the party. The inability of the center to extend its economic vision to the state was noticeable in the Third Five-Year Plan where, as Frankel notes, "the final version . . . revealed that the Planning Commission had been completely unsuccessful in convincing state leaders to accept an accelerated pace of agrarian reorganization" (183). This was especially true of land reform where the national leadership was completely unable to enlist the support of state leaders for effective reform (190), and state governments with few exceptions made little effort to stop abuses of land reform legislation (194). This defiance over agricultural policy extended to the Parliament where, in May 1963, a large number of Congress MPs failed to support the government on a constitutional amendment placing ceilings on landholding in agriculture. In this period, the central government still retained an advantage in economic matters largely because of its greater access to resources. As Franda (1968, 35–128) notes, the center could, however, be resisted once it came to issues that concerned a state or a set of states such as interstate cooperation for development projects like river valley projects.

From 1978 to 1991 there were some movements toward provincialization, but the center still had the upper hand in many policy areas. Thus it is not clear whether the central or state government was more salient for voters in that era.

The excessive centralization of the early and mid-1970s ended after a political transition in 1978. The dominant role of the central government in the economy was reassessed in the early 1980s. There were attempts made to reduce the role of the central government in industrial licensing and a larger attempt at provincialization was made in the mid-1980s. Twenty-five broad categories of industries were "delicensed" (or, no licenses or permission from the central government was required) in March 1985. In June 1985 delicensing was extended to a large part of the pharmaceutical industry, and in December 1985 twenty-two industries that were closely watched because of their monopoly characteristics were also delicensed. Further, in 1986 companies that still required licenses were allowed to "broadband," that is, make changes to their product mix without seeking fresh licenses, something that had previously been required (India, Ministry of Finance 1986, 29).[21] An extremely liberalized environment with virtually no capacity restrictions

---

[21]For reasons this liberalization did not succeed, see Kohli (1989).

and liberal import policies was created for the electronics industry and that set the stage for the contemporary success of information technology (IT) companies in India. The gradual delicensing and broadbanding of industry continued for much of the 1980s, albeit at a slower pace than was the intent when the policies were first announced.

### SIZE OF GOVERNMENTS

While the central government was attempting to reduce its role in the economy in some areas, state governments continued to play a significant role in their economies. The general expansion of the role of government in the 1970s gave the state governments the chance to expand their role. The larger role of the state governments can be seen in the number of public-sector organizations run by state governments. Before 1970 there were only 200 state-level public-sector undertakings distinct from India's government-run public-sector companies (SLPEs). During the 1970s, 300 new units were added, and in the period from 1980 to 1987, another 350 were added. These gave state governments control over large swaths of their economies. Further, subsidies given by state governments for social and economic services "grew phenomenally over the decade 1977–78 to 1987–88" (Rao and Mundle 1992, 112).

Further evidence of the increasing importance of state governments in this period is reflected in employment growth and trends in central government spending. As Figure 5.4 shows, the number of state government employees increased dramatically between 1973 and 1991, with the largest increase coming between 1978 to 1991. Between 1973 and 1997 the number of state government employees increased by almost 10 percent, whereas in the period 1977 to 1982 the increase was 16 percent. Between 1982 and 1990 there was a 20 percent increase in the number of state government employees. Similarly, trends in the proportion of government spending from the national level largely correspond to these patterns—note the increase in the 1970s and the overall decline in the 1990s—although the large increase in this proportion in the 1980s resulted from payments on debt and not from centralization of authority.

## UNITED STATES

The United States started its political life as a fairly decentralized union of states. Over time, the expansion of the U.S. economy and the ever increasing need to provide for a national solution to regulating and encouraging market forces led to the centralization of authority in Washington, D.C. The major centralization began at the end of the nineteenth

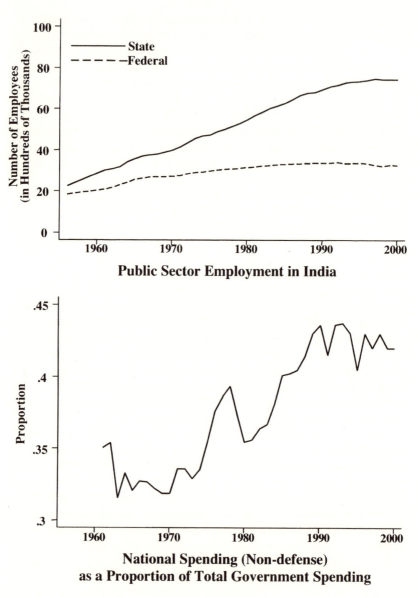

Figure 5.4. National and State Government in India

century. The centralization process was almost completed by the middle of the twentieth century, especially with the adoption of the New Deal, which gave the federal government more authority relative to state governments than it had ever had since the adoption of the Constitution in 1788.

Southern secession constituted a major threat to United States national integrity, and while the Civil War did centralize authority for a brief period in the 1860s, states nevertheless gradually regained their rights to regulate political and economic life in their territories.

## Centralizing Periods, 1860–1876, 1932-

Two eras—the Civil War and post–New Deal—were the most important periods of political and economic centralization in American history. Another period, the Progressive Era, especially 1900–1910, was somewhat centralizing, although important elements of policy making remained the preserve of the state governments.

### CONSTITUTIONAL AND LEGAL AUTHORITY

The centralization of authority that followed the Civil War was reflected in changes to the Constitution. In 1868 the Fourteenth Amendment was adopted and "unlike the pre–Civil War Constitution, whose first ten amendments provided rights enforceable against the national government, the Constitution after Reconstruction provided rights for citizens enforceable against the states" (Eskridge and Ferejohn 1994, 1377). The Supreme Court, in this period, also dealt state authority over individual rights a blow when the court, in two important decisions, *Crandall v. Nevada* and *Strauder v. West Virginia*, struck down state laws that limited individual action. One state law imposed a capitation fee on any person leaving the state, and the second excluded black citizens from juries (1377).

The hand of the federal government was further strengthened by the Supreme Court after the New Deal when it issued a series of rulings that upheld the authority of the federal government. The Court in its rulings in *NLRB v. Jones & Laughlin Steel Corp.* upheld National Labor Relations Act's regulation of unfair labor practices (Eskridge and Ferejohn 1994, 1385); and in *United States v. Darby* the Fair Labor Standards Act's regulation of hours, wages, and other conditions of employment was upheld (1386). It was only after the New Deal that the "Court's dormant Commerce Clause jurisprudence received its mature development" because the United States economy was a "national one in ways it had not been before the *Lochner* era" and because the "Depression had indicated the need for federal rather than just state-by-state regulation of these increasingly nationalized (and transnationalized) features of the economy. Starting with *Jones & Laughlin,* the new Court repeatedly sanctioned these national development policies, though carefully preserving state prerogatives to pursue local development objectives as well" (1387). The Supreme Court also "upheld federal statutes redistributing wealth through a system of social security and welfare, and social power through a string of civil rights laws" (1388). The Court's judgments also affected the authority of Congress to "impose regulatory obligations directly on the states" (1391). In *Maryland v. Wirtz,* the Court upheld amendments to the Fair Labor Standards Act, which extended rules on minimum wages and maximum hours to employees of states, their political subdivisions, and state enterprises (1391).

THREAT TO NATIONAL INTEGRITY

The centralization that was initiated by the Civil War lasted until the mid-1870s, when the national government ended the policies of southern reconstruction. For nearly two decades, the national government encroached into areas that it had never before, federalizing lands in some states and taking over the functions of government in many local areas. It created the war machinery, including the promotion of industries geared toward making metal products, gunpowder, guns and bombs, ships, railroads and trains, wagons, tents, housing and clothing for soldiers, easily transportable foods, and wooden coffins. It adopted policies related to civil liberties and to rights that were either blatantly or arguably unconstitutional, not only in the treatment of prisoners (suspension of habeas corpus) but also in the overpowering authority of the national government relative to the states. And it routinely overturned government policies (even some election results in the South following the war) that were at odds with national government priorities. Not only did the Civil War create in the United States a sense of nationality, it also generated a "broad constituency committed to maintaining the integrity of the national state (at least as far as its ability to raise revenue was concerned)" (Foner 2002, 23).

While the courts and other observers granted President Lincoln wide latitude because of powers assumed under his role as commander in chief, it was widely held after that war that the United States Constitution could not survive unless greater levels of state sovereignty were restored. Immediately after the war, the northern states demanded the authority to deal with their own internal issues, asking for veterans benefits from the national government and not much else. In the southern states, the national government dominated state and local politics for approximately ten years following the war, but by the late 1870s the national government's authority had receded. The year 1877, according to Foner

(2002), "marked a decisive retreat from the idea, born during the civil war, of a powerful national state protecting the fundamental rights of American citizens" (582). Even the Enforcement Acts, which were adopted by Congress to address violence in the states, were repealed using a states' rights argument (455).

DEVELOPMENT POLICIES

There is little doubt that a major expansion of government activity in the economy, especially by the federal government, happened throughout the twentieth century, but it occurred especially after the New Deal. Engerman (2000, vii) in a survey of United States economic history observes that "the expanded nature of fiscal and monetary institutions, the greater use of deliberative policy controls, and the increased regulation of business and individual behavior were among the most dramatic changes of this century, making the United States economy of the year 2000 very different from the economy of 1900." Much of this regulation came from the federal government. In 1902, for example, "public sector expenditures were about two-thirds state and local . . . but [were] less than one-third in 1970" (Brownlee 2000, 1015).

On the whole, prior to the New Deal, governance in the United States was quite decentralized, with the states controlling most areas of policies about which voters cared. There were various spasms of centralization prior to the New Deal. None was as enduring as the New Deal, although at least one was arguably as intense. Centralization of authority to the national government following the onset of the Civil War in 1860 was abrupt and monumental. Freyer (2000, 436), in an exhaustive study of government regulation of business in the nineteenth century, notes that "the peacetime operation of the Constitution's federal system ensured that the rules governing property and contract rights varied from state to state. Moreover, different rules governing identical property or contract claims frequently existed side by side in the same place, making conflicted outcomes virtually inevitable."

Prior to the Civil War the "federal government was in a 'state of incompetence,' its conception of duties little changed since the days of Washington and Jefferson. Most functions of government were handled at the state and local level; one could live out one's life without ever encountering an official representative of national authority" (Foner 2002, 23). The Civil War changed all that. As Foner (2002) notes, "to mobilize the financial resources of the Union, the government created a national paper currency, an enormous national debt, and a national banking system" (21). Second, the federal budget expanded—from $63 million in 1860 to more than $1 billion by 1865 (23). This, however, does not imply that there was a consensus on an expansion of the role of government. Even the Republican Party "proved reluctant to promote the state's expansion into new realms. Measured by the magnitude of the federal budget, the size of the bureaucracy, and the number of bills brought before Congress, the scope of national authority far exceeded antebellum levels. . . . Yet, even among Republicans, doubts about the activist state persisted" (451). The expansion of the federal state was limited in this period and efforts to form national bureaus of health, federal railroad commissions, and nationalization of the telegraph industry died in Congress, while the creation of a Weather Bureau was accepted (451–52).

### SIZE OF GOVERNMENTS

The New Deal era in the United States presents perhaps the canonical case of a change in the size of the central government. During the 1930s the national government, in many ways, set in motion a dramatic centralization of authority over public taxation, borrowing, and expenditures. The era was also the culmination of a process begun around the turn of the new century to increase the authority of the national government to regulate commerce, banking, transportation, and communications. Following the Depression the federal government adopted a series of acts that increased the regulatory authority of the federal government: the Federal Home Loan Bank Act of 1932, the Banking Act of 1933, the Securities Act of 1933, the Securities Exchange Act of 1934, the Federal Credit Union Act of 1934, the Banking Act of 1935, and the Investment Company Act of 1940 (Vietor 2000, 978). Not only did the federal government adopt these acts but "new federal agencies were vested with extraordinary powers to restrict competition, control monopoly, and intervene directly in the details of managerial decision-making. *The authority of the states, relative to Washington, was diminished*" (986; emphasis added).

The expansion of the role of the federal government continued unabated after the New Deal especially between 1964 and 1977 when "Congress adopted nearly three dozen major regulatory laws pertaining to environmental, health, and safety matters" (Vietor 2000, 988). New regulatory agencies, such as the Equal Employment Opportunity Commission, the National Highway Traffic Safety Administration, the Occupational Safety and Health Administration, the Consumer Product Safety Commission, and the Environmental Agency were also created in this period. Vietor notes that "the federal budget for regulation *tripled* in constant 1970 dollars from less than $800 million in 1964 to more than $2.6 billion by 1977" (988; emphasis added).

Many steps were taken before the 1930s to increase national authority over redistributive taxations and social programs, including the introduction of the income tax after 1913 and the extension of the veterans' pensions to include widows and family members (Skocpol 1992). Yet the overwhelming electoral victories of the Roosevelt Democrats, his so-called New Deal Coalition, followed by a series of court decisions and government spending policies to boost the economy, plus the mobilization of the country for war in the early 1940s, brought national politics to every electoral district in the country. There were farm subsidies and programs, as well as work projects funded by the national government to build parks, roads, dams, bridges, canals, locks, harbors, and electric grids. And, of course, there was the Social Security Act, and the acts establishing the Medicare and Medicaid programs, which nationalized pensions and medical care for the elderly and poor. Above all, it was the adoption as policy of the notion that the national government was an important, if not the most important, actor responsible for the economic health of the country. The economic health of local areas now depended on the policies of the national government to a degree far beyond what had been the case. The New Deal also created a more uniform national market than had ever existed in the United States.

Without a doubt, states after the New Deal retained authority over many policy areas that voters cared about, such as schools, prisons and crime control, and regulations in certain industries such as insurance and the professions. State politics still mattered, and state-level political parties still mattered. We are not arguing that policy making in the United States became completely centralized or that voters only cared about national politics in choosing congressional candidates. Rather, in comparison with previous eras, there was simply no period in American history that matched or exceeded the degree of political and economic centralization as put into place following the New Deal. Consider social spending by states and localities in Table 5.1. There was a major drop-off in the 1930s as the national government took up that task. The states and localities gradually increased their spending in current dollars (though a smaller proportion of total government spending), although the degree of autonomy they had in spending in the latter half of the twentieth century is debatable (see Wildavsky 1984).

The data on central-government spending demonstrate the increasing dominance of the national government after 1932, both over the state and local governments and over the economy as a whole. As Figure 5.5 shows, national expenditures rose dramatically, after subtracting defense spending. There was also a large expansion of the federal bureaucracy after the New Deal. The total number of federal government employees (neither in defense nor the post office) between 1932 and 1936 more than doubled from 202,821 to 420,712 (U.S. Department of Commerce 1975, 1102). This is the single largest increase in a three-year span in

TABLE 5.1
Total Subnational-Government Expenditure
Devoted to Social Services in the United States
(figures in current dollars)

| Year | Expenditure |
| --- | --- |
| 1902 | 80,718,133 |
| 1913 | 158,331,348 |
| 1932 | 459,713 |
| 1942 | 1,222,198 |
| 1962 | 9,048,090 |
| 1972 | 32,263,348 |
| 1982 | 82,706,570 |

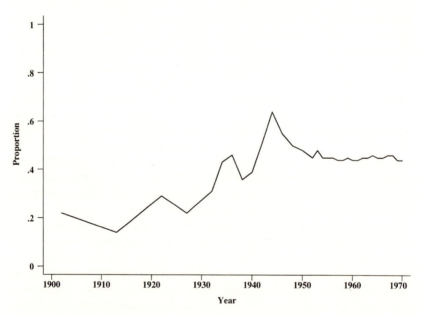

Figure 5.5. National-Government Spending as a Proportion of Total Government (Nondefense) Spending in the United States

the federal bureaucracy in the twentieth century. It took almost three decades in the period prior to 1930s and another three decades after 1936, for the number of federal employees to double (1102).

Some would say that another period of centralization began in the late 1890s, with the biggest boost coming upon the election of Theodore Roosevelt in 1900. Civil service reform had begun ten years before, but it culminated in the creation of new federal bureaucratic agencies after the turn of the century to wrest control of government administration from partisan appointments. Roosevelt, a strong-willed, assertive leader, believed in the need to rationalize and standardize government, and he felt that the only way for this to succeed was to centralize the movement at the national level. Decentralized civil service reform would not work, he thought. Coming out of the period of party spoils in the 1870s and 1880s, when government jobs went directly to supporters of election victors, this centralization in the early twentieth century was intended to take power away from the states, which were seen to be dominated by local party bosses. As Skowronek (1982, 177) writes of the new bureaucracies, "The titles alone suggest something of an obsession with the rationalization of governmental forms and procedures. . . . The Commission on Department Methods, the Commission on Economy and Efficiency, the Bureau of Efficiency, the Central Bureau of Planning and Statistics, the Bureau of the Budget, the General Accounting Office, the Personnel Classification Board."

Indeed, Roosevelt's 1904 reelection effort centered on revitalizing the Interstate Commerce Commission to regulate the conduct of the country's largest business corporations, especially the railroads. In this he largely succeeded after election day (Skowronek 1982). Upon leaving office in 1909, he had built an administrative apparatus to regulate rail transport that touched every single congressional district in the country. While this and other bureaus were sometimes incapacitated by court decisions and interinstitutional conflict between presidents and congresses over the next twenty years, an important threshold had been passed. The structures in place by the beginning of World War I, followed by the mobilization for that war, laid the groundwork for the massive centralization of authority in the 1930s.

The Progressive Era centralization slowed to a crawl after 1911, when the Democrats regained control of the House of Representatives. As avid states' rights advocates in the early twentieth century, the Democrats in the House thwarted any efforts by William Howard Taft, Roosevelt's successor, to build on Roosevelt's legacy. In truth Taft was not overly enthusiastic about continuing Roosevelt's centralizing reforms. Taft believed in the value of a strict interpretation of the Constitution, which meant that he generally favored giving the national government limited authority to regulate commerce, promote economic development, and set standards.

We are more comfortable typing this era (1900–1910) as ambiguous, though it is a close call. It is true that Roosevelt centralized authority through state building. It is not the case, however, that the national government was more important in people's lives than state governments, nor that the national government was more involved in regulations of economic activity than were the state governments. In fact, Roosevelt still believed in laissez-faire government and had Supreme Court decisions to help him, with some exceptions related to trusts and price gouging.

## Decentralized Period, 1800–1854

The presidential administration under George Washington contained within it the seeds of the first American party system, consisting of the Federalists and Jeffersonians (Democratic-Republicans). There was a great deal of animosity and intra-administration conflict between the two main protagonists, Alexander Hamilton and Thomas Jefferson, over the proper role of the national government in the new nation. Hamilton, who advocated a strong, centralizing national government that would be able to set the economic course for the country, certainly had the upper hand in the Washington administration and in the Adams administration that followed. For the first decade of American history, there was a concerted effort by the president and his administration to unify and coordinate the goals of the states and their new federal government.

When Jefferson won the presidency and his new party won control of both legislative chambers in 1800, however, the tide had turned, and turned significantly. The Democratic-Republicans (which became the Democrats in the 1830s) controlled, in one form or another, the national government for over fifty of the next sixty years. It is not hyperbole to say that political economy of first half of the nineteenth century in the United States was dominated by the philosophy of the Jeffersonian, then Jacksonian, then antebellum Democratic Party. Ironically, that philosophy and the policies that gave it heft, while they came from the national government, were intended to preserve the sovereignty and political authority of the states relative to the national government. This philosophy dominated the political economy of the new nation, with roots predating the Constitution.

### CONSTITUTIONAL AND LEGAL AUTHORITY

Eskridge and Ferejohn (1994) note that because of the nation's experience under the Articles of Confederation "there was a consensus after the adoption of the Constitution that the federal government should be able to exercise national authority to facilitate a national market. . . . The Court's federalism decisions in this period relentlessly pursued this developmental objective, but without violating the original promise that state governments would be left free to follow local developmental policies" (1369). Even in *Gibbons v. Ogden,* which struck down a New York law to license steamboats between New York and New Jersey because it was inconsistent with a federal statute, the court, nevertheless, left open the "possibility of state regulation of the coastal trade" (1370). A case that ostensibly federalized commercial law, *Swift v. Tyson* was overruled in *Erie Railroad Co. v. Tompkins.* In contrast to the Marshall Court, the Taney Court allowed the "states to pursue local development objectives, even in cases where the Marshall Court may have considered these objectives to have trenched upon national authority or private property" (1373). "An exemplar was *Mayor of the City of New York v. Miln* which upheld a New York law screening immigrants coming into the city from overseas and barring entry of immigrants the mayor felt were likely to become dependent upon the city. . . . in *Cooley v. Board of Wardens* the court upheld Pennsylvania statute requiring vessels entering and leaving the port of Philadelphia to engage local pilots to navigate then through the harbor" (1374).

The Supreme Court accommodated and sustained the states' policy-making dominance (Freyer 2000, 448). This is apparent in the operation of contract law. "State courts generally enforced commercial contract law leniently, especially where nonresident merchants or corporations challenged local business. The emergence of the federal judiciary's general commercial law culminating in the *Swift v. Tyson* (1842) did not destroy local control of negotiable credit paper. On the contrary, it created a dual credit market: the federal courts aided interstate credit transactions while state legal institutions protected locally oriented market relations" (456). The Court also expanded the ability of states to "promote new technologies such as railroads while also protecting local producer interests" (458).

THREATS TO NATIONAL INTEGRITY

Three exceptions to the pattern of provincialization occurred during this time. For all three, the national government was expected to, threatened to, or actually did take actions that mattered a great deal to ordinary citizens. The first two kinds were sporadic throughout the era, and the third kind was a constant.

First, when war broke out with Britain in 1812 and Mexico in 1846 or when periodic wars were waged against the Native American nations, national issues came to the forefront, and ordinary citizens were confronted with military recruiters, the loss of sons to war, and dangers from foreign and Native American militaries. Second, when the economy entered a downturn, which was mainly when prices for agricultural products were low, such as in the recessions of the 1830s and 1840s, attention tended to shift toward higher levels of government, especially the national government. Third, sectional conflict over slavery was always lurking underneath decentralized America as the one issue that ultimately led to centralization in the 1860s. A large motivation for many Democrats to maintain decentralized authority in the United States in the 1840s and 1850s was the belief that centralization would lead to one or more of the following outcomes, any of which was bad for Democrats: it would split apart the Democratic Party, it would split apart the country, or it would lead to intrusion in the southern political economy by a northern-led national government. Thus, a national issue was always present below the surface, although neither major political party nor politicians in many key states found it in their interests to make that issue more important than the local and state-based policy issues that were the standard foci of political campaigns. When the issue of slavery in the new territories finally broke into the open with the Nebraska Act of 1854, the most decentralized political era in American history ended.

## DEVELOPMENT POLICIES

Between independence and prior to the adoption of the constitution in 1787, each state had a peculiar mix of "promotional and protectionist mercantile policies" (Freyer 2000, 438). Massachusetts "gave bounties to producers of lumber, fish, and potash while facilitating small-scale manufacturing through a combination of import duties, grants to individuals, and public aid to private enterprise"; New York, in contrast, used tariffs and bounties to encourage the production of hemp and iron (438). The southern states instituted systems of public warehouses and offered subsidies to preferred crops and prohibited certain exports: "During the 1780s these states also provided inducements for the construction of their own fleet of ships to overcome dependence upon the foreign carrying trade" (438). These "mercantile regulations nonetheless stimulated each state's productive enterprise sufficiently that local rather than national economic development prevailed" (439). States also defended their debtors not only against foreign creditors but also from creditors from other states.

Freyer (2000) attributes a larger role to state governments for economic development in the first seventy years or so after the ratification of the Constitution. He observes that "as the new American brand of federalism evolved state and local governments established wider direct influence over the economic order than did the national government. . . . After 1815, the states replaced the federal government as the primary stimulators of economic development" (447–48).

### SIZE OF GOVERNMENTS

From 1790 to about 1860, federal government expenditures accounted for less than 2 percent of the national income (Freyer 2000). Estimates of real per-capita federal spending show that federal monies remained well below the $3 per capita mark until the Civil War and did not rise above the $5 per capita mark till 1915 when it spent between $7 and $8 per head (Sylla 2000, 505). As for state governments, their aggregate spending was at its highest between 1820 and 1840 when states borrowed nearly $200 million for development investments (Sylla 2000, 506, 521). In 1853 state and local governments were recipients of 36 percent of all foreign investment in the United States when the federal government's share was only 7 percent. (For 1843, state and local governments received 65 percent of total foreign investment in the United States, whereas the federal government got 0 percent.) (See Davis and Cull 2000, 741–42.)

Jefferson's legacy lived well into the late nineteenth century in the party he had spawned. Compared with its main competitors, the Federalists and then the Whigs, the Democratic party stood for provincialization. They worked to inhibit the power of the national government to intrude into state and local matters, to restrict the power of the federal courts to override state laws and actions, and to use the federal government as the protector of state interests—by collecting tariffs on foreign goods, for example. Only on issues of war with Britain and war against the natives, and on building trade barriers against other nations, were the Democrats much interested as a party in centralizing authority to the national government, and even then they were often divided.

As a result, during these early decades the United States was truly a nation of states, where the national government collected no taxes directly from citizens, had no permanent bureaucratic agencies, and had very limited reach and authority. What money it spent went to the military, diplomacy, exploration, new purchases of land in the West, salaries for postal workers and other federal employees, and internal improvements such as canals, land clearing, and roads. The federal government, through its employees, hardly interacted with ordinary citizens at all, except perhaps through the postal system or military recruiters, and even these latter were typically state-based. In contrast, the states actually spent some money, albeit not a great deal, on social services and welfare (see Sylla 2000). Cities, towns, and states sometimes paid for poorhouses, orphanages, and the building of hospitals. Local and state governments played a much more integral role in the lives of ordinary citizens than did the national government during this time. The same could be said in most other eras until the 1930s, but undoubtedly it was to a greater degree before the Civil War than any time thereafter.

## Ambiguous Period, 1876–1932

### CONSTITUTIONAL AND LEGAL AUTHORITY

The period between the Civil War and the New Deal saw a struggle between which level of government had more authority. It is difficult to categorize it as either centralizing or provincializing. The Supreme Court protected provincialization in *Munn v. Illinois* (1877), unholding the use of the state's police powers to control businesses with a public interest; it also sanctioned state authority over out-of-state corporations, and allowed "states wide discretion over eminent domain" (Freyer 2000, 464). "Simultaneously, however, the Court and Congress enlarged national authority by upholding congressional power over new technologies such as the telegraph (*Pensacola Telegraph Co. v. Western Union* in 1877), and the justices affirmed as constitutional the use of federal taxing power for regulatory purposes. On the whole, especially after the mid-1880s, the Court construed the commerce clause in favor of increased federal power" (Freyer 2000, 464).

The Supreme Court continued its trend of protecting some states' rights while allowing an expansion of federal authority. In 1873 the Supreme Court in "The Slaughter House Cases . . . refused to apply the various clauses of the fourteenth amendment to strike down a Louisiana statute vesting a monopoly in one butcher's establishment in the city of New Orleans" (Eskridge and Ferejohn 1994, 1378). States' rights prevailed during the Chase (1864–73) and the Waite (1874–88) Courts. Between 1895 and 1896, the judges staked out an agenda that had three features, according to Eskridge and Ferejohn. First, the court decision meant that the "federal government should enjoy virtually plenary power to regulate interstate railway transportation" (1380). Second, the court continued to insist that the "federal government had no authority to invade the state's autonomy or their local development prerogatives, even under the 'pretext' of their established constitutional powers" (1381). And, third, neither the states nor the federal government had the authority to engage in economic redistribution from the haves to have-nots. The court struck down the federal income tax as it violated, in the court's judgment, "Article 1's requirement that such taxes be apportioned among the states" (1382). Simultaneously the Supreme Court in *Nebbia v. New York* in 1934 affirmed the authority of state legislatures over intrastate commerce (Vietor 2000, 974).

### DEVELOPMENT POLICIES

Like all major wars, World War I influenced the relationship of the federal government to business. The war "confirmed the importance of national industrial coordination and established the legitimacy of large-scale enterprise. It yielded successful examples of cooperation among firms and between business and government . . . [and] federal regulatory authority, especially regarding banking, competition policy, and transportation was overhauled at the outset of this period" (Vietor 2000, 971–72). While the federal government enacted the Federal Reserve Act (1913), the Clayton and Federal Trade Commission Act (1914), and the Transportation Act (1920), state governments also expanded their role in this period. From 1914 to 1932 "regulatory responsibilities in most other areas of the economy were still decentralized"; most essential services were provided by either the state or the localities, and it was in this period that public utility commissions came to supervise public services (Vietor 2000, 973).

State governments played an important but different role in this period. By the 1870s the role of the government in creating the basic economic infrastructure had been largely completed (Sylla 2000, 536). Industrialization created the demand for regulation, and there was a persistent demand for regulatory and social interventions from the government in this period. The state was the level of government to deal with on issues of regulation. As Woodrow Wilson noted, "the great bulk of the business of the government still rests with state authorities . . . they determine the power of masters over servants and the whole law of principal and agent, . . . they regulate partnerships, debt and credit, and insurance; they constitute all corporations, both private and municipal. . . . Space would fail in which to enumerate the particular items of this vast range of power; to detail its parts would be to catalogue all social and business relationships, to set forth all foundations of law and order" (cited in Sylla 2000, 510–11). State legislation, then, dealt with the new issues of regulation. "By 1887, when the federal Interstate Commerce Commission came in, twenty-nine states already had railroad commissions. By World War I, 44 of 48 states had such commissions. In 1914, twenty-three states regulated most public utilities, and thirty-five regulated telephone companies. Milk inspection was practiced by forty-six states" (Sylla 2000, 537). Child labor was limited by twenty-eight states in 1900, thirty-nine states limited women's hours of work in 1917, worker accident compensation was available in thirty-one states by

1916, and all states by World War I had laws for compulsory education (537–38). Argersinger (2001) too observes that state governments were far more important in making social policy and regulating of economic activity in the second half of the nineteenth century.

SIZE OF GOVERNMENTS

The Civil War had a major impact on government finances as it allowed the federal government to "set precedents that had consequences long after the war ended. They came in each of the three means by which government, any government, can gain control over resources, mainly taxation, printing money and borrowing" (Sylla 2000, 527). The federal government increased the rates on tariffs, which were the mainstay of federal government finance. Internal taxation such as excise taxes on consumer goods or stamp taxes on legal documents was levied, as were federal direct taxes on property (that had been eliminated in 1812). The income tax, which was first levied in the Civil War (though it was phased out by 1872) established an important precedent. Attempts to introduce the income tax failed until 1894, two years after the Democrats had captured both houses of Congress. The Democrats revived the income tax, with a large exemption ($4,000) and a low rate (2 percent), but the tax was held unconstitutional by the Supreme Court. The income tax was finally levied in 1913, after the adoption of the Sixteenth Amendment (528).

The introduction of direct federal payments to veterans was the other major change resulting from the Civil War. It established the role of entitlements from the federal government. Payments to veterans had been a component of every federal budget since 1789, but the numbers had been very small (between $1 million and $3 million between 1815 to 1860). These payments increased after the Civil War to between $25 million and $30 million, but the monies were allocated only to those who had been disabled in the line of duty (Sylla 2000, 534). In 1879, after budget surpluses had reemerged, Congress passed the Pension Arrears Act that increased the number of pensioners. As a consequence, pension payments constituted almost 20 percent of federal spending in 1885 (535). The pension plans were further liberalized in 1890, and as the number of beneficiaries rose to nearly a million in 1893 pension payments were almost 40 percent of the federal budget (535). Despite a gradual decrease over time in veterans' benefits as a the proportion of the federal budget, in 1914 such payments to veterans still amounted to almost 25 percent.

The expansion of the role of the federal government after the Civil War did not intrude on the authority of state governments to "control local governments, family and criminal law, and (to a degree) commercial credit" (Freyer 2000, 462). In many respects, during and shortly after the Progressive Era the role of government in the economy began to increase quite dramatically. Government expenditures as a proportion of GNP rose from about 7 percent in 1900 to about 40 percent in 1990. This involved a relative expansion of federal expenditures, from "35 percent of all government expenditures in 1900 to 45 percent in 1940, and 60 percent by 1990" (474). State and federal governments increased their role in the period preceding the New Deal. Moreover, "the Supreme Court sanctioned increased, if decentralized, state and federal regulatory activism" (475). State governments continued to exercise authority in the area of commercial law. There were attempts to make uniform state laws on negotiable paper—but all states did not play along. Few legislatures had adopted, by 1916, the set of model laws for all aspects of negotiable paper and by World War I at least "two-thirds of the states had no laws against commercial bribery" (478–79). In this period even though "commercial law underwent increased rationalization, federalism nevertheless enmeshed it in contentiousness" (478).

State government expenditures grew most dramatically during the 1920s (Brownlee 2000, 1015). Between 1913 and 1932 state government expenditures as a proportion of GNP grew from 1 percent to almost 5 percent. No other level of government grew so rapidly in these twenty years. Federal government expenditures tripled, fueled largely by defense spending. Local government expenditures over this period merely doubled (1014). This increase in state expenditures is not surprising since the state governments in the first part of the twentieth century had to address social issues and infrastructural needs such as transit systems, waterworks, sewer systems, parks, and the like (1025). In the 1920s it was state and local governments that faced increased expectations from the populace, and as a result of this pressure on their revenues state governments introduced such enduring new taxes as the sales tax and user charges (1035).

Some may argue that the current era, especially since 1980, has been an era of provincialization and deregulation in the years following the Reagan presidency. Beginning with the Nixon administration, in fact, political rhetoric from both Republicans and Democrats has continued to extol the virtues of giving power back to the states. In some cases, such as the 1996 welfare reforms under the Clinton administration (Democratic) and Republican Congress, there actually was a ceding of authority from the national government to the state governments. Nevertheless, examples of such provincialization are modest in comparison with the overwhelming authority of the national government to determine the economic well-being of individuals and communities. This national authority has been in place since the New Deal and has only been enhanced by the growth of social insurance programs and other forms of direct national assistance to individuals and communities. Moreover, many of the provincializing moves by the national government have been laden with restrictions and oversight on the states, so these are sometimes less provincializing than they appear at first glance. Consider, for example, the continuing role of national government spending on research and development, natural resource management, weapons purchases, military bases, and salaries for federal workers and military personnel. All of these expenditures affect the economies of local areas throughout the country, and the fundamental fact about American political life that voters hold the national government most responsible among all the levels of government for the health of the economy has changed little since the 1930s.

## CONCLUSION

There have been periods of centralization and provincialization in all four nations, and in those periods either the central or provincial governments had more power or trends were moving in one direction or another. The extent of centralization or provincialization is a matter of degree, and in a modern democracy no level of government can ever be void of decision-making authority.

There are, however, as we discuss in more detail in the next chapter, key differences between Canada and India and the United States in the powers of state and provincial governments. In Canada and India, state or provincial governments have played a far larger role in their economies than state governments in the United States in the latter half of the twentieth century. This is most apparent in the large number of public-sector corporations and organizations that the Canadian and Indian state governments ran in earlier decades. Such public ownership was never as extensive in the United States, where, for a variety of historical reasons, states never had the same degree of control over economic activity within their boundaries as did states and provinces in India and Canada.

# Chapter 6

## DYNAMICS OF PARTY AGGREGATION

IN THIS CHAPTER and the next, we summarize data from hundreds of national elections and tens of thousands of district elections in our four countries to make the case that changes in party aggregation relate systematically to changes in political authority across different levels of government. We take a broad view of party systems in this chapter, focusing on changes over time in the degree to which party systems are national and comparing party systems across countries. In the next chapter we devote closer attention to our specific cases of Canada, Great Britain, India, and the United States.

For party aggregation to occur, voters and candidates have to be partisan in two distinct ways. First, voters must show a preference for choosing candidates with party labels over independent candidates, and candidates have to prefer running under party labels over running as independents. Second, voters and candidates must show partisanship of a more specific kind by demonstrating a preference or loyalty toward particular party labels. In order for voters to have the latter kind of partisanship, they must exhibit the first.

The first version of partisanship—a preference for party-affiliated candidates over independents—is a necessary condition for party aggregation, and, as demonstrated in chapter 4, with few exceptions candidates and voters in the four countries use party labels either to run for office or to vote for candidates. Supporting modern party systems is a shared belief by voters that candidates with party labels are more likely to win and will be more effective in office than those without such labels. Party labels that have meaning across vast reaches of the country—such as the Congress Party in India, the Liberal Party in Canada, the Conservative and Labour parties in Great Britain, and the Democratic and Republican parties in the United States—exist because voters believe that coordination at election time around a party label with voters in other regions, among other things, will make the processes of forming intragovernmental coalitions easier, will ease the difficulties of managing large and far-flung national bureaucracies, and will enable voters in future elections to know which collective group of politicians was responsible for the national policies previously adopted. In federal systems, voters may reason that common party labels not only help politicians from different regions within the national government work together but also help politicians across levels of government work better together.

This elemental reasoning would be hard to detect from survey data or from analyzing campaign rhetoric or local political commentary and is merely implied in the actions of voters when they support candidates with *any* party labels that have meaning outside of their electoral districts. Voters from British Columbia do not tell pollsters that they voted for the Liberals because voters in Ontario are doing likewise. It is taken for granted that the labels have meaning across geographic space.

To the extent that parties are discussed at all, voters focus instead on the policies and competencies associated with specific parties. Liberal voters in Canada will say how the Conservatives have failed or will fail, how the Liberals have succeeded or will succeed, in making people's lives better. Liberal candidates tell voters to support Liberals because it is the only way to defeat those in the Conservative Party and their policies. Public conversations that mention parties at election time typically are not about the importance of party labels in and of themselves, or about partisan versus nonpartisan candidates, but rather are about about party X versus party Y, or party X versus all the other parties.

The second, more specific kind of partisanship by candidates and voters gives a party system its distinctive characteristics. Party systems are ultimately the products of various decisions by different kinds of actors: the reactions and counterreactions of party leaders to each other and to the problems facing the nation, voters' responses to the candidates running under the party labels, and the actions of party organizations that are designed to hold in place the aggregation of votes across regions.

Our argument is that those decisions are shaped by how candidates and voters understand the nature of governance in the country. Specific decisions made over *which* party labels might make politicians more or less effective in providing public services, prosperity, and peace will depend considerably on the answers to the following kinds of questions. Where, in voters' minds, are the important decisions made? Is public authority dominated by the national government? Do state or provincial governments have a large role to play in the creation of jobs, the establishment of schools, the development and enforcement of business regulations, and the licensing of food products and alcohol? Answers to these questions will help determine how much support specific kinds of parties will gain at the expense of other kinds of parties. In particular, it will help determine how much support minor and regional parties will be able to maintain in opposition to national parties. Minor and regional parties should be more viable when a country is somewhat provincialized, and their support should be less during periods of centralization.

In other words, national party systems are more likely to occur when central governments have authority over the issues voters care about.

### REVIEW OF DIFFERENT ERAS

In the previous chapter we identified the eras in our four countries when centralization and provincialization occurred. A summary of that discussion is displayed in Table 6.1, which shows the eras and their categories. In Canada, for example, the overall pattern for the years between the British North American Act of 1867 and 1921 was one of increasing centralization, whereas for the years after 1960 the overall tendency was toward provincialization. In Great Britain, centralization of authority took place mostly after the Second World War when Westminster estab-

TABLE 6.1
Summary of Periods

|  | Centralizing or Centralized Periods | Decentralizing or Decentralized Periods | Ambiguous Periods |
|---|---|---|---|
| Canada | 1867–1921 *Dominion Control* | 1960– *Provincialization and Post–Meech Lake* | 1921–1960 *Federated Welfare State* |
| Great Britain | 1940–70 *Creating the Welfare State* | 1970– *Increasing Regionalism* | 1890–1940 *Political Centralization, Economic Decentralization* |
| India | 1952–57 *Unifying the Nation* <br><br>1970–77 *Indira Gandhi's Authority* | 1964–69; 1991– *State-Level Regulation* | 1957–64; 1978–91 *Devolution, but Center Holds Resources* |
| United States | 1860–76 *Civil War* <br><br>1932– *Post–New Deal* | 1800–54 *Jeffersonian Government* | 1876–1932 *End of Reconstruction, Gradual State Building* |

lished, and continued to build, a comparatively generous welfare state, whereas in recent decades it has been devolving authority toward the regions. India experienced centralization during the 1970s, as Indira Gandhi took powers away from the state governments, waged war on Pakistan, and put in place a state of emergency. The state governments have regained their authority and even exert more authority than ever before over key aspects of economic activity. Finally, the United States has had spasms of centralization, the most important occurring in the eras during and following the Civil War and during the Progressive Era, that culminated in the overwhelming changes in authority over economic policy during and following the New Deal programs of the 1930s.

If our analysis of the formation of national party systems is correct, then we should observe a dynamic relationship between the degree of political and economic centralization in a country and the nature of the party aggregation. In particular, it should be easier for parties to aggregate to the national level as a country experiences political and economic centralization. Moreover, it should be easier for minor and regional parties to survive the more a country is decentralized or provincialized politically and economically. Both of these effects should be more pronounced if the country is federal.

While we acknowledge the possibility that we have the causal story backward, and that party system changes drive centralization and decentralization rather than the reverse, we believe that our evidence shows otherwise, and we address this possibility in detail in Chapter 8.

MEASURES

We use various measures in this chapter and the next to demonstrate the dynamics of party systems in these countries. The different measures are like pieces of a puzzle that, when put together, reveal a picture. No one measure can provide a complete picture of a country's party system. Moreover, it would be tedious to report all the measures for all four countries in all eras in this chapter and the next, so we restrict the reporting of data to those necessary to provide an accurate picture of the process of party aggregation in Canada, Great Britain, India, and the United States.

One crucial measure has already been shown and discussed briefly in the first chapter, the effective number of political parties at the national level in lower-house elections (Figures 1.1–1.4). The measure for the effective number of parties, N, offers an indication of the concentration of votes across parties. The number is higher when votes are more fragmented or widely distributed among parties, and the number is lower the more those votes are concentrated on a small number of parties. Fewer political parties winning substantial votes means that party aggregation has been more effective. Therefore, all other things being equal, that measure should decrease under centralization if our explanation is correct. This is especially true in single-member, simple-plurality systems where two parties get votes in the district. If two and only two parties get votes in the districts and the number of parties getting votes in the nation is greater than two, then it has to be the case that the same two parties are not competing in all districts.

In chapter 2, we reported the average effective number of parties in the districts for the lower-house elections. Using this measure and the number of national parties, we can combine them to understand the degree to which party aggregation leads to a fully nationalized party system, as opposed to a regionalized party system. Once again, by nationalized we mean that party systems at the district, state or province, or regional level are similar to the party systems at the national level. Note that if Duverger's Law works at the district level and 2 parties get all the votes in district elections, then two-partism nationally means a fully aggregated, national party system. As we saw in chapter 2, Duverger's Law does not always work at the district level. In Canada and Great Britain, the average effective number of parties in the districts has been above 2.5 in recent decades, so full party aggregation could mean having a national party system with more than two parties.

We focus attention, therefore, on the difference between the effective number of parties at the national level and the average effective number of parties in the districts. Figure 6.1 shows the trends in this measure for our four countries. We call this the measure of party aggregation. If that number is 0, party systems in the districts mirror party systems nationally.[1] Numbers above 0 mean that there are more parties nationally than there are in the districts, and some parties are competing and winning votes in only a portion of the districts. Generally, the lower the number, the better parties aggregate and the more nationalized the party system. (The number can be below 0 only if there are gaps in the data,

---

[1] This conclusion assumes several things: (1) in the district elections it is not the case that on average many minor parties are receiving very small proportions of the vote (as we showed in chapter 2, this assumption makes sense given our data); (2) the standard deviation of N across the districts is relatively small (it is for our countries); and (3) the districts are of roughly equal size by population (this does not hold for some eras for our countries, but it turns out that the consequences for our conclusions are insignificant because there is no evidence of systematic differences in our measures between small districts and large districts in any of our countries in these eras).

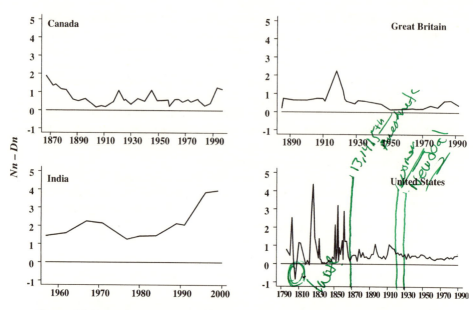

Figure 6.1. Party Aggregation: Difference between National N and Average District N (*Nn–Dn*)

something we discuss later.) These figures on party aggregation provide the basis for our main conclusions on the dynamics in party systems, which we discuss shortly.

We report, in Figures 6.2–6.5, the effective number of parties at the state, provincial, or regional levels, in combination with the effective number of parties at the district and national levels. These are worth examining in detail, as they are instructive regarding the formation of national party systems. Using these data, we can calculate a revealing and, for many of our arguments, decisive statistic. Figure 6.6 shows the proportion of the party aggregation disparity between districts and nation that is taken up by the difference between the state-level measure and the national measure. This statistic demonstrates how much of the *lack of* party aggregation at the national level is due to state- or provincial-level parties failing to coordinate across those units, and how much of the lack of party aggregation at the national level is attributable to the failure of voters or candidates to aggregate votes across districts to the state or provincial level. When that statistic is above .5, then more of the total lack of aggregation is due to a failure of parties to aggregate across states, provinces, or regions rather than across districts within states, provinces, or regions. As we see in Figure 6.6, there are interest-

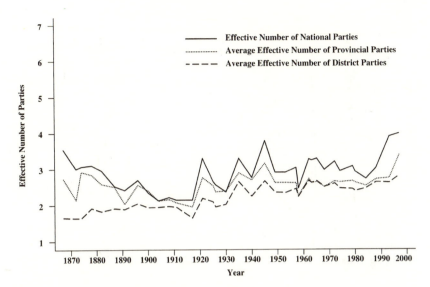

Figure 6.2. Effective Number of Parties in Canada

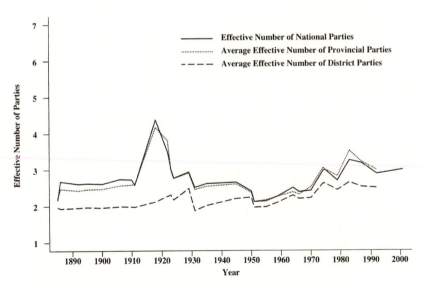

Figure 6.3. Effective Number of Parties in Great Britain

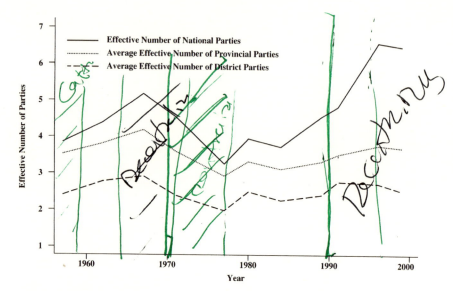

Figure 6.4. Effective Number of Parties in India

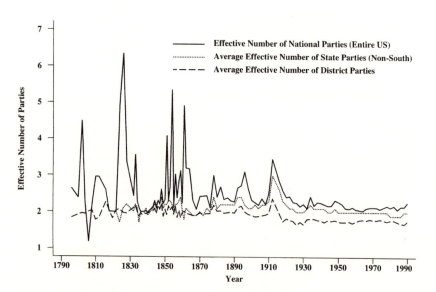

Figure 6.5. Effective Number of Parties in the United States

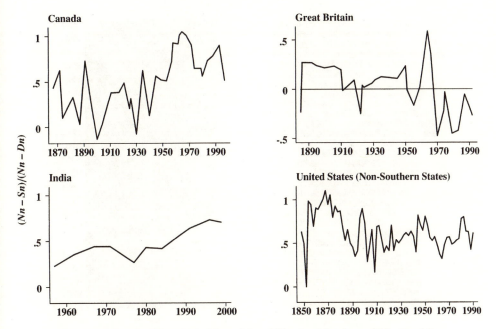

Figure 6.6. $(Nn–Sn)/(Nn–Dn)$. *Note:* $Nn$ = Effective Number of National Parties; $Sn$ = Average Effective Number of State Parties; $Dn$ = Average Effective Number of District Parties

ing patterns in this statistic that require explanation to understand cross-national differences and over-time differences within countries.

Several other measures of party fragmentation can be useful in describing the nature of party systems. We report, in Figures 6.7 and 6.8, the proportion of the vote obtained by the top two parties, and the effective number of minor parties—N calculated with all parties other than the top two parties in votes. These measures, respectively, provide an indication of the overall strength of minor parties and the concentration of strength among the minor parties.

We also wish to know about the presence or absence of national strength among the major parties, and the presence or absence of strong regional parties. Thus, we rely on four measures of national reach and strength of parties. While we measure these for specific parties—the top four parties by votes in any given election—we are interested in how these combined party features form the nature of the party system. These measures are the proportion of states or provinces in which the party contests at least one seat, the proportion of states or provinces in which the party wins at least one seat, the average proportion of districts within

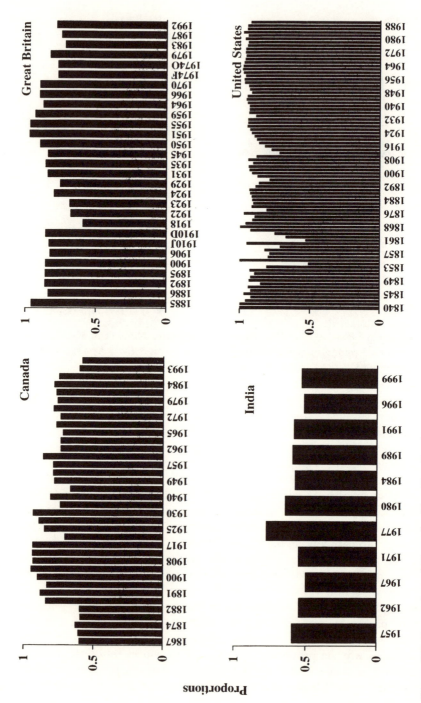

Figure 6.7. Proportion of Votes for Top Two Parties

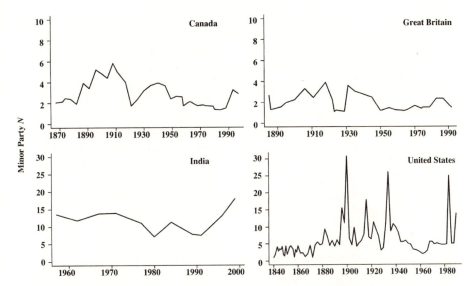

Figure 6.8. Minor Party $N$ (Effective Number of Parties for All but the Top Two Vote-Winning Parties). *Note*: The scales are different for the top panels and the bottom panels.

the states or provinces the party contests, and the average proportion of districts within the states or provinces the party wins. We do not show all of these data for all four countries but rather highlight relevant features for our arguments.

By nationalization we do not mean that all parties are national and that there are no regional parties. A highly nationalized party system can contain regional parties. It is a matter of degree; if a large proportion of votes are going to regional parties, then a party system is not very nationalized. Moreover, in drawing conclusions about specific parties, one needs to be careful not to conclude that each political party that has won a substantial portion of votes in lower-house elections in our four countries belongs in one of two categories—primarily either a regional party or a national party.

Similar to drawing conclusions about the party system as a whole, the issue of what makes a political party regional as opposed to national is not straightforward. Any such classification of a political organization can be misleading by forcing a dichotomy. Measuring the regional concentration of a party's appeal and electoral support is a matter of degree. Moreover, the type of measurement used is important. A single measure, such as the number of regions within which a party wins votes, may not provide the entire picture. A party may not necessary be considered regional simply because it receives most of its support from one or two regions and does poorly in other regions. It may field candidates in every district in every region of the country, and its trajectory may be upward everywhere, indicating that it may be in the process of nationalizing. For example, the New Democratic Party (NDP) in Canada was considered by some to be a regional party even though it gradually grew to win substantial votes in most regions (Carty, Cross, and Young 2000). When it became a national party depends on one's threshold, and whether one focuses on where the party fields candidates, how many votes it receives in each region, and where it wins seats. Party reputations, and even scholarly classifications based on them, may not be entirely accurate and may fail to detect subtleties or changes in the regional or national strength of parties.

## OVERALL PATTERNS OF PARTY AGGREGATION

As Figure 6.1 shows, trends in the degree of party aggregation are identifiable in all four countries. The lowest levels of the party aggregation measure correspond to periods of centralization, whereas the highest levels of the party aggregation measure correspond to periods of decentralization. For the ambiguous periods, the data are more mixed, but this is perhaps to be expected. In some eras, such as in Canada from 1867 to 1917, a period of centralization, there is an unmistakable downward trend in the party aggregation measure. The same can be said for Britain from 1930 to the early 1950s. While the average measure over these years may not be low compared with those of other eras—because, for example, the party aggregation measure is high in Canada in 1870—the trends show the response of the party system to centralization. From these data, the inference is clear: it becomes increasingly easier to aggregate votes across districts under party labels as countries centralize. On the flip side, decentralization or provincialization creates the space for local or regional parties to form and survive.

For example, Canada's party aggregation measure drops from near 2 in the 1860s to close to 0 by 1910. Indeed, Figure 6.2 indicates that Canada experienced pure two-partism for approximately a decade and a half, from 1904 to 1920. Then, beginning in 1921, regional parties came to be important and the number of parties fluctuated until the 1980s, when problems of party aggregation became serious. These problems of party aggregation, we argue, occurred because of the failure of aggregation across provinces, rather than within provinces, as Figure 6.6 shows, and this is especially true after the 1960s. The statistic in Figure 6.6 is above .5 after 1960. Essentially, the provincialization in recent decades in Canada has given rise to regionally specific parties and brought about a level of *provincial party fragmentation* unprecedented in Canadian history. In contemporary Canadian politics increasing numbers of voters and candidates, especially those who oppose the Liberals, have not found it essential to be part of national parties that have the potential to govern alone.

In Great Britain, parties aggregated most effectively, and the country experienced two-partism, during the 1950s, precisely when Duverger was writing about single-member plurality systems leading to two-partism. Otherwise, British parties have aggregated reasonably well, though not perfectly. During the period of decentralization since 1970, the party aggregation measure is relatively low, even though the number of national parties has shot upward. This results from the rise in the number of parties at the district level (see Figure 2.4).

India has never experienced two-partism, although the number of parties and the measure of party aggregation dropped precipitously in the 1970s. At its lowest point, India was a three-party system, as measured by the effective number of national parties. In recent decades, party aggregation has not been successful, as the party system in India has fragmented into state-level parties. Figure 6.6 shows how in recent years most of the party aggregation problems stem from the failure of state-level parties to coordinate. The measure of party aggregation from Figure 6.1 is highest in India in 2000 among all the elections reported, save the United States in 1820, for which data problems (lack of party labels for many candidates) limit the ability to draw reliable inferences from these numbers.

Finally, party aggregation in the United States has been relatively successful since the 1870s. It blips upward several times during the 1890s and the 1910s, but it is quite low otherwise. Interestingly, while the United States has had probably the world's purest two-partism since the 1930s, the party aggregation measure does not drop to 0. This is largely due to the high numbers of uncontested elections to the lower house for most of the twentieth century, thus making the average effective number of parties at the district level lower than 2. When districts are uncontested, the effective number of parties is 1, so the average for this measure over all districts will be lower than 2 in the United States. Consequently, the party aggregation measure, which results from subtracting the national measure from the district-level measure, is greater than 0.

A striking conclusion from Figure 6.1 is that, for the most part, in three of the four countries, parties aggregate quite well, and that these countries have experienced highly nationalized party systems. If we make the arbitrary designation that a party aggregation measure below 1 indicates a well-aggregated, nationalized party system, then Canada since the 1890s, Great Britain throughout its history since the 1880s (except for 1917), and the United States since the 1870s, all qualify. In fact, one can only conclude that if party aggregation is a good measure of the degree to which district-level elections reflect national party competition, these three countries are remarkably similar. The measure fluctuates between 0 and 1 (with the exception of 1917 in Britain) for the entire twentieth century for all three countries.

From another angle, however, an examination of Figures 6.2–6.5 on the effective number of national parties, the United States from 1870 to 1932 looks quite similar to Canada and Great Britain during long portions of their histories. For all three countries in those eras, there are occasional spikes upward to above three effective parties nationally, with troughs down to two-partism.

Given these data, we must revisit the widespread conclusion that the United States is inherently or stubbornly a two-party system. From the data on lower-house elections, one would be hard put to sustain the view of American exceptionalism: the United States is hardly a two-party system prior to 1930 and hardly exceptional in its party competition to lower-house elections in comparison with our other single-member, simple-plurality countries. To maintain the conclusion of American two-partism, one must emphasize at least one of three other patterns. First, in presidential politics throughout American history, two candidates (even in much of the nineteenth century) routinely received the vast majority of votes (though there are plenty of exceptions as well). Second, post-1932 congressional elections, as shown in Figure 6.5, were unambiguously two-party. Third, party competition for majority status within the Congress has always been between the two major parties. Members of Congress in the nineteenth century often ran on one party label and adopted one of the two major party labels upon taking office.

India, however, *is* exceptional among our four countries, and while it flirted with a party aggregation measure of 1 in 1977, for the most part, it has a highly fragmented, regionalized, disaggregated party system, and increasingly so in recent times. It is tempting, and probably not altogether wrong, when explaining why India is an outlier to emphasize how much more diverse India is culturally, linguistically, and religiously in comparison with the other three countries. In India, the number of parties and party aggregation have fluctutated, although there have not been concomitant changes in India's religious, linguistic, and caste diversity. The latter can, therefore, not be the sole explanation for changes in the party system. As one might imagine, we believe that India's status as an outlier has to do at least as much with the role of the national government in people's lives as it does with diversity, something we discuss further in the next chapter.

## Supportive Evidence Using a Different Measure

We have adopted one notion of what it means to say that a party system is "national," or "nationalized," but ours is not the only possible measure of the nationalization of the party system. There are different, yet related, notions in the literature. Some (e.g., Sundquist 1973; Claggett, Flanigan, and Zingale 1984; Kawato 1987) have considered the degree to which subunit (state or district) electorates show similar voting patterns as the national electorate, paying close attention to levels of support for the major parties. Others (Claggett, Flanigan, and Zingale 1984; Kawato 1987; Brady 1985; Bawn, Cox, and Rosenbluth 1999) focus on how changes in support for parties or presidential candidates among subunit electorates mirror changes in national support for those parties or candidates. Taken as a whole, these arguments support our periodization of the nationalization of party systems. For example, many researchers have identified and quantified the substantial nationalization of the American party system after the New Deal. This is consistent with our claims. This literature has, however, little analysis of time-series data from Canada, Great Britain, and India.

Jones and Mainwaring (2003) examine both party system nationalization and party nationalization using an innovative measure. They are interested in the degree of similarity of party support in geographic subunits to nationwide party support. They rely on a version of the Gini index, which is a common measure of income inequality, to quantify levels of inequality of vote shares for parties across states or provinces. For their purposes, a Gini coefficient of 0 for a party means that the party received equal vote shares in every state or province, while a coefficient approaching 1 means that a party won all its votes in one state or province and none in any other. The degree of nationalization, then, is the weighted average of the Gini coefficients across all the parties in the country. They report party system measures for Canada and the United States back to 1980, and most Latin American democracies in recent decades. According to their data and formulas, Canada has relatively low nationalization in its party system compared with Latin American countries, while the United States has an intermediate level of nationalization.

It is worth comparing the Jones and Mainwaring measures to our own, and we report their measure of party system nationalization using our data on our three federal countries, Canada, India, and the United States. By analyzing the data with an alternative measure reflecting a slightly different notion of nationalization, we can conduct a valuable test of the robustness of our claims. Our party aggregation measure as shown in Figure 6.1—the national N minus the average district N—is lower the more the party system is nationalized. While they report 1 minus the Gini coefficient as their measure of nationalization for a party—higher values mean more nationalization—for comparison purposes we report the reverse of their formula so that it coincides better with our party aggregation measure. In reproducing the Jones and Mainwaring measure we report the Gini coefficient (instead of 1 minus the Gini coefficient); the two measures should move in the same direction over time if our claims are robust.

The specific means of calculating the Jones and Mainwaring measure are described in the appendix. For now, we note that their measure of party nationalization uses states or provinces as the units of analysis, whereas our measure uses electoral constituencies or districts. Thus our measure is a bit more fine-grained, and in combination with some specific features of their measure, this distinction turns out to make a slight difference in the results.

By any standard test of correlation of time-series data, the two measures are highly correlated. Figure 6.9 shows the two trend lines for our three federal countries, and we can see that in general, the two measures of party systems nationalization are related—they essentially measure similar processes and outcomes. Using our own measure, we have shown

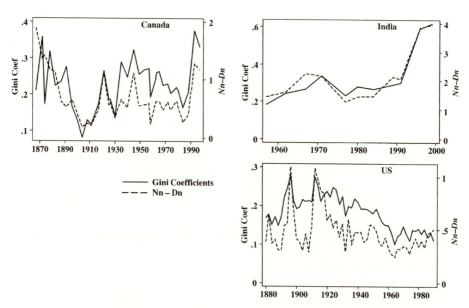

Figure 6.9. Comparison of Gini Coefficient to the Party Aggregation Measure

that the Canadian party system had no clear pattern of nationalization or fragmentation from 1910 to 1980, and then it experienced a clear move away from nationalization beginning in the 1980s. For the United States we have shown that since the New Deal, the American system has become quite nationalized, and that in India the system was most nationalized in the 1970s and early 1980s with high fractionalization starting in the late 1980s. If we were to rely solely on the Jones and Mainwaring measure, we would be led to similar conclusions. When our measure slopes up or down, the Jones and Mainwaring measure slopes up or down. The troughs and peaks take place at similar intervals.

The levels to which the measures drop or rise, and the timing of the changes, however, are not completely commensurate for Canada since the 1930s and for the United States in all periods. Roughly speaking, the (inverse of the) Jones and Mainwaring measure rises to "higher" levels than our measure. Our countries appear less nationalized using their data. Why the difference? The answers lie in the differences between the two formulas, and in the difference between district to national comparisons, and state or province to national comparisons.

The Jones and Mainwaring measure is sensitive to the number of states or provinces in a country, especially if there is a correlation between the population sizes of the states or provinces and party support, and this can explain why their measure reports less nationalization for the United States than our measure. All things being equal, under their measure countries with a large number of states or provinces will appear less nationalized than countries with a small number of states or provinces.[2] Moreover, their party nationalization measure does not weight states or provinces by population size, yet their party system nationalization measure weights parties by vote size. In the United States, for example (which has relatively many states), if smaller population states support Republicans more than larger population states, the distributions for both Democrats and Republicans across the states will be unequal, and the Gini index will be high for both major parties, leading to a relatively low nationalization measure for the United States.

It is also relevant that we measure district-level data, whereas they rely on state- or province-level data. Recall that in Figure 6.6, we show a measure of the degree of the failure of district to national party aggregation that is attributable to the failure of state-to-national party aggregation. When that number is above .5, it means that most of the gap

[2]If there are two countries of similar size with similar vote shares given to the various types of parties, but one has a small number of states and the other has a large number of states, then, all things being equal, the voting patterns in the states in the country with the small number of states will reflect the national pattern more so than the patterns in the states in the country with the larger number of states.

between the average district N and the national N comes from the failure of parties to aggregate across states or provinces. And note that the measure in Figure 6.6 is above .5 for Canada for most of the post-1930s era and .5 for nearly all of American history. This means that there are substantial differences across states or provinces in party competition (especially in the strength of minor parties), more than there are differences across districts within the states or provinces. Jones and Mainwaring are correct to conclude that, judging from the differences across the states or provinces, Canada and the United States do not appear highly nationalized. From our perspective, however, relying on comparisons between national- and district-party competition, the countries appear more nationalized in some eras.

This comparison and explanation of the difference between these measures does not alter the main point, which is that the two measures trend in similar ways. Therefore, one would be led to similar conclusions using either approach.

## THE INFLUENCE OF CENTRALIZATION AND PROVINCIALIZATION ON POLITICAL PARTIES

If our argument linking party formation to centralization and provincialization is correct, we should see the formation of political parties responding to trends in federal relations in a nation-state. One way to assess the validity of this claim is to find instances when the support offered by particular groups of voters to specific political parties varies depending on which level of government has more authority. We provide two cases of how voter responses to changes in federal relations had an influence on the kind of political party—national or regional—they supported.

In India the backward- or middle-caste groups have varied their support for national or regional parties. The backward classes in the North Indian states of Bihar and Uttar Pradesh supported the socialist parties—the Praja Socialist Party (PSP) and the Samyukta Socialist Party (SSP). Both parties wanted preferential treatment for the backward classes of Indian society (Fickett 1968, 831; Brass 1981); the most appealing "campaign platform in Bihar, however, was the demand for the reservation of 60 percent of government jobs and places in educational institutions for the 'backward classes.' . . . This slogan was a great rallying cry among Bihar's lower castes and was unquestionably a major contributing factor in the SSP success in that state" (Fickett 1968, 491). In 1964 the two parties decided to merge and contest elections under one common label. In the 1990s, a period of provincialization, the backward castes in Bihar and Uttar Pradesh still supported a policy platform in which they were looking for preferential treatment in educational institutions and government jobs *yet* they supported their own parties in Bihar and Uttar Pradesh. In Bihar the backward classes support the Rashtriya Janata Dal of Laloo Yadav and in Uttar Pradesh the backward classes support a Uttar Pradesh party—the Samajwadi Party—led by Mulayam Singh Yadav.

Similarly, in the Canadian province of Alberta, farmers supported either national or regional parties, depending on which party better represented their interests. Farmers in Alberta were Liberal voters during the period of centralization through 1921. In 1921, however, things changed. Wheat storage and prices were an important issue. Farmers needed government support. The role of the Dominion government in agriculture was limited under the British North American Act, and the provincial government was supposed to make most decisions relating to agriculture. With provincial authority increasing, Alberta decided to take an active role in protecting farmer rights, especially those of wheat farmers. Unlike other provinces, for example, Alberta decided to build and own grain elevators that would store the wheat produced by farmers. The province was forced into action by the rise of the United Farmers of Alberta (UFA), a party that made an alliance with the Progressives for the elections of 1921. When the Liberals lost to the UFA in Alberta in 1921, the UFA came to control the provincial government. UFA candidates, however, ran under the Progressive label for the national elections in Alberta, and, not surprisingly, the Progressive Party in Alberta did much better than the Liberals. The Progressive Party, however, focused on national issues, although, in this period of provincialization they could not hold the attention of the Alberta farmers around issues that the national government should have dealt with. As a result, the party's vote share dropped in the 1925 national elections, and the UFA, seeing no point in supporting a national party, decided to run its own candidates for the national elections in Alberta. Following the 1926 national elections, the UFA emerged as the third largest party in the House of Commons.

*Chapter 7*

---

# PARTY AGGREGATION IN FOUR COUNTRIES

CHAPTER SIX DEMONSTRATED the broad patterns of party aggregation in our four countries, and offered specific examples of party system change in response to centralization and decentralization. In this chapter we expand our discussion of party aggregation, taking a more systematic approach to the history in each country. These cases support our evidence from the previous chapter and add considerable weight to our arguments.

## PARTY SYSTEM DYNAMICS IN CANADA

In some ways, the Canadian party system has seen very little stasis. Minor and regional parties have come and gone, and there have been several dramatic and rapid fluctuations in the fortunes of the major and the minor parties. No one could reasonably conclude that Canada has had a two-party system or a fully national system, except for a brief interlude from 1904 to 1920. This is in spite of the fact that it has had, for the most part, a single-member, simple-plurality electoral system since the Dominion's founding.

Despite the instability in some party system measures for Canada, there has been remarkable stability in the identity of the two major parties, the Liberals and the Conservatives.[1] Only in the 1990s have one of these two, the Conservatives, begun to show signs of perilous health. Otherwise, these two parties have consistently won the most votes in

---

[1]Johnston (2000) has a slightly different interpretation of the Canadian party system. He observes that Canada, like India, has seen the dominance of one party, the Liberals. He argues they have dominated Canadian elections much like the Congress Party has done in India. If one examines national-level data, as Johnston (2000) does, the Liberals do appear as the dominant party post-1935. But national-level data mask the fact that the Liberals faced more severe competition in the provinces, and, like the Congress Party of India, the Liberals were opposed by different parties in the various provinces. As the opposition to the Liberals varied by province (as it did for the Congress in India), the difference between the vote share of the Liberals and their closest competitor at the national level had to be larger than the differences in the vote share of the Liberals and their main opponents in each of the provinces.

every election, traded off (or even shared in) governing the dominion, and together maintained the loyalties of more voters than all other parties combined from 1867 to 1993. The most important minor parties in national elections, the Progressives, Social Credit, the Co-operative Commonwealth Federation (CCF), the New Democratic Party (NDP), the Bloc Quebecois, Reform, and the Alliance, have all presented serious challenges to the major parties, either by draining votes away or by winning seats outright. Only the Reform Party has ever finished among the top two parties in votes in any given election, effectively replacing the Conservatives in many regions in recent years.

Canada is also well known for its independent provincial party systems. They are independent in several ways. Sometimes the parties in the provinces are completely independent from their national party cousins with the same names. Thus, for many years, the Liberals in Ontario and Quebec have been barely linked—in ideology, personnel, organization, and levels of coordinated action—to the Liberal Party in national elections.[2] In other provinces, the party systems at the provincial level are vastly different. In British Columbia, for example, the "two big provincial parties [Social Credit and the NDP] shared 75 percent of the total vote" in 1953, and the combined vote has been very high ever since, even gaining over 90 percent between them after the 1986 elections (Blake, Carty, and Erickson 1991, 11). These two parties were the most important minor parties nationally, but they were not competitive for control of the national parliament, which has been dominated by the Liberals and Conservatives in much of the remainder of the country. There are also provincial-level parties that are independent of the major national parties, but not necessarily independent of the groups under the same name, that seek to win national seats. The Social Credit Party from Alberta, which was strong from the 1930s to the 1970s, is an example of how the two levels of party organization were in close cooperation. We recognize that these kinds of independent provincial parties are both symptomatic of the relatively provincialized nature of the Canadian state and consequential for national-party politics.

Consider our theoretical argument from chapter 3, and our discussion of the Canadian welfare state from chapter 5. If the federal government in Canada had a greater role to play in providing welfare directly to the citizens, or greater say in economic development or industrial relations (i.e., the state was more centralized than provincialized), voters would believe that having provincial parties with little national representation and national parliamentary seats filled by provincial parties would not

---

[2]For the breakup of the provincial and federal Liberals in Quebec, see Rayside (1978) and Ullman (1983).

benefit them much. The situation is different, however, when the operation of the welfare state and economic regulation are delicately balanced
between province and national authority, and especially when there is
intense bargaining between provinces and the national government over
the design of these policies, as there was in the 1930s and 1940s during
the establishment of the Canadian welfare state. Some voters are more
comfortable voting for these provincial parties in national parliamentary
elections. These voters are also more comfortable voting for the provincial parties in provincial elections than they would be if the Canadian
state were more centralized. Under conditions where the provinces have
real authority over economic policies, provincial politics opens a space
for such provincial-level parties as Social Credit to form and endure.
When provincial politics matters and provincial leaders bargain with
national leaders regularly, these parties can survive because enough voters want their provincial parties to have national representation and
their national parties to have provincial power.

It is interesting to contrast Canada with Great Britain and the United
States on this point. In Great Britain prior to the 1990s, there was no
explicitly authorized, constitutionally mandated space for regional-level
parties to gain local power and bargain with the national government
over the proper role for regions in making social and economic policies.
The only means was for regional or nationalist parties to contest national parliamentary seats and pressure the major national parties to pay
attention to regional concerns. Thus, the regional or nationalist parties
in Great Britain did not have a large impact on the party system relative
to the regional parties in Canada, which could gain real political authority at the provincial level. This is not to say that they had a small impact
on British politics. In fact, they had a significant impact mainly in forcing the major parties to pay more attention to regional grievances. In
Great Britain, it was not until in the 1970s and 1980s that a *national*
minor party, the Liberals/Social Democrats, won seats and votes in many
regions that the number of parties in Britain crept upward and the party
system fundamentally changed from a largely two-party system to a
three-party system.

State-level parties that have no connection to major parties do not
exist in the United States, at least at the level of competing seriously for
state office and for national representation in Congress. This is probably
due to the combined effects of two factors: the United States national
government's domination of the states on economic policies, and the
existence of presidential elections. Voters and candidates see the obvious
benefits of having state-level parties with connections to national parties,
whether those connections are merely to have voice in presidential nominations or to play a role in national policy making. There were some

small regional parties in the early 1800s in the United States, but none that received substantial congressional votes specific to a single state.

To offer a sense of the changes over time in the Canadian party system, it will be helpful to focus our attention on several types of data. These data are summarized in various figures across various chapters. Besides the graphs we have already mentioned, from chapters 1, 2, and 6, Figure 7.1 shows selected measures of the geographic spread of the top four parties.

We identified the fifty years following Confederation from 1867 to 1921 as one of centralization, and the period from 1921 to 1960 as ambiguous. As already mentioned, the data from the former period display a clear pattern indicating party aggregation toward nationalization of the party system. As shown in Figure 6.2, the earlier period corresponds to the lowest ebb in the effective number of parties in Canada and the lowest measure of party aggregation. By 1904 and until 1921, Canada was as much a two-party system as the United States has been

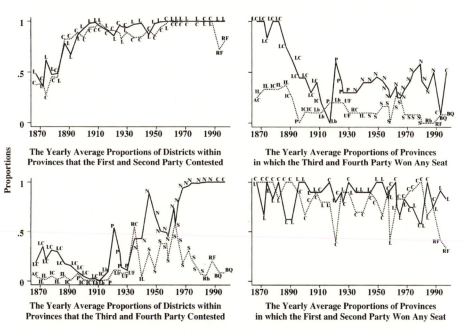

The Yearly Average Proportions of Districts within Provinces that the First and Second Party Contested

The Yearly Average Proportions of Provinces in which the Third and Fourth Party Won Any Seat

The Yearly Average Proportions of Districts within Provinces that the Third and Fourth Party Contested

The Yearly Average Proportions of Provinces in which the First and Second Party Won Any Seat

Figure 7.1. Selected Regional Patterns in Canadian Party Politics. *Note:* AC = All Canadian Party; BQ = Bloc Quebecois; C = Conservative; IC = Independent Conservative; IL = Independent Liberal; L = Liberal; Lb = Labour; LC = Liberal Conservative; N = New Democratic Party; P = Progressives; RC = Radical; RF = Reform Party; Rh = Rhinoceros; S = Social Credit; UF = United Farmers

since the 1930s. The Liberals and Conservatives together dominated Canadian national politics with no prominent minor party capturing much of the parliamentary vote.

There is widespread agreement that the party system was more national and Canadian government more centralized in the years from Confederation to the end of World War I than in other eras. Johnston (2000) and Johnston et al. (1992), in characterizing the evolution of the Canadian party system, recognize the period between 1896 and 1917 as one in which there was robust two-party competition in Canada. In this period there were two parties that competed and won most of the votes, and the parties were closer in their vote shares than at any other time in Canadian history; further, both parties were not as concentrated regionally (Johnston 2000, 5–6).[3] Carty, Cross, and Young (2000, 5; 2001) also see the period between 1896 and 1921 as one that was more centralized than any system that followed. Bickerton, Gagnon, and Smith (1999, 25) characterize this first party system as one in which the Conservatives, reflecting the view of those wanting to protect the status quo, preferred a "strong central government entrusted with sufficient powers to build and maintain a transcontinental political unit." Given the power of the federal government and its impact on economic development (Royal Commission on Dominion-Provincial Relations 1940), it is no surprise that provincial politicians aligned themselves with federal parties. In British Columbia, for example, it was provincial self-interest—the need to obtain federal largesse—that dictated the federal party to which provincial politicians aligned themselves (Blake 1985, 11–14).

Over this period, the effective number of national parties was between 2 and 3, but the average number of district parties was less than 2 (Figure 6.2). Many district elections were either uncontested or uncompetitive, and the two major parties did not compete in every district in every province (as shown in Figure 7.1, top left panel). Furthermore, there was a notable lack of coordination among candidates on party labels, with many local notables choosing any number of labels, Liberal, Conservative, Liberal Conservative, Independent Liberal, and Independent Conservative. In fact, candidates with the Liberal Conservative label ran and won in every province in the early elections, as shown in Figure 7.1, top right panel.

Over time, the parties aggregated, labels became more consolidated, and local notables lost their clout relative to parties and were less free to adopt whichever label suited them. There was marked movement

[3]Johnston et al. (1992) also offer a similar typology of the various party systems in Canada.

from 1880 to 1900 toward a system in which the two major party labels dominated; every district in every province ran candidates with both labels, and both parties won at least one seat in most provinces (see Figure 7.1, top left panel). Ironically, the number of minor parties increased, but each of these minor parties received fewer and fewer votes over the late nineteenth century. Consider Figures 6.7 and 6.8. By 1900 the two major parties received more than 90 percent of the national vote, but the effective number of minor parties rose to near five.

In 1921 the two-party system was shattered by two interrelated processes. First, there was the brief, but explosive, emergence of the Progressive vote. The Progressives represented the interests of western farmers discontented with, among other things, the high tariffs adopted by the Conservative government and supported implicitly by the opposition Liberals. They received 23 percent of the national vote in the first election they contested in 1921. Second, the major parties became more regional, with the Conservatives losing their national character and becoming more the party of Ontario and the Liberals becoming more a party of Quebec and the Maritime provinces. The election of 1921 marked the beginning of a more regional party system. Bickerton, Gagnon, and Smith (1999, 30) note that the "election heralded a transition from a party system based on a classic two-party competition with an intensely local or constituency focus to a system based on regional brokerage." Carty, Cross, and Young (2000, 5) also observe that the "first party system collapse in Canadian History occurred during and after the First World War as this era of the historic parties of Confederation ended and a new, more democratic, more regionalized, party politics emerged. The Canada of regional brokerage that this second party system served lasted until about 1960."

The first change, and the resulting spasm of fragmentation in Canadian party politics, did not in themselves last long, as the next two elections saw the demise of the Progressives. By 1935, as most of the "moderate Progressives had returned to the Liberal fold, the radicals became the nucleus of the CCF party" (Wearing 1981, 5). Two-partism in Canada never returned, however, coming close only in 1958 when the major parties received over 85 percent of the national vote.[4] Note the transition here. From 1887 to 1930, the top two parties generally received over 80 percent of the national vote, with the 1921 election as the major exception (see Figure 6.7). Starting in 1935, the top two parties in Canada received less than 80 percent of the national vote in every year except

---

[4]Johnston (2000, 5) sees this as the period of one-party dominance by the Liberals dominating national electoral politics.

one (1958). The minor parties together received between one-quarter to one-third of the national vote from then on.

As we discussed in chapter 6, the departure of two-partism in Canada corresponds precisely to the time when the provinces began to take on substantial roles in worker's compensation programs and when the courts were granting greater leeway to the provinces. The 1930s Depression hit Canada hard. As in the United States, calls by Canadians across the political spectrum for government action to relieve unemployment, support farmers, protect industry, and regulate business activities grew loud and angry. Provincial governments reacted both by blaming Ottawa for not doing enough and by demanding that Ottawa give them funds to spend on their citizens at their own discretion. The provinces also sought to relieve economic suffering, and relied on constitutional authority to define their responsibilities. The process of building the Canadian welfare state during this time was neither purely provincialization nor absolute centralization. Voters could not be certain whether it was better to press for provincial solutions or to seek national solutions to the Depression.

Thus, the number of national parties (Figure 6.2) and the party aggregation measure (Figure 6.1) from 1935 to 1988 do not stabilize or follow a monotonic trend over the next fifty years. It was neither fully fragmenting nor fully aggregating, but changing from election to election with minor parties often showing temporary strength only to be followed by decline and then resurgence later. It is safe to conclude, regardless, that Canada was nowhere near a fully national party system during this period. Note again Figure 6.2, which shows the effective number of parties at three levels: national, provincial, and district level. The provinces for the most part had 2.5 party systems in the late twentieth century, well below the national number, but above the district average. Parties were not aggregating as they had before.

The data on the Canadian party system show some interesting, and somewhat contradictory, patterns over this period. On the one hand, after the 1960s, most of the fragmentation in the national party system was due to the failure to aggregate votes across provinces. As seen in Figure 6.6, the reported statistic remains below .5 prior to the 1960s but is above .5 after the 1960s. In most of the latter half of the twentieth century, the district-to-state aggregation occurs smoothly in Canada, while the province-to-nation aggregation was less smooth. The disjuncture between federal and provincial parties has been noted quite widely in Canada. Blake (1985) and Blake, Carty, and Erickson (1991) cite, for example, that British Columbia voters inhabited separate federal and provincial worlds and that "Federal politics in B.C. take place in a dif-

ferent world . . . [with] Social Credit and the NDP [dominating] the provincial system, but the federal stage is shared by three parties, and only
the NDP performs on both" (Blake 1985, 4).[5] Blake (1985) attributes
this disjuncture between provincial and federal politics in part to the
federal system. British Columbia voters feel that they have a limited impact on federal politics because of the smaller size of the province relative to Ontario and Quebec. The province has, however, responsibility
for the "pace and direction of economic development" (5) and this responsibility is manifested in provincial politics more than in federal
party politics in British Columbia. Blake goes on to argue that "institutional incentives for class politics are stronger at the provincial level
given the primary importance of provincial governments in the provision of social services, determination of the conditions of work and
. . . the centrality of economic development questions on provincial
agendas" (6).

Wilson and Hoffman (1970, 178) also point to differential federal-
provincial voting in the Canadian provinces. They argue that the federal
system allows "these groups . . . to elect their own people to provincial
legislatures and, with control of the government, to bargain with Ottawa from a powerful provincial base." The extreme case was perhaps
that of Ross Thatcher, the Saskatchewan provincial Liberal leader.
Thatcher "had rebuilt the party from its grassroots base," and was sus-
pected by the Liberal leaders in Ottawa of having made deals with the
federal Conservatives, of "deliberately getting inferior candidates to
stand in the 1962 election, and of putting federal campaign money into
provincial party coffers" (Wearing 1981, 28).

Not surprisingly, the ideological self- perceptions of provincial legislators also varies by province. In British Columbia, for example, Liberal
legislators in a survey in the 1970s saw themselves as centrist (all 100
percent of the respondents said they were centrist), whereas Liberal legislators in Ontario perceived themselves as moderately left (with 50 percent identifying themselves as to the left) (Clarke 1978, 623).[6] Clarke
and Stewart (1987, 395) note that party attachments in Canada vary
across provincial and federal levels because "federalism permits voters

---

[5]The Conservatives and Liberals folded into regional parties in British Columbia quite
effectively, though the Liberals managed to maintain somewhat of an independent existence (Blake, Carty, and Erickson, 1991).

[6]Similar differences certainly have existed and still exist across states or regions in the
United States, with vast differences most notably among Democrats in the mid-twentieth
century. The strong provincial powers in Canada, however, as opposed to the post–New
Deal centralization in the United States, opened up more space for provincial-level parties
to form and be completely separate from national parties in Canada.

to form attachments with different parties and different levels of government or to do so at one level only."[7] In British Columbia the provincial and federal party systems separated in the 1940s, and "after 1953, the fortunes of the Liberal and Conservative parties in federal politics fluctuated independently of the level of support achieved by their provincial counterparts" (Blake 1985, 17, 19).

On the other hand, there were some signs of decreasing regionalism in this era. In the 1930s and 1940s, the minor parties were fragmented and primarily regional. The two major parties were often seen in the West as favoring the interests of the eastern provinces, especially on trade matters, and when natural disasters and rising unemployment compounded the frustration of many western Canadians with their government, they responded by abandoning the major parties in favor of regional parties such as Social Credit, the Reconstruction Party (in 1935), and the Cooperative Commonwealth Federation (CCF). These regional parties also had an ideological component to their appeal, and they did win votes in Ontario. The CCF, Canada's socialist party, had substantial support in the East, winning up to one-third of the provincial and national vote in Ontario in some elections. Nevertheless, its strength was mostly in the West. Over time, these minor parties became less fragmented, and only a few minor parties received substantial votes in later elections in this period.

By 1984 there was only one important minor party, the New Democrats (NDP), as the successor to the CCF. Figure 6.8 shows the trend, as the minor-party N declines markedly from 1940 to 1984. Thus, while the major parties received about three-quarters of the vote in the 1960s and 1970s, the minor parties were, intentionally or not, consolidating into one important party. Note the corresponding data in Figure 7.1, bottom left panel, which shows that the NDP increasingly became a national party. These trends could be attributed to what Carty, Cross, and Young (2000, 5) term the "existential and constitutional angst . . . [in] attempting to marry Keynesian politics with the practices of executive federalism."

By the 1980s the party system had all the signs of being relatively national, though not two-party. The most important minor party, the NDP, was national in scope, and receiving approximately one-fifth of the national vote and about 11 percent of the seats in Parliament. The two major parties split most of the remaining 80 percent of the vote between them, leaving a few votes to insignificant minor parties. In 1984 the party aggregation measure troughs, largely because in many districts, voters were not following the assumptions used in models of Duverger's

---

[7]Similar claims were made by Seymour Martin Lipset (1954) in his discussion of Alberta.

Law (see chapter 2). The NDP was receiving substantial votes locally and nationally, so that the effective number of parties was relatively high, while the party aggregation measure was low. District politics mirrored national politics on average.

Regional voting had ebbed, but provincial voting had not, and there are signs the latter was increasing. This is largely because Canada was experiencing a remarkable mixture of federalism on economic and social policy that made provincial-level politics and parties increasingly important, with the recognition among all that decisions over the Canadian federation required national solutions. By the 1980s the national deliberations taking place over possible devolution of authority, and even the secession of Quebec, had stalled. Canadian policy making had not become unambiguously more centralized; however, solutions to various crises in Canadian politics—what to do about Quebec separatism, and how to manage trade with the United States—were widely seen as requiring national solutions. By the late 1980s, solving Canada's problems with federalism became imperative with the failure of the Meech Lake Accord, the rise of aboriginal issues, and rise of the new Quebecois separatism.

The growing momentum for provincialization in Canada had reached a breaking point by the 1980s. The deliberations and political bargains that eventually resulted in the Charlottetown Accord in 1992 fragmented the Canadian party system more than at any time in its history. Quebec nationalism rose to the surface in national parliamentary elections, and the various Quebecois parties consolidated under the Bloc Quebecois to run for national parliamentary seats. Western regionalism both expanded the vote of the NDP and, most crucially, made the Reform Party into the primary rightist party west of Ontario. The Conservatives lost badly in the 1990s in Quebec and in the West. Figure 7.1, bottom right panel, shows that the Reform Party wins in less than half the provinces, but in the same figure, upper left panel, it competes in most provinces. Carty, Cross, and Young (2000, 6) regard the representation of regional interests as one of the reasons for the emergence of the Bloc and Reform as powerful political forces in the 1990s.

The party system fragmentation had an unusual character. The effective number of national parties in the two elections prior to this writing was around 4, the highest ever in Canadian history. Yet because the fragmented party voting occurred also at the district level, the party aggregation measure in Figure 6.1 is only just above 1. As chapter 2 discusses at length, Canadians in district elections were voting for more than two parties and violating the assumptions of Duverger's Law in the 1980s and 1990s. As a result, Canadians by the end of the century had a curiously nationalized system because most districts were seeing three parties receive substantial votes, although the party system was still quite fragmented, with some regional voting, lack of cross-provincial coordination, and many parties.

The legislative experience of the members of the House of Commons provides further evidence of the provincialization of the Canadian party system that follows the changing nature of federal-provincial relations in Canada. If the federal government were more important than the provincial government, it would stand to reason that politicians would want to be active at the federal level. A career path would then take a politician from the provincial to the federal level. If, however, the federal government shares authority with the provincial government or is less important within a province than the provincial government, legislators may not find it in their interest to move to the federal level. In Canada, as Figure 7.2 shows, during the period of centralization, from Confederation to almost 1921, more than one-third of the members of the House of Commons had provincial legislative experience. Starting in the 1960s, the proportion of MPs with some provincial legislative experience drops to less than one-sixth.

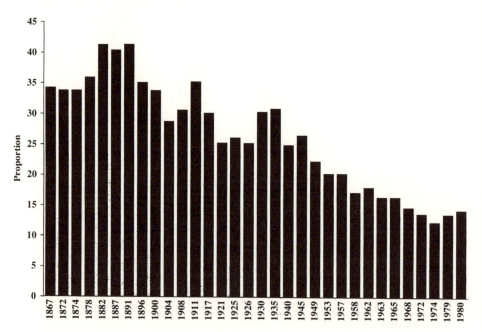

Figure 7.2. Members of House of Commons with Experience in Provincial Politics in Canada

By 2001 "Canadian voters in each of the country's traditional regions now face different choices. . . . Genuinely national contests that engage the parties and the electorate in debate . . . seem unlikely" (Carty, Cross, and Young 2001, 28). "Thus in November 2000, the polls showed the following regional contests: Atlantic Canadians had a realistic choice between Liberals and Conservatives; Quebecers chose between the Bloc and the Liberals; Ontarians selected between Liberals and the Alliance; voters in Manitoba and Saskatchewan could choose among the Alliance, New Democrats and Liberals; Albertans chose between the Alliance and the Liberals; and in British Columbia the voters selected among the Alliance, Liberals and New Democrats." Reform that morphed itself into the Alliance in 2000, like the Bloc, had "as their very raison d'être, the articulation of regional grievances" (29). Similarly, the "New Democrats have always been a special kind of national party, a federation of provincial organizations, its life and strength depending on the health of its provincial parties." Ironically, as Carty, Cross, and Young observe, the "Liberals have survived as a national governing party by becoming the party of a region, Ontario" (30).

The regionalism that characterizes contemporary Canadian party politics stands in sharp contrast to the half-century following Confederation when two parties that were national in scope received most of the votes. The major difference between the two eras is the dramatically different role played by the federal government in relation to the authority exercised by provincial governments. From 1867 to 1917, the Dominion government was the engine of economic development in Canada and made policies that had a large bearing on the life of most Canadians. At the end of the twentieth century this was not true to the same degree. Provincial governments had much more authority than they did 100 years earlier. The provincialization of the Canadian party system resulted primarily from the changes in Canadian federalism. While Quebecois voting and western regionalism occurred during the entire process of negotiations that led up to Meech Lake, with the two processes feeding off one another, it would be misleading to infer that the process of provincialization in the 1980s and 1990s was caused by the actions of these regional parties. The frequency and amount of regional voting and the fragmentation of the party system both shot upward in the 1990s after Canada had become politically more provincialized.

Let us now return to the issue of province-level party systems to test further our arguments for Canada. Under conditions where the provinces have real authority over economic policies, provincial politics opens a space for such provincial-level parties as Social Credit to form and endure. When provincial politics matters and provincial leaders bargain with national leaders regularly, enough voters want their provincial parties to have national representation and their national parties to have provincial power so that these parties can survive.

Atlantic Canada, however, is different. In contrast to the other provinces, the Atlantic provinces are dependent upon the federal government for much of their budgets. In fact, up to 50 percent of the resources available to the provincial governments in Atlantic Canada come from Ottawa, and these provinces are far more reliant on the federal government and federal transfer payments (Dyck 1986, 28). If our argument is correct, then there should be better party aggregation to national vote totals in Atlantic Canada than in the rest of the country.

First, each of the four provinces in Atlantic Canada has had, for the most part, a two-party system, with third parties being notoriously unsuccessful (Dyck 1986, 29). Bickerton (1994, 434) agrees that "the historic affinity of the four Atlantic Provinces for traditional two-party politics is arguably not unrelated to this regional political economy." Not only is there a two-party system in these provinces that mirrors the national parties, but federal and provincial party organizations also are more closely integrated in these provinces than in the rest of Canada (Dyck 1986, 29). Not surprisingly, the average combined vote for the major national parties between 1905 and 1984 in provincial elections was higher in the Atlantic provinces than in the rest of Canada. The vote share of federal parties in provincial elections was 51.6 percent in Prince Edward Island, 45.6 percent in Nova Scotia, 48.3 percent in Newfoundland, and 47.1 percent in New Brunswick. Quebec was the only other province with a greater than 40 percent vote for a major national party in provincial elections (44 percent), while in all other provinces the major national parties received less than 35 percent of the vote in provincial elections (I. Stewart 1986, 131).

Other compelling evidence for successful party aggregation across the provincial and federal levels in Atlantic Canada comes from the number of MPs who have provincial experience. It stands to reason that when parties are more aggregated there should be a greater flow of legislators from the province to the nation. Forty percent of the MPs elected from Atlantic Canada since 1867 had some provincial political experience, whereas only 20 percent of the MPs from the rest of the country had provincial experience (see Table 7.1).

This finding is corroborated by a survey of provincial legislators conducted in British Columbia, Saskatechwan, Ontario, Quebec, and Nova Scotia. The survey revealed that none of the Nova Scotians, in stark contrast to legislators from other provinces, were province-oriented

TABLE 7.1

Proportion of MPs in Canada with Provincial Experience
(all figures in percentages)

|  | No Provincial Experience | Provincial Experience |
|---|---|---|
| Atlantic Canada | 60 | 40 |
| Rest of Canada | 79 | 21 |

$N = 3,807$

(Clarke, Price, and Krause 1975, 225). Kornberg, Clarke, and Stewart (1979, 895, 896) also noted that in Atlantic Canada support for federal political authorities is highest among the regions of Canada, while the perceived costs of federalism were the lowest for Atlantic provinces.

A detailed analysis of politics in Prince Edward Island supports our argument that the federal government's larger role is the cause of successful party aggregation. Ian Stewart (1986, 128) notes that in sixteen of twenty-one elections between 1905 and 1984 voters in Prince Edward Island ensured that partisan complexion of provincial administration would conform to that of the existing federal government. Stewart also reports that 80 percent of survey respondents in Prince Edward Island said it is important to have a provincial government of the same party as the federal government because of the large role played by the federal government in the economic life of the province (140).

The *Prince Edward Patriot* on the eve of the 1921 provincial elections proclaimed "'Electors! Keep the Two Governments in Line, and Prince Edward Island will be in a Better Position to Get Aid from Ottawa.' The Two Governments were in Line on Each Occasion and increase was granted" (cited in I. Stewart 1986, 133). The opposition conservatives in their campaign stressed that the Islanders were not receiving many benefits from the federal government. The Liberal Party, which governed Prince Edward Island for much of this period, pointed to its success in getting largesse from the federal government as a reason for voters to continue to support it, and in 1943 when the Liberals were in power in Ottawa, the Prince Edward Island Liberal Party said, "During the last year we have received from the Dominion Government in one way or another $2,250,000. Yesterday we received a further $75,000 for a wing to the Sanatorium" (cited in I. Stewart 1986, 135).

PARTY SYSTEM DYNAMICS IN GREAT BRITAIN

Like Canada, Great Britain has seen some elements of stasis and some elements of continuity in its party system. A glance at Figure 6.1 indicates, however, that Britain exhibits more stability when compared with Canada. Other than the sharp increase around the First World War, the transitions in the party aggregation measure in Britain from election to election are smoother, and the changes not as dramatic, in comparison with the transitions in Canada. Regional parties and national minor parties in Britain do not typically appear and then disappear from one election to the next, as with the Canadian Progressives in 1921, which did well in that election and then quickly vanished from the electoral scene, or as with the NDP, whose fortunes fluctuated quite rapidly in the 1950s and 1960s. The British Liberals lived through ups and downs, but the changes, with a few exceptions, were less abrupt than those of the NDP in Canada.

As in Canada, Great Britain has generally had two major parties that have competed for majority control of the parliament. And similar to Canada, there have been a relatively small number of minor parties also winning substantial votes. Compare the minor party N from Figure 6.8 for the two countries. These numbers are considerably lower than the minor party Ns in both India and the United States.

Two factors have largely defined the dynamics of the British party system since the 1880s, the political health and aggregation success of the Liberals/Social Democrats, and the nationalist voting patterns of citizens in Scotland and Wales. The former has had a much larger effect on our primary measures, the effective number of national parties and party aggregation. The latter, however, has been an important marker of the progress of British political devolution.

As mentioned, two-partism existed in Britain only in the 1950s, when the Liberals lost the battle for relevance in British politics and policy making in the Commons. There were two abrupt changes to start and end the temporary two-party period. In the 1950 election, the Liberals received 2.6 million votes, or 9 percent of the national vote. In 1951, they received 730,000 votes, or about 2.5 percent of the national vote, with similar totals for the next election in 1955. In 1959, they doubled their vote total, and then doubled it once again in 1964. They regained status later by the 1970s, but the period when the Liberals were at their lowest ebb is precisely the period when both party aggregation and the effective number of national parties ebbed.

It is worth noting that the 1950s are widely regarded as the period in British history with the most class-based voting and the least amount of nationalist voting in Scotland and Wales. This was no accident because it followed the most rapid escalation of central government activity in setting up the British welfare state and was prior to a period of serious discussions about devolution toward the regions.

We can use the 1950s as a marker in the history of British party aggregation. Before the 1950s, the Liberal Party did not aggregate effectively relative to other periods, as seen in the upper panels of Figure 7.3. From 1885 until the First World War, of course, the Liberals were not only one of the two major parties; they were also the primary governing party, sometimes in coalition. Yet they were divided into various party groups, with distinct party labels for elections. Candidates received votes under such names as Independent Liberal, Liberal Unionist, National Liberal, and Liberal/Labour Alliance. These labels indicated policy differences and were well understood by informed voters. Their adoption by candidates was correlated with geographic region.

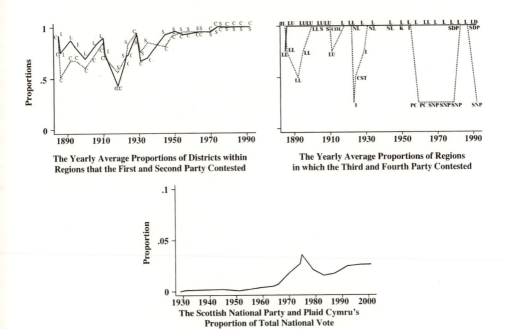

The Yearly Average Proportions of Districts within Regions that the First and Second Party Contested

The Yearly Average Proportions of Regions in which the Third and Fourth Party Contested

The Scottish National Party and Plaid Cymru's Proportion of Total National Vote

Figure 7.3. Selected Regional Patterns in British Party Politics. *Note*: C = Conservatives; COC = Conservative Coalition; COL = Liberal Coalition; CST = Constitutionalists; I = Independents; IL = Independent Liberal-Labour; K = Communist Party; L = Liberals; LD = Liberal Democrat; LL = Liberal-Labour Alliance; LU = Liberal Unionists; NL = National Liberals; S = Labour Party; SDP = Social Democratic Party; SNP = Scottish National Party

By 1922 Labour had replaced the Liberals as the major opposition party to the Conservatives. The transition from a Liberal-Conservative to Labour-Conservative system caused serious disruptions in both the left and right sides of the British political spectrum, but the turmoil, at least as measured by the lack of party aggregation, was brief. During the war the election of 1918 had an unusual fragmentation of both the Liberals and the Conservatives, and the effective number of national parties surged to above four. Data from that election, however, make the case an outlier, and the processes of party fragmentation from the election did not lead to a general trend, as Figure 6.3 shows.

Britain was essentially a 3-party system through the 1920s, although the 1922 election saw the Liberal candidates split between two labels: the Liberal and the National Liberal. All three parties, Labour, Conservative, and Liberal, fluctuated in strength, until there was a precipitous drop in Liberal votes beginning in 1931. While through the 1930s the Labour and Conservative together captured over 80 percent of the national vote, the votes of the Liberals made it a 2.5-party system, not unlike how they would later in the 1960s and 1970s. An abrupt drop in the Liberal vote occurred in the early 1950s as Britain entered the period of two-partism that Duverger said represented a pattern for single-member, simple-plurality systems.

For the thirty years after the 1950s, the Liberals either received few votes or aggregated well. In the 1980s the aggregation measure creeps back up to the pre-1950s range. In both the pre-1950s era and the post-1983 era, the fragmentation of the Liberals/Social Democrats was the primary cause of the increase in the measure.

To see this, compare the district N and the national N in Figure 6.3, and look also at the data in Figure 6.6. Prior to the 1950s, both the effective number of national parties and the party aggregation measure are relatively high compared with those figures in the 1950s. The same could be said for the 1980s and later. But in the 1960s and 1970s the party aggregation measure is low while the effective number of parties is relatively high. This means that in the 1960s and 1970s (much as in Canada in later years), the Liberals were not fragmented and were getting substantial votes nationally and in many districts. In other words, the district party systems were very similar to the national party systems, enabling us to conclude that the British had a more nationalized party system during that time than in other periods, even though the number of national parties was relatively high.

Not until the 1974 elections (there were two, one in February and one October), when the two most important minor parties, the Liberals and the Scottish National Party (SNP), more than doubled their previous votes, do we see an increase again in the party aggregation measure. The

Liberals went from 2.1 million votes in 1970 to 6 million votes in 1974. Likewise, the SNP went from 309,000 in 1970 to 635,000 in 1974, while the Plaid Cyrmu (PC, the Welsh nationalist party) held its own with about 175,000 votes in both elections. These changes increased the effective number of parties nationally and increased it locally at the district level, but not as much. Thus the party aggregation measure goes up only slightly.

In the 1980s, when the so-called moderate vote was split between the Liberals and Social Democrats, the party aggregation measure rises to levels similar to those prior to the 1950s. Once again, the Liberal vote was fragmented. Social Democrats and Liberals did not aggregate effectively into a single party. While the nationalist votes by the Scots and Welsh declined somewhat in the 1980s, the total effect was an increase in both the number of national parties, and an increase in the party aggregation measure, as seen in Figures 6.3 and 6.6. Britain had a less nationalized party system than before this period.

Let us now take a closer look at the voting for the Scottish and Welsh nationalist parties over time and compare changes in party support to British devolution. The lower panel of Figure 7.3 shows the patterns in the parties' votes.

There is little doubt that increasing votes for the nationalist parties through the 1970s put pressure on the major parties and the governments to consider and debate devolution to the regions. The relationship between election returns and efforts to devolve was certainly reciprocal. Our belief is that small amounts of nationalist voting in the 1960s put a real scare into the major parties, resulting in discussions on devolution at the highest levels of government in London. These discussions, as they became more public, only fueled the nationalism, which increased the votes for the SNP and PC, which then increased the incentives for the major parties to devise plans for devolution, and so on. For both regions, but for slightly different reasons, much of the increase in support for these parties *followed* the beginnings of serious deliberations over decentralization at the national level and attempts by the national government to pass devolution measures. By no means was party politics irrelevant to the decisions by the major party leaders to engage in such deliberations, although the party politics (i.e., increase in nationalist voting) certainly resulted from the deliberations.

Discussions about establishing Scottish and Welsh autonomy, and some real changes in policy implementation that gave more power to local governments, occurred throughout the 1960s and 1970s. They were most pronounced and publicized in Scotland in the 1970s, as voting for the SNP reached its peak (see Figure 7.3, bottom left panel), and just after voting for the PC leveled off. Many observers (see, e.g., Bogdanor 1999) credit two main reasons for the increased nationalist voting in Scotland in the 1970s: the discovery of oil in the North Sea and the United Kingdom joining the European Community. Both events made it seem to many in Scotland that they could go it alone without being part of the United Kingdom, that they had the resources (oil) to do so, and that they could just as well be connected to Brussels as to London. "With important areas of decision-making being removed from London to Brussels, Edinburgh would become even more remote from the centres of power. Scotland was already part of the British periphery; how much more peripheral it would be when viewed from Brussels" (Bogdanor 1999, 126).

Change was dramatic in Scotland in 1974 as the SNP increased its share of the vote from 22 percent in February to 30 percent in October. More impressive, the average vote share across the districts in Scotland for the SNP went from 12 percent in February to 28 percent in October. What happened in the interim? The February election was fought mostly over a miner's strike and the flagging British economy. Regionalism was not a big issue in that election. In June 1974, however, the Royal Commission published *Devolution within the United Kingdom: Some Alternatives for Discussion.* Another white paper by the government, *Democracy and Devolution,* which laid out concrete proposals for directly elected regional assemblies, and which eventually was the cornerstone for the Scotland and Wales Act of 1978 that passed and was then scuttled by the new Thatcher government in 1979, was published in September 1974. Increased voting for the SNP in Scotland followed these two dramatic, government-sponsored documents, which laid out the case for devolution. Voting for the SNP peaked in 1974 (October), when it received 840,000 votes, or 3 percent of the national vote.

The proportion of the vote for the SNP has been more varied over time than votes for the PC. Votes for the PC increased dramatically in the 1970s and stayed steady into the 1990s. The voting patterns for the PC followed serious discussions and true reform toward devolution in the 1960s. "[I]n Wales, unlike in Scotland, devolution could be linked to local government reform, and *the case for devolution was first presented in the mid-1960s* as part of a broader argument for reform of Welsh local government." Furthermore, "the idea of an all-Wales body was put forward some time *before* Plaid Cymru appeared to threaten Labour [in Wales]" (Bogdanor 1999, 162–63; emphasis added).

There is one more issue to discuss regarding British party politics and regionalism. It is sometimes said that even the major British parties, the Conservative and Labour parties, are essentially regional parties, and that the only truly national party is the Liberals/Social Democrats. The claim is that in many regions there is two-partism, the Liberals/Social Democrats and one of the two major parties.

The data do not bear this out. The regional Ns, as shown in Figure 6.3, indicate that these data track the national N very closely. Just recently in Scotland has the number of parties been systematically higher in one region than in the nation as a whole, and this is because of the votes going to the SNP over and above the votes to the three other major parties in that region.

As that figure and other data not shown indicate, all three parties compete quite well in both Wales and Scotland. We have examined data that show the proportion of constituencies in which each of the three parties come in first, second, or third place in Scotland and Wales. Most revealing are the data that indicate the proportion of districts in Wales and Scotland for which the Liberals/Social Democrats come in third place. The party comes in third place in about the same proportion in Scotland and Wales as it does in London and in the rest of England. It is one thing to say there are some indications of regional voting patterns, and some parties run better in Scotland than others. It is another thing to say that the regions are two-party, which is not the case. In Britain, we do not see the same kind of pattern of lower numbers of parties in the states, provinces, or regions that we tend to see in Canada (Figure 6.2) and India (Figure 6.4).

One might respond that there are pockets of two-partism within the regions. That may be true, but those pockets do not correspond to well-defined political areas, unlike a Canadian province or even a British region such as Wales or Scotland. There are pockets of one-party dominance in all the countries, including the United States, and finding these is just a matter of focusing attention on smaller and smaller geographic areas. This is far from saying that, because there are geographic correlations in voting data, the major parties are regional.

To summarize our view of the dynamics of the British party system, the underlying patterns of voting for Scottish and Welsh national parties correspond to moves toward devolution in Great Britain, although these patterns are not the major force of change in the party system. Rather, the strength of the Liberals/Social Democrats and the ability of those parties to aggregate their votes effectively create the most movement in the measures of interest here, the number of parties nationally and the relationship of that measure to the average effective number of parties at the district level. Those changes in party aggregation correspond well to the centralization and (serious, high level discussions about) decentralization of the British state.

## PARTY SYSTEM DYNAMICS IN INDIA

The party aggregation measure for India in Figure 6.1 indicates that the lowest ebb was during the 1970s, and the highest point occurred in the most recent elections in the 1990s and 2000. Parties aggregated most effectively during the centralization under Indira Gandhi and least effectively in recent elections, when the Indian nation was perhaps at its most decentralized period ever. As is the case for Canada and Great Britain, comparing Table 6.1 with Figure 6.1 shows a close correspondence between the levels of centralization and party aggregation.

Given the reputation, and to some extent the reality, of Indian party politics, it is remarkable that the party aggregation measure was as low as it was until the 1990s. It is true that the measure is systematically higher for India than for any of our other countries, as discussed before. For most years prior to 1991, it was between 1 and 2, while for the other countries in the twentieth century, it was typically below 1. In the first few elections in India, and in 1977, it was barely above 1, our threshold for a nationalized party system. No doubt, however, something systematic and palpable occurred in the 1990s when the aggregation measure shot up to the levels not seen in the other countries in the twentieth century.

Why does India not only have more parties than the other countries, but also have the highest measure of party aggregation on average? Compared with figures in the other countries, India's top two parties receive far smaller proportions of the national vote, typically less than two-thirds in national elections (see Figure 6.7). At the same time, its minor party N is quite high. In short, India has considerably more parties than these other countries, especially in recent years.

The ethnic, linguistic, and religious diversity of India certainly plays a role in causing the number of parties. Throughout recent Indian history, small ethnic parties have been competitive in elections and have garnered representation in the Lok Sabha. As Cox (1997) argues, "strong" electoral systems, such as the single-member, simple-plurality systems, can significantly lower the number of parties, while population diversity can increase the number of parties, leading to results that are not consistent with Duvergerian predictions, even at the district level. Ethnicity and caste are important factors in any full explanation of electoral and political outcomes in India, but they cannot explain the dynamics in the party system over the past fifty years.

India's central government is less involved in economic decisions that affect voters at the local level than are national governments in Canada, Great Britain, and the United States. For example, to use a simple measure of federal intrusion, direct taxes levied by the national government as a proportion of GNP are much lower in India (around .02 in recent decades) than in the other three (approximately .12 in Canada, .19 in Great Britain, and .13 in the United States). The other countries, even provincialized Canada, have a far better developed welfare state and accompanying national bureaucracy than India. The average Indian has less contact with the central government than the average Canadian, British, and American citizens do with theirs. To assess whether our claim that the role of the central government in India is limited, especially when contrasted to the state governments, we asked respondents in a national survey conducted in 2001 which level of government they thought was responsible for providing a set of public goods that they cared about. The findings from the survey, reported in Table 7.2, make it quite clear that citizens in contemporary India look to the state, not the national government, to address their main concerns. This is consistent with contemporary federal arrangements in India, where it is the state governments that have greater authority than the central government (chapter 5). So, while the dynamics of Indian party politics offer the most convincing evidence about the true cause of party aggregation and fragmentation, the cross-national comparison is consistent with the main idea in this book—that party systems follow the relative authority of different levels of government.

In earlier times, India was widely classified as a one-party dominant system (Kothari 1964; Riker 1982), and the Congress Party undoubtedly dominated government for many decades, as Figure 7.4 shows. It received votes and seats in every state, and thus gained the most seats in the Lok Sabha, forming governments with coalition partners only in the 1990s. The Congress Party dominated the electoral landscape until recently, mainly because it was given the reigns of power upon independence in 1947. It completely controlled the resources of the national state for forty years, could spend resources to undercut efforts by state and local parties to build opposing coalitions with industry and local

TABLE 7.2
Citizens' Perception of the Role of Different Levels of Government
in Providing Public Goods in India, 2001 (all figures in percentages)

|  | Central | State | Local |
|---|---|---|---|
| Electricity | 11 | 74 | 15 |
| Controlling criminal activities | 12 | 74 | 14 |
| Education facilities | 11 | 72 | 17 |
| Medical facilities | 13 | 70 | 17 |
| Ration supply | 13 | 67 | 20 |
| Roads | 11 | 57 | 32 |
| Pollution | 14 | 53 | 33 |
| Drinking water | 9 | 50 | 41 |
| Cleanliness | 7 | 37 | 56 |

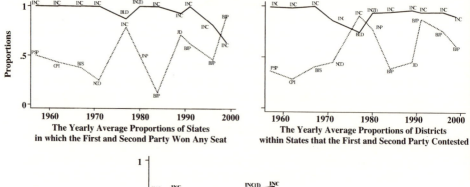

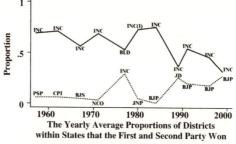

Figure 7.4. Selected Regional Patterns in Indian Party Politics. *Note*: INC, INC(I) = Congress; NCO = Congress(O); BJP = Bharatiya Janata; BJS = Jana Sangh; BLD = Lok Dal; CPI = Communist; JD = Janata; PSP = Praja Socialist

elites, and had the prestige associated with the movement to establish a new, independent, viable, democratic nation.

Given all this, it shared national standing only with the Communist and Socialist parties (CPI and PSP, respectively). These parties contested in nearly every state, although they did not win seats in many states. In addition to these left parties, the Congress Party in all cases had to fight vigorously for seats against candidates representing state-based parties and independent candidates everywhere. The top two parties, at the height of the Congress Party's power in the 1957 election, received only 60 percent of the national vote (Figure 6.7).

Although one party dominated Indian government, the country was not a one-party state electorally. In fact, according to Figure 6.4, it was almost a four-party country in 1957, as measured by the effective number of national parties. The Congress party won national elections with approximately two-fifths of the vote because, as Riker (1982) and Chhibber and Petrocik (1989) note, the opposition to Congress could not overcome its differences to unite. For most of India's democratic history, political parties built electoral coalitions around state government policy. The federal division of power led each of the state Congress parties to mobilize its own distinct bases of support, a move made easier by the fact that some important preexisting social divisions, such as those based on language, rarely crossed state boundaries. The Congress Party maintained its electoral dominance insofar as those who joined the party did so to gain access to the state. For at least two decades following independence when the Congress was seen as electorally invincible, the party was the vehicle for providing access to public resources. Congress politicians were able to exercise a significant influence over the allocation of resources and regulation of economic activity by gaining access to the resources of the state.

From the 1950s to the 1960s, the effective number of national parties increased from less than four to more than five, as the country decentralized. The first serious threat to the electoral dominance of the Congress Party came with the general election of 1967, in which the party lost electoral majorities in eight states and was returned to national power with a reduced majority in Parliament.[8] The Congress Party suffered electoral setbacks in almost all of the states when compared with 1962 election results. Not only did it have a lower overall vote share, but it also lost seats in the state assemblies and in the Lok Sabha in almost all states. The party's vote share for the Lok Sabha, when compared with the 1962 election results, dropped by 22 percent in Orissa and between 5 and 10 percent in Bihar, Gujarat, Uttar Pradesh, and West Bengal. Its vote shares for the state assemblies also registered a decline in every state but Kerala, Madhya Pradesh, and Rajasthan. This trend was repeated in the number of seats the party held in the Vidhan Sabhas (state assemblies). Congress lost eighty-nine seats in Tamilnadu, and more than fifty seats in each of the Bihar, Orissa, and Uttar Pradesh assemblies. For the Lok Sabha the party did better in 1967 only in Andhra Pradesh and Assam, where it managed to gain just one seat more than it did in 1962.

The major source of electoral competition to the Congress in the years leading to and including the 1967 election occurred at the state level. In Punjab and Tamil Nadu, regional parties—the Akali Dal and Dravida Munnetra Kazhagzam, respectively—provided opposition to the Congress and emerged as political forces in their own right. Opposition parties also emerged in Gujarat, in the form of the Congress (O) and the Swatantra Party, and in Maharashtra, in the form of the Republican parties, the Shiv Sena, and the Congress Party breakaways. Madhya Pradesh has been the scene of ongoing political battles between the erstwhile Jan Sangh, now the Bharatiya Janata Party (BJP), and the Congress. Kerala politics has long been characterized by multiparty electoral battles, with the CPI(M), the Muslim League, the Congress Party, and

---

[8]Robins (1979) offers a comprehensive analysis of the relationship between seats and votes analysis for the 1967 elections.

the Kerala Congress as the major contestants. Orissa was initially the home of the Ganatantra Parishad; later it became a stronghold of the Swatantra Party and subsequently saw the ascendance of a regional party, the Utkal Congress. Bihar and eastern Uttar Pradesh have been influenced by a variant of the socialist parties, while western Uttar Pradesh and Haryana has been home to the Bharatiya Kranti Dal and its successor, the Lok Dal. Rajasthan at independence was home to an informal Rajput coalition that subsequently merged with the Congress. Over the years, however, the state has provided the Bharatiya Janata Party and the Swatantra Party with substantial support. West Bengal saw the ascendance of the CPI(M), along with a host of smaller leftist parties, such as the Forward Bloc. Each is state-specific.[9]

The centralization of economic policy making and political authority began in the early 1970s (Rudolph and Rudolph 1987; Kohli 1990). Prime Minister Indira Gandhi called the 1971 national election separately from the state elections. The immediate impact of this decision was to separate local issues—an important basis of voter mobilization— from national ones and to buffer national politics from state-level factional conflict. A demobilization of the electorate followed. In contrast to 1967, when 62 percent of eligible voters turned out in the national election, in 1971 only 55 percent of the voting population exercised the franchise. In these elections, the Congress (R) was returned with a two-thirds parliamentary majority, having gotten 44 percent of the vote. It benefited from the "multiplier effect" associated with single-member systems, in which large parties receive a greater proportion of seats than their vote share. With this parliamentary majority, the Congress government at the center [mis]used its constitutional position and centralized authority leading, first, to the "restoration" of the Congress Party in 1972 and, second, to the winning of elections to all state assemblies. India in 1972 looked like India in the early 1960s when the Congress Party controlled the central government and all state governments as well.[10]

In 1975 there was a further and dramatic centralization when the Indira Gandhi government accumulated political and economic power by invoking a national "emergency" under which even basic civil rights were suspended. This political centralization led to a coalesence of the opposition parties to the Congress and the number of national parties in the elections of 1977 plunged.

In 1977 Congress actually lost the popular vote to the Janata coalition (see Figure 7.4, top left panel). Centralization under Gandhi had reduced

[9]Roy (1969) makes a similar observation.
[10]For the "restoration" argument, see Weiner (1989). The 1984 national elections were an exception to this. Those elections followed the assassination of Indira Gandhi, and Congress won on a wave of sympathy.

the political issues down to one, namely whether the candidate opposed or supported Gandhi's policies. The party labels communicated the answer to this question, and voters and candidates responded by aggregating their votes across districts, states, and regions more effectively than ever before or since. Never before had India had such a nationalized party system.

The coalition to oppose Gandhi was so diverse that it could not hold, and once the coalition came to power it fragmented. While the effective number of parties stayed below four until the 1990s, it moved upward under Rajiv Gandhi's prime ministership in the 1980s. Rajiv Gandhi did not continue his mother's centralizing policies. He simply could not sustain his mother's strong policies against the state governments and local elites. Much of this is discussed in the previous chapter. What is notable here is how the political processes taking place in India by the late 1980s and especially by the early 1990s, as the country was rapidly decentralizing authority to the states, moved India into a system of state-based, Duvergerian party systems. This was a new pattern and a different party system (Yadav 1996). India thus has a multitude of political parties in the Lok Sabha, many representing state-level parties. The legislative coalition politics are very tricky, as governing coalitions have to make these state-based representatives happy with various redistributive, distributive, and pork barrel schemes. This kind of bargaining across state-level parties was not always so pronounced and consequential, especially when governance was more centralized.

Consider Figures 6.4 and 6.6 again, within which the data for India represents some of the most dramatic illustrations of our explanation. The state-level measure in Figure 6.4 is for Lok Sabha elections. Before 1977 this middle line largely tracked the national measure, though one notch lower. After 1980, it tracks the district level measure, and departs from the national measure. The separation from the national measure after 1980 indicates that the states had mostly three-party systems—remarkably low given the diversity in some Indian states, many of which have tens of millions of people—while the national measure leaps to six and seven parties. In the late 1990s, the state-level measure actually drops. What this means is that starting in the 1980s, and gaining momentum by the early 1990s, when power was rapidly devolving to the states, the party system was fragmenting into many state-level party systems with little aggregation across these states. The state-specific nature of party competition in the major Indian states is depicted in Table 7.3, and the overall pattern is caused by the decentralization of authority that has occurred over the past decade in India.

Figure 6.6 effectively summarizes this pattern. The measure is above .5 after the mid-1980s. Previous to that turning point, the failure to

TABLE 7.3
Party Competition in the Large States of India, 2002

| State | Major Parties |
| --- | --- |
| Andhra Pradesh | *Telugu Desam*, Congress |
| Assam | Congress, *Asam Gano Parishad*, BJP |
| Bihar | *Rashtriya Janata Dal*, BJP, Congress |
| Gujarat | BJP, Congress, *All India Rashtriya Janata Party* |
| Haryana | *Indian National Lok Dal*, Congress, BJP, Bahujan Samaj Party |
| Karnataka | Congress, BJP, *Janata Dal (S), Janata Dal (U)* |
| Kerala | CPI (M), Congress, CPI, *Muslim League*, BJP |
| Madhya Pradesh | Congress, BJP |
| Maharashtra | Congress, *Nationalist Congress Party, Shiv Sena*, BJP |
| Orissa | Congress, *Biju Janata Dal*, BJP |
| Punjab | Congress, *Akali Dal*, BJP |
| Rajasthan | Congress, BJP |
| Tamil Nadu | *Dravida Munnetra Kazhagam, All-India Dravida Munnetra Kazhagam* |
| Uttar Pradesh | *Samjawadi Party, Bahujan Samaj Party*, BJP, Congress |
| West Bengal | Communist Party of India (Marxist), *All-India Trinamool Congress*, Congress, BJP |

*Note:* State parties are in italics. The parties are listed in order of the votes they received in the last state assembly elections held in the state. Only parties that received more than 5 percent of the vote are listed.

aggregate for Indian parties had as much to do with the failure to aggregate across districts as it did with the failure to aggregate across states. The figure shows that fragmentation in the Indian party system in recent decades is due to the failure of state-level parties to coordinate across state-boundaries.

We add more evidence to support our claims for the Indian case, much as we did for the Canadian case, by taking a closer look at the role of central government finances in special Indian geographic subunits. In some Indian territorial jurisdictions the central government continues to play a large role. There are three kinds of political geographic units: states, special-category states, and union territories. The central government has a much larger role to play in the union territories and special category states (with union territories under the direct governance of the national government) than in the rest of the states. If our thesis is correct, then the problem of party aggregation should also be less severe in the union territories than special-category states with the largest problem of party aggregation occurring in the rest of the states where the role of the central government is most limited.

In 1999 when there were more than seven national parties in the Lok Sabha the union territories typically returned Congress and BJP candidates to the national parliament. The Congress or the BJP won all of the thirteen seats in the union territories of the Andaman Islands in the Bay of Bengal (parts of which are closer to Indonesia than India) and Lakshadweep in the Arabian Sea. Even if one excludes Delhi (which provides six of the thirteen members elected to the Lok Sabha from the union territories) the Congress or the BJP were the main competitors in four of the six union territories—Andaman and Nicobar Islands, Chandigarh, Dadra and Nagar Haveli, and Daman and Diu. In two other union territories, Pondicherry and Lakshadweep, the Congress won the elections and was opposed by a regional party only in Pondicherry. Figure 7.5 shows that regional or local parties have little presence in the

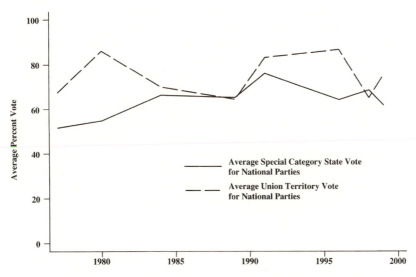

Figure 7.5. Average Percent Vote for National Parties in Special Category States and Union Territories in India

union territories (excluding Delhi and Chandigarh). The most telling example of voters and candidate lining up behind winning national parties in the union territories comes from the Andaman and Nicobar Islands. In the 1991 elections the BJP received less than 5 percent of the vote in the Andaman and Nicobar Island electoral district. This was about par for the BJP. After the 1991 elections, when the BJP emerged as the second largest party in the nation, the BJP managed to draw voters in the Andaman and Nicobar Islands and in the 1996 elections it received 24 percent of the vote and, after it came to govern the nation in 1998, the Andaman and Nicobar Islands, for the first time, elected a BJP candidate.

Among the Indian states, some are more dependent upon the central government for budgetary support. These states include Jammu and Kashmir, Himachal Pradesh, and the states of the Northeast, Assam, Arunachal Pradesh, Meghapalya, Manipur, Mizoram, Nagaland, and Tripura. The states of the Northeast, in particular the smaller states of Arunachal Pradesh, Meghapalya, Manipur, Mizoram, Nagaland, and Tripura, were not part of India until the British completed annexing this region in 1898. In some of these states the very question of integration into India is a matter of discussion. In Nagaland, for the first time in independent India, an ethnic minority refused citizenship of the Indian state (Hussain 2003). Despite this lack of integration the party system in these states aggregates quite well. Jyotindra Dasgupta notes that per capita plan outlay allocations made by the central government are higher in the northeastern states. While the average for India in 1990–91 was Rs. 288, Arunachal Pradesh got 2,288, Mizoran 1,786, Nagaland 1,318, Meghalaya 1,029, Manipur 1,000, and Tripura 800. We would expect that in these states national parties would do well despite their lack of integration into India. As Dasgupta (2001, 326) notes, "By 1997, when so many large states and the center in India have been ruled by regional parties or coalitions of national and regional parties, it so happens that almost all the Northeastern states have continued to be controlled by the national secular parties like the Congress Party and the Communist Party of India, Marxist (CPI[M]). It is rarely recognized that the smaller and the newer states of the region need the collective resources of the nation more than most of the larger states." Not only in 1997 but even in previous elections, national parties have done remarkably well in these northeastern states.

## PARTY SYSTEM DYNAMICS IN THE UNITED STATES

In some respects, the United States presents the most straightforward case. When it comes to relating the dynamics of centralization and provincialization to the dynamics of the party system, a simple glance at Figures 6.1 and 6.5 in combination, and at Table 6.1, offers a good summary of the basic pattern. There was a major transition that occurred in the United States in the 1920s and 1930s, where the effective number of parties nationally dropped to 2 and stayed there, and thus the party aggregation measure drops to low levels and does not rise again. Great surges in third- and fourth-party strength at the national level ceased by the 1930s. Prior to that, the same measure fluctuates from near 2 to as high as 6.5 in the early nineteenth century. A closer look at these data reveals the major moments in American political history. For example, the periods corresponding to the Populist and Progressive movements show expected punctuations.

Meanwhile, unlike the national measure, the average effective number of parties in the districts (Figures 2.4 and 6.5) has been near 2 for the most part throughout American history. The measure dips slightly below 2 starting around the First World War because of uncontested races. Many, but not all, of these uncontested races occurred in the South. Likewise, other than 1912, the state-level measure also hovers around 2. Fragmentation in the United States occurs because of the failure of state-level parties to coordinate across their borders. Holt (1999), in his study of the rise and decline of the Whig Party, sees the emergence of state parties as a direct result of the larger role played by state governments as compared to the federal government. Holt states that "For most of the 19th Century, *state governments addressed more matters that affected people's everyday lives than did Congress or the president.* As a result, many people cared about controlling state governments than the national regime" (12; emphasis added). The rise of state parties was also facilitated by the fact that since a state party "could distribute ballots more easily for a single state than for the entire nation, the possibility of starting new parties oriented toward state issues always existed" (12).

In the early part of the nineteenth century, at least until the removal of property qualifications for suffrage and the waning of the practice of allowing the state legislature to chose presidential electors, "national leaders, to construct winning coalitions, forged alliance with members of local elites within their own states and coalesced with national leaders from other states who had built similar alliances" (Holt 1999, 8). State organizations were critical to winning elections as they "purchased existing newspapers or established new ones . . . [and] aroused public interest with mass rallies, parades, barbecues, and pole raisings" (9). The rise of the Whigs in the 1830s, following the denunciation by President Jackson of the nullification law passed by South Carolina (South Carolina nullified the tariffs of 1828 and 1832 and defied the federal government to collect taxes after February 1, 1833), was, in part, the effort of those who wished to protect states' rights (20). For the Whigs, however, "rallying voters against Jackson proved insufficient to launch successful state organizations. Transplanting a nationally oriented party to the states required more than the nutrient of national issues, especially when those issues began to lose their sustaining power. To sink permanent roots in the state the Whig party had to address matters of state political concern so that citizens would vote Whig in state as well as presidential elections" (33). Between 1832 and 1836 the Whigs won legislative or gubernatorial elections only in those states "where the party inherited a National Republican majority or where they carved out a distinctive and advantageous position on salient state issues—that is, where they demonstrated that Whig ideas were relevant to the needs of a state's voters. Where *Whigs relied solely on the presidential question in campaigns for state offices or took unpopular stands on state issues, they made their poorest showings, no matter how well their presidential candidates ran*" (49; emphasis added) This, of course, is radically different from the situation today, when parties win elections based mostly on national issues, and a campaign for the House on state-specific matters is usually not sufficient to win a seat.

Because the district-level measure stays largely constant, the measure of party aggregation in Figure 6.1 changes largely in accordance with the national measure. From the measure in Figure 6.1, we can actually discern three general periods: prior to the Civil War, when the party system was quite regionalized and fragmented; after the Civil War but before the New Deal, when there were periodic surges in minor-party support; and then after the New Deal, when such surges stopped. As mentioned, the reason the party aggregation measure is not 0 after the 1920s is because of the uncontested district races that cause the district-level measure to fall below 2. From Figure 6.5, we see that the effective number of parties nationally stays right at 2 or slightly below.

The upward spikes in the party aggregation measure reflect the state, regional, or local bases of minor parties in the United States historically. In some regions in the late nineteenth century, for example, Republicans faced their most significant opposition from Populists, while in other regions the threat came mostly from Democrats. Both Populists and Democrats aggregated substantial votes, causing the effective number of parties at the national level to increase and the party aggregation measure to increase. It was rare for both Populists and Democrats to have a substantial share of votes in the same district or in the same region.

Figure 7.6 provides more detail on changes in elections to the House of Representatives. The upper left panel shows the two parties that received the third and fourth number of votes nationally in any given year.

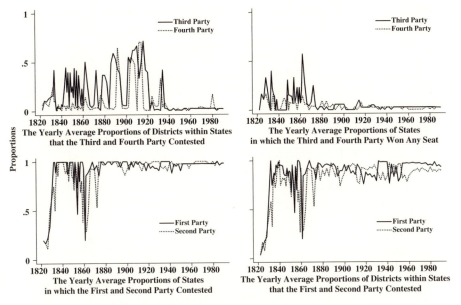

Figure 7.6. Selected Regional Patterns in American Party Politics

Once again, the 1930s ushered in major changes. Prior to that point, third and fourth parties contested in at least one district in one-third to three-quarters of the states in most elections years.

The upper right panel in Figure 7.6 summarizes the results of these elections. After the 1870s, very few minor-party candidates won seats to the lower house. Contrary to the previous figure, the line flattens in the latter half of the nineteenth century instead of in the 1930s. So, while minor parties after the 1870s are running candidates, and in some cases winning substantial votes—they might be the second largest vote getter within a district—they are not winning many seats. And to repeat an often-made point, two-partism in the United States, as interpreted by political scientists, at least prior to the New Deal, is much more about who wins elections than about who runs and who wins substantial votes. Although we do not interpret the United States before the New Deal as constituting a two-party system, it is true that two parties did win most of the seats to the Congress.

Minor parties in the United States have never been able to unite in opposition to the two major parties. Their reputations in recent decades are as holding grounds for cranks and misfits. The same cannot be concluded for those who ran under minor-party labels in the nineteenth century. Not only did many serious candidates run under minor-party labels, but those labels were often threatening to the major parties in large parts of the country.

Regardless of the reputations of minor-party candidates, the data clearly show that they are an extremely fragmented and varied group. Consider Figures 6.7 and 6.8. The large spikes upward in the minor-party N (to as many as thirty parties!) come in years when the major parties get nearly all the vote. So the spikes refer to situations where many, many minor candidates are splitting a very small proportion of the national vote. The two measures are, in fact, negatively related in the post–New Deal era, with a −.58 Pearson correlation coefficient. When the two parties get more of the vote, the minor-party N increases.

There are notable exceptions to this pattern. As an example, the year 1912 has a small, minor-party N, the smallest in all the years since the 1870s, but also the lowest measure in the proportion of the vote for the top two parties. These two measures are related in this instance. The minor-party N is low in 1912 because the Progressives received many more votes than any other minor-party, dwarfing the effect of other parties in the calculation of the minor party N. This, however, is not typical in the American data after the 1870s.

The fact that the United States has a very fragmented set of minor parties relative to Canada and Great Britain is also noteworthy. Even though the scaling makes the numbers look small, the effective number of minor parties in the United States is typically around 5 since the New Deal. Once again, the major parties are getting nearly all the vote, so many minor parties are splitting a small piece of the pie. Remember that both Canada and Great Britain had minor-party Ns around 2 or 3 in the late twentieth century.

While our focus is on using broad brushes to paint the picture of party system history, and on the whole our description is quite simple in dividing American political history into pre– and post–New Deal, two other aspects of the American case are worth discussing. First, we turn our attention to some of the dynamics of the nineteenth- and early twentieth-century party politics. Second, we examine the role of the South and southern politics in the national party system.

Figure 6.5 shows that during the nineteenth century there were wild fluctuations in the number of national parties receiving substantial votes in elections for the lower house. In some years, the United States was a two-party system in lower-house elections—in 1840, for example— whereas in the 1850s there were as many as five effective parties. Our argument is that a decentralized political and economic system does not necessarily lead to many parties, but that it opens the gates to having regionally based parties leading to large spikes in our measures. Thus, the existence of two-partism in some years in a decentralized era is not a disconfirmation of our theoretical argument.

There are several things to note about these data. For one, the spikes are not caused by small numbers of randomly unrepresentative, off-year elections. We do not include data from years in which there were fewer than thirty elections. Throughout the nineteenth century, elections to the lower house were not synchronized across states and could occur in any year, as long as each district held an election every two years. Elections were spread fairly evenly across even- and odd-numbered years. This is in contrast with most of the twentieth century, when elections were synchronized to be in even-numbered years across the states, while in odd-numbered years elections held were to fill vacated seats only.

For another, the data on party labels for candidates for the years prior to 1830 are not complete, whereas for the years after 1830 they are virtually complete. This has implications for how we interpret Figure 6.5 and Figure 6.1 on party aggregation. For example, in 1806 we only have data on party labels from one state, Vermont, where all the winners were from the same party, the Old Republicans. In fact, that year has the least amount of complete data. For candidates in the other states, and for candidates facing the Old Republicans in Vermont, party labels are not available. In that year, however, as in other years, we have quite good data on most races in terms of the number of votes that each candidate received in elections in that year. Note that to make the district-level measure we do not need party labels, only the vote totals of the candidates. So the district-level measure in Figures 2.4 and 6.5 is around 2, but the national measure is at 1, so the party aggregation measure is actually below 0. With complete data on party labels, that measure of party aggregation cannot go below 0. We report that number in Figure 6.1 precisely to make this point and to show that the measure can only go below 0 in the absence of party label data.

More important for our argument, if we focus attention on the years following 1830 when the data are much more complete, we see that the most activity for minor parties in the United States, and the most volatility in our measures from election to election, occurs in the 1850s and 1860s. In the 1850s, congressional election politics was a complicated mixture of state-level issues such as the regulation of alcohol and controversies over Catholic schools and immigration and national-level issues such as slavery, Western expansion, and tariff policies. A number of scholars, especially Gienapp (1987) and Holt (1999), have documented the overwhelmingly state-based and local nature of congressional elections in the 1850s, even following the Nebraska Act in 1854 that brought the issue of slavery to the forefront of national politics.

The 1850s was a time of transition, when national issues began to intrude on local politics, although the local issues did not wane in importance until late in the decade on the eve of war. Different regions had candidates running under different labels, and parties did not aggregate votes nationally very effectively. There were Soft Democrats, Hard Democrats, Free-Soilers, Whigs, Democrats, Americans (Know-Nothings), Unionists, and Independent Democrats. Most of these parties gained votes in one or a few states. The Know-Nothings, for example, had their greatest success in Massachusetts because of a confluence of local factors (Haynes 1897). The decline of the Whigs was in large part due to state-specific and local factors (Holt 1999, 780–99). In most states the Whigs "failed to find a distinctive issue," and there was a "seepage of some Whig voters toward new parties" (Holt 1999, 799, 800). By 1856 the Republicans emerged from the many opponents to the Democrats, and they actually aggregated antislavery votes reasonably well—note the drop in the number of national parties in the late 1850s—but once war broke out between North and South, the party system fragmented again badly, if only temporarily.

By the mid-1860s the fragmentation was not quite as severe, and while the Unionists and Conservatives split the anti-Democratic vote enough to give the United States about three effective national parties, it was considerably less fragmented than before. The centralization surrounding the Civil War definitely reduced the number of parties in the United States, as the large spikes observed in the 1850s did not return. From the end of the Civil War to the 1930s, compared with the period prior to the Civil War, the United States is more like a two-party system in congressional elections interrupted only by occasional surges of support for minor, more regionally based parties. These minor parties included the Greenbacks, the Liberal Republicans, the Union Laborites, the Populists, the Prohibitionists, and socialists of various stripes.

The relationship between recession and voting for minor parties is a recurring theme in the electoral history of this period. In some cases, recessions in the nineteenth century led to an increase in votes for minor parties, especially when that party had a strong economics program. One vivid example is the rise of the Greenbacks in the 1870s, a decade of severe economic hardship for many Americans. Greenback support surged in 1876 and 1878 when the recession of that time was most serious. This is not entirely consistent with our explanation. One would think recessions might undercut votes for minor parties because national issues—how the national government ought to change tariff policies, or print more money, or break up the monopoly trusts in response to bad economic times—might make voters turn more toward the national parties and away from more regionally based parties.

The Greenbacks, however, were an exception, and their electoral success is not actually inconsistent with our argument. Historians of party competition in the nineteenth century focus considerable attention on the overwhelmingly local nature of congressional races, and the irrelevance of national issues in many of these campaigns. Voters in good economic times voted on the basis of which local politician was more or less corrupt, the religion of the candidate, and the reputation of that candidate on state-level politics. All in all, the candidates' and state parties' positions on national issues were not all that important once those other factors were taken into account. Of course, for the variety of reasons discussed in chapter 4, virtually every candidate had a party affiliation.

When economic times were bad, however, voters focused more attention on the national government. It is telling that the Greenbacks fought for national policy changes, and votes for the party rose during recessions. But other parties' vote totals, the parties that focused attention on more regional or local issues, such as Prohibition, Farmer-Labor, and Progressives in the late nineteenth century, typically dropped during the recessions of the 1870s and 1890s.[11]

There is more to say about the 1870s. Upon closer inspection of Figure 7.6, this decade marks a turning point. The most likely interpretation of the pattern in Figures 6.5 and 7.5 is that, prior to the 1880s but after the Civil War, many politicians, especially those on the non-Democratic side of the political spectrum, were aligned politically to politicians in other parts of the country but did not aggregate votes effectively among themselves because they took on different party labels. For example, in the 1860s, there were the Modern Republicans, the Union Republicans, and Union candidates. In the 1870s, there were the Liberal Republicans and the Modern Republicans. They never ran against each other within districts, but opposed the Democrats in various parts of the country. After the 1870s, the two major parties stamped out the proliferation of labels and both coalesced under singular labels. Thus, in nearly every district, starting in the 1880s, there were two candidates, one each from the Democrats and Republicans, and then others for the Greenbacks, Prohibition, Union Labor, Populists, and other labels. Then finally, in the 1930s, these minor parties began receiving very few votes.

In the early twentieth century, there was another surge in minor-party support. The Progressives were largely a collection of locally based parties that did not necessarily coordinate their efforts across districts and

---

[11]The base of Prohibitionists' support was found in the state-specific Temperance conventions (Kleppner 1987).

even had slightly different labels in neighboring states (Shefter 1994).[12] Before the New Deal, even the national parties were more locally based. The parties gathered and "handed out divisible economic benefits to meet their patronage requirements" (Finegold and Skocpol 1995, 54). While these local parties were often labeled Democrat or Republican, in some places parties such as Labor, Progressive, Socialist, Prohibitionist, or Farmer were one of the two locally dominant political organizations.[13]

The political and economic centralization of the 1930s had a profound effect on local politics and local political economies. The New Deal not only centralized public taxing and spending decisions but had the effect of centralizing political authority. According to Milkis (1993, 9), it brought about the "nationalization of the political system . . . [and] established conditions for the emergence of a more national and programmatic party system." The new policies in some cases weakened more conservative Democratic machines in big cities, such as New York (Erie 1988). But they also brought into the Democratic fold the Republican Progressives in Minnesota and the Farmer-Labor members in Wisconsin (Milkis 1993). They strengthened local Democratic machines in Chicago and Pittsburgh and maintained the Democratic hold on many parts of the South. The centralizing policies put into place caused voters and politicians to orient their party affiliations either in support of or in opposition to them. Nearly all viable legislative candidates, in response to national centralization, found it increasingly in their interests to affiliate with one of the two major parties, and voters increasingly considered national policies when choosing to support partisan candidates. As Schattschneider ([1960] 1975, 88) states, the elections of the 1930s and 1940s were "completely dominated by national influences."

In similar fashion, congressional elections since the New Deal have been completely dominated by the two major parties, as the data summarized in these figures indicate. While it is true that candidates retain local ties and cultivate relationships with constituents that are somewhat independent of party labels in many cases, it is also true that just about any serious candidate for Congress has to run under a major party label to win office. This has not always been the case, but it has been the case since the 1930s. The exceptions, such as the occasional independents, the Minnesota Farmer-Labor candidates, and the rising Greens in parts of the West, and the attention they gain, prove the rule. The spikes in the 1970s and 1980s in Figure 7.5 are the Conservative Party and the

---

[12]The collapse of the Progressive Party has been attributed, in a very particular rendition by Ickes (1941), to the leadership of George Perkins, who was an insider in Progressive politics. For a more complete discussion of the failure of the Progressives, see Link (1959).
[13]The collapse of the Progressive Party after 1912 could be attributed to its inability to coordinate state-level and local-level party ballots (Mowry 1983).

Libertarian Party, respectively. Other parties that finish lower than fourth nationally, and are thus not depicted in the figure, are noteworthy. For example, prior to the 1930s, the Prohibition Party fielded candidates in almost every state, but few won many votes and not a single Prohibition candidate won a seat. The names of the parties that in any given year fielded many candidates across the country, but never made much of a dent, varied: National Progressive, Socialist Labor, People's, Independent (the party, not running as an independent), Republican-Democrat.

The correlation between the dramatic changes in the early half of the twentieth century in both political outcomes and economic policy making is hard to refute. Centralization happened prior to and during the changes in the party system. In no way do the data support the idea that party system changes caused the centralization. In a previously published article (Chhibber and Kollman 1998), we report statistical results that support the relationship between centralization and party aggregation in the United States. We regressed the number of national parties on central government spending (minus defense) as a proportion of gross national product (GNP) for the years 1880 to 1970. Under various specifications and time-series procedures, the results clearly show that there is a negative correlation in these data between the number of national parties and fiscal centralization. The statistical results further show that party system changes lag in time in relation to changes in fiscal centralization. Thus, when American public finances centralize, the number of national parties declines, and when American public finances decentralize, the number of national parties increases.

We now turn our attention to the most distinctive region in American political history. No study claiming to explain interesting patterns in American national parties can ignore the role of the South. How do the historical patterns associated with partisanship and party strength in the South fit with our argument?

The South was predominantly a one-party region for approximately eighty years, from the 1890s to the 1970s. As numerous scholars have argued, most famously V. O. Key, one-partism in the South during this era was a regional reaction by state-level politicians and economic elites to the threat of national interference in the way southern societies were operated. Voters—those who were not disenfranchised—aggregated their votes effectively because of a widely recognized threat. The threat they perceived, and their response to it, are not altogether different from the perceived threats that unified voters and candidates in Wales and Scotland, in Quebec, and among some regional parties like the DMK and the Akali Dal in India. Only in a few cases are opposition parties in these regions perceived as lowly as Republicans were in the South, and pure one-partism of the kind practiced in the South required help to enforce it from extralegal, nondemocratic measures, such as poll taxes, violence, and intimidation of potential voters. Nevertheless, this is consistent with our overall explanation, that voters paying attention to higher levels of government will support candidates with party labels that have meaning at those higher levels of government.

It is misleading to try to understand one-partism in the South in the absence of national politics. Granted, and as Key makes clear, local issues mattered in the South, and they played out electorally, often in the Democratic primaries and caucuses, the intraparty factional battles that animate Key's famous book, *Southern Politics* (1949). As we know from Key, the South did have electoral competition in the primaries, and some states even had vigorous two-party competition between Republican and Democrats. Yet when party labels mattered to voters, in the general elections, the many southern voters who pulled for Democrats would not think of voting for Republicans because they felt to do so would bring upon southern society a centralized force in the national government.

Why southern elites did not separate from the Democratic Party following Reconstruction in the 1870s and form a new, Southern political party is an intriguing question. Why did they rejoin forces with northern and western Democrats? Our answer is that this is where the American presidential system has had its most potent effect in its history. Voting for Democrats was the southern elites' way of making sure they had a unified voice in presidential politics—the unified South had a veto on Democratic presidential candidates because of voting rules in the nominating conventions—and a way of countering a centralized threat through unified voting and scuttling of action on racial matters in the Congress. The president was the one actor who could use his bureaucracy and his enforcement powers to pressure the South. That was the office from which national politicians lifted the Reconstruction policies, threatened the South with ideas about full, nonracialized democracy, and chose to turn the Justice Department's blind eye to violations of the post–Civil War civil rights amendments. By bolting from the Democratic Party, the South would have reduced its role in choosing presidents. Consider how much Democratic presidents like Cleveland and Wilson had to cater to the South because they needed southern delegates to win within their own party.

In principle, it would have been possible for a "Southern Party" to form, and to play kingmaker between the two major parties. Some southern Populists advocated this role for its newfound party in the 1890s. However, the strategy taken—to stay within the Democratic Party—paid off by influencing the Democrats' presidential candidate and especially in ascending to the top of the seniority rankings in the

Congress to maintain control over key committees. This latter effect would have been hard to achieve if a unified, separate southern party had formed to represent southern elite, white interests.

Our data comparing the South and the rest of the country underscore much of what we already know about regional voting patterns and party competition. Figure 7.7 shows the effective number of parties in the districts and in the states in the South, in the rest of the country, and combined. The South's measures in both cases are much lower during the era of Jim Crow and into the 1970s. Because of the population differences between the regions, however (and because so few southerners voted in the early twentieth century), including or excluding the South makes little difference in the overall national measure, as these figures, and Figure 6.5, indicate.

Republicans did win some seats in many southern states before World War I and after the 1940s. Consider the bottom panel in Figure 7.7. The period from 1900 to the First World War, and the period from 1950 to 1990 show a highly nationalized party system. Both parties are winning seats in almost every state. The parties are stronger in some regions than in others, but it is not as pronounced as one would believe from impressions of the one-party South. The data from the 1930s and 1940s,

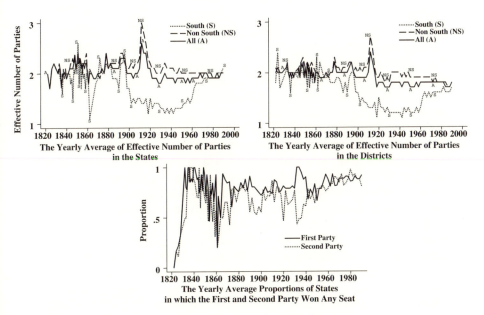

Figure 7.7. Distinctive Southern Politics in the United States

however, show that the Republicans were winning seats in only half to two-thirds of the states. The South had completely shut the door on the Republicans for about twenty years, and the party system was more regionalized than at any time since the 1870s. (Note that the 1890s looks the same in these data, but it is misleading, not because any one region was one-party, but rather because the Populists took votes away from the Democrats, even in the South.)

Figure 6.5, which shows the effective number of parties in the states, is worth another final look. It shows quite clearly that state-level party systems have been overwhelmingly two-party—with the exception of the South in some periods. Yet we do not see the same change in the 1920s and 1930s in the state-level data that we see in the national level data. Most striking, the volatility in the 1850s and 1860s in the national data comes from state-level parties failing to aggregate votes across states, not from many parties within the states. This merely confirms what we have been saying all along. Votes will aggregate up to the level where policy-making authority lies. It rested mostly with the states in the nineteenth and early twentieth centuries, and then migrated to the national level in the 1920s and 1930s. The linkages that occurred, as discussed in Cox (1997), happen in the post–New Deal era across states, not across districts. The district-level linkages happened from the very beginning.

## CONCLUSION

The data from these cases point in the same direction. For all four countries, periods of centralization correspond to more effective party aggregation and periods of provincialization correspond to periods of more party fragmentation and regionalism. The most difficult case among the four is certainly Canada, because of the long stretch of time in the twentieth century when federalism there was in flux. Authority not only moved back and forth in court decisions, accords among the provinces, and policy making by the national government, but there was a great deal of ambiguity about which direction the wind was blowing at any point in time. The party system appropriately shows the same degree of indecisiveness over time. The fluctuations in the strength of the minor and regional parties could be dramatic. Given the nature of Canadian federal relations during this time, is it any wonder that Canadians might have been torn from time to time over whether it was better for their interests to support one of the two major parties or support a minor party?

The British case also is not altogether straightforward because it is not federal in the same way that the other countries are. The fluctuations are not as dramatic in Britain, and the movements up and down in the party measures are not as steep. All in all, federalism seems to enhance the effects of centralization and provincialization on the party system. We say this somewhat cautiously given that we only have one case of a nonfederal system in this study.

# Chapter 8

# CONCLUSION

IN THIS CHAPTER WE SUMMARIZE our argument and the evidence on party aggregation, discuss alternative ideas about party system change, and provide evidence that our basic argument applies to cases that are not single-member, simple-plurality systems.

## SUMMARY

We have emphasized that political parties aggregate votes and coordinate political activity across geographic space. The policies of the government, the distribution of authority across levels of government, and the trends in the migration of that authority affect how well that party aggregation occurs and the exact results of that aggregation for the party system.

More specifically, we use data from four countries with similar electoral systems—attempting as best we can to control for electoral system effects across our countries—to examine the dynamics of party system change. We have sought to understand why party systems in single-member, simple-plurality systems sometimes fragment into many parties and sometimes aggregate into small numbers of parties. Our four cases are Canada, Great Britain, India, and the United States. In all four, there have been changes in the degree to which minor and regional parties have won substantial votes in elections to the lower house of parliament in the national government.

The basic argument is straightforward. Voters are more likely to support national political parties as the national government becomes more important in their lives. As this happens, candidates also are more likely to forsake local parties and assume the labels of national parties. These two effects are especially true in federal systems where there can be a real back-and-forth between the authority of states or provinces and the national government. As voters and candidates abandon local parties, those parties become less competitive locally, and the decline spirals downward to the point where the local parties are abandoned altogether and disappear. Or, moving in the opposite direction, as authority devolves to lower levels of government, state-based, province-based, or even region-based parties can gain increasing votes at the expense of the national parties.

The cumulative effect of having voters and candidates who are motivated by the nature of political authority in the country is that party systems—the number of parties and the link between local-level elections and national elections—respond to the degree of political and economic centralization in the country. More provincialization leads to greater party system fragmentation, especially along geographic lines, and more centralization leads to more consolidation of votes into national party labels.

Data support our argument in these four countries. A few figures and one table tell the primary story. Table 6.1 lists the periods in each country when centralization and provincialization occurred. We rely on historical materials and public finance and employment data to type these periods. Figures 6.1–6.5 show the party system dynamics. First, in Figures 6.2–6.5, the average effective number of parties in the electoral districts are shown for each year. Immediately noticeable is that, for the most part, these numbers are low. While they approach 3 in some years in Canada, Great Britain, and India, and while they do fluctuate and even trend over long spans of time, they nevertheless stay somewhere near the number 2, corresponding for the most part to the main prediction from the political science literature regarding these kinds of electoral systems. Duverger's famous law, and the body of follow-up research that surrounds it, as summarized in chapter 2, predict that single-member district rules will lead to two part-ism. As shown in chapter 2, these data fit the predictions from Duverger's Law reasonably well *at the district level*. There are systematic departures from these predictions, mainly in the many, but by no means majority, of British and Canadian district elections where three or more parties win substantial votes. We cannot comfortably offer an explanation for these exceptions because of a lack of district-level, nonelectoral data, such as demographic or public opinion data.

After chapter 2, the focus is on the systemic level rather than the district level. Duverger's Law, as many others have pointed out, is a theoretical instrument that is too simple, and perhaps too blunt, to understand party system dynamics in our four countries. The many studies reporting the correlations between party system characteristics and electoral systems also use aggregate measures that overlook the temporal dimensions of party system change in Canada, Great Britain, India, and the United States. Cox's book, *Making Votes Count*, which appropriately emphasizes the difference between district-level electoral patterns and system-level patterns, left the reader with some provocative ideas on how local elections piece together into national party systems. In perhaps his most original contribution to the study of national party systems, Cox, following Shugart and Carey, focuses attention on the relationship between executive-level elections and legislative elections. This is not only an important step theoretically but also improves the fit of statistical models on cross-national data. Nevertheless, the executive electoral institutions cannot be the answer to why party system characteristics fluctuate, because those institutions typically do not change over time.

This book fleshes out an aspect of what was left unsaid in the second half of Cox's book, in which his tenth chapter is titled, "Putting the Constituencies Together," and in which he devotes attention to national party systems as they relate to electoral rules and political institutions. Our entry into this literature is by paying attention to change and to stasis. What stays the same and what changes in countries and their party systems? Population diversity and electoral systems largely stay the same, while political centralization, provincialization, and the role of the government in people's lives changes over time.

Comparing the periods in Table 6.1 to the data in Figures 6.2–6.5 and especially Figure 6.1, we see that centralized periods correspond to better party aggregation (lower values in Figure 6.1) and usually (though not always) lower numbers of effective parties nationally. The exact opposite is true for provincialized or provincializing periods, when the number of national parties increases for the most part, or there are periodic spikes in the number of national parties.

We also sought to clarify with our data the distinctions between nationalized party systems, national parties, regional parties, and regionalized party systems. By nationalized party system, we mean lower values in our party aggregation measure in Figure 6.1. Lower values in that measure mean that district-level election results look similar to national election results. In a perfectly nationalized party system, that measure would be zero, whereas in the perfectly fragmented (by geography) party system, when two parties receive all the vote in each of the districts, that measure would be two multiplied by the number of districts. Note that if district-level elections tend to have three parties receiving all the votes, and those parties also split the national vote in ways similar to the typical district, then that measure could be zero as well. In other words, the connection between Duverger's Law and a nationalized party system is not a given. If there are more than two parties at various levels of aggregation, but those parties correspond, then the system could be quite nationalized, irrespective of Duvergerian pressures for reductions in the number of candidates or parties receiving votes.

By national parties we mean those parties that contest elections and win votes in many regions, many states or provinces, and many districts in the country. Regional parties are those that compete in elections and win votes in smaller numbers of regions, states, provinces, or districts. Clearly, this is a matter of degree, and highly nationalized party systems can contain some regional parties, but as those parties gain higher proportions of the national vote, the party system will become less and less nationalized. The more the national votes are fragmented among regionalized parties, the more regionalized is the party system. Consider Figure 6.4, which shows the effective number of Indian parties at the district, state, and national levels. There is little doubt that starting in the 1990s, India moved up a notch, becoming an extremely fragmented, state-based (or regionalized) party system. In contrast, the United States after the 1930s, Canada in the 1910s, and Britain in the 1950s were not highly fragmented and regionalized. And to reiterate a point we make more extensively in chapter 6, this is not the same as saying that parties do not do well in some regions and poorly in others, as is true almost everywhere in the world. That pattern can coexist with the determination that a party system is highly nationalized (though it is granted that with perfect nationalization, a party aggregation measure of zero, would not be possible under that condition.)[1]

The book offers several claims or findings that cut against previous research, and even common wisdom about politics in these countries. Perhaps most surprising is the finding that the United States has not been a pure two-party system until the 1930s. As demonstrated, many American voters supported minor parties for congressional elections in the nineteenth century and into the early twentieth century.

Furthermore, the finding on Duverger's Law in the district elections is true even in countries like India where the heterogeneity of the population within districts, based on class, religion, language, wealth, status, and education, is among the highest anywhere in the world. Even in some remarkably diverse constituencies, for example, most elections to the Indian lower house of parliament result in two parties receiving nearly all the votes. This challenges general claims that party divisions necessarily reflect social cleavages.

Finally, the book shows that it is highly misleading to draw direct causal links between electoral systems and the number of political par-

---

[1]Ours is not a detailed historical account of how the party systems changed, although we rely on historical facts and certainly historical data to make our case. One will have to look elsewhere for specific historical material on how the political party systems of these four countries came about. We have read and relied on many of these fine accounts, and they are extremely valuable for our enterprise and wonderfully instructive for scholars of political parties. Here we are trying to understand general relationships between political institutions, government policy, and political party competition through mass elections, and our four countries stand as our test cases.

ties at the national level. In all four of our countries, the number of parties competing for national-level representation has fluctuated over time, while the electoral systems have stayed virtually constant. We demonstrated that at a minimum, electoral rules interact with other important factors—namely, the degree of political and fiscal authority wielded by lower-level governments—to shape party systems and that we must focus on factors that change over time to explain party systems that change over time.

## ALTERNATIVE EXPLANATIONS

Various other explanations can be offered for the levels of party aggregation found in these four countries, or in any country. One explanation for the correlations found in our data, and perhaps the most serious challenge to our explanation, is that we have the story backward. This deserves considerable attention.

It could be argued that party system change causes centralization or provincialization, and not vice versa. Given the research on the influence of parties on economic policy making (Alesina, Roubini, and Cohen 1999; Boix 1998; Persson and Tabellini 1999), it could be that any correlations found in our data result from the fact that many of the governing parties in these four countries throughout their histories advocated and carried out reforms of government that centralized or moved authority away from the center. Perhaps national parties, upon winning office, take power away from lower levels of government to accomplish national goals. Or, likewise, regionalization of party systems could cause authority to migrate toward lower levels of government, as regional-based parties pressure national governments to cede authority.

Undoubtedly, there is some truth to this alternative argument. In some periods, regional parties, or even threats of the rise of regional parties, do spur national governments to pay more attention to pressures for devolution. In Great Britain, for example, the major parties responded to electoral threats from the Welsh and Scottish nationalist parties in the 1960s and 1970s by offering to grant more spending authority to those regions. There were serious discussions in Westminster throughout the latter half of the twentieth century about creating more federalism in Britain,. These discussions occurred against the backdrop of rising nationalism in the regions. It would also be incorrect to claim that party politics, the electoral contests and their results, and the ideologies promulgated and policies enacted by parties once in office are irrelevant as causes of centralization or provincialization. The Democratic Party in the United States, prior to the Civil War, governed for most of five decades under the guiding philosophies of Thomas Jefferson and Andrew Jackson, who shared the belief that limited national government was the fundamental pillar of the United States Constitution. Indeed, many of the governing parties in these four countries throughout their histories have advocated and carried out reforms of government that centralized or moved authority away from the center. Because the governments of these four countries were controlled by parties and party politicians, how could it not be otherwise?

To admit this is a far cry from saying that centralization or provincialization occurs mostly, or solely, as a result of the nationalization or regionalization of the party systems respectively, and that our claims are wrong because the causal direction we posit is backward. Our claim is that the changing relationships of national governments to lower levels of government themselves cause changes in the party systems, regardless of how the changes in the degree of centralization occur. Those changes in political authority could result from changes in party systems, but most often the changes in party systems were not the primary cause of changes in the policy-making system. Moreover, as results in chapters 6 and 7 show, the broad processes of centralization and provincialization have nearly always begun prior to changes in party systems. The timing of these changes suggests that while there can be reciprocal causation, it is typically the changing nature of political authority that initiates changes in party systems, and not the other way around. Finally, without exception, the policies that led to centralization and provincialization in all four of our countries were the ambit of the major, national parties. National parties did not always centralize when they were in power, while regional parties moved authority to the provinces when they were in power. Instead, provincialization sometimes occurred in response to threats from regional parties, but it would be misleading to say that regional parties carried out the reforms to devolve authority.

This naturally begs the question of what events, if not party system changes, lead to centralization and provincialization. In our four countries, the periods of centralization occur around four types of events: war or the threat of war, economic depression, nation building, or the development of the welfare state. While the leaders of political parties, and partisan voters, respond to these events by pressuring for policies that affect the distribution of authority across levels of government, and so their actions can be said to cause government action that might lead to centralization, the root causes are typically larger in scope than the electoral politics surrounding an election or a string of elections. Throughout the histories of these countries, it is often the case that partisan proposals from both of the major parties to deal with crises call for centralization of authority. To say that party leaders adopt policies that centralize authority is not the same as saying that centralization does not cause party system changes.

There have been various studies of centralization of government activity and the expansion of the role of the national government. None of them attribute centralization solely to party politics. In Canada, the centralization that occurred immediately after Confederation and during World Wars I and II was not a result of party politics, although some politicians did use the opportunity to expand the role of the national government. Centralization in both eras was rooted in various processes, including efforts to link together more concretely the various parts of Canada, especially French and English Canada. "As far as the assimilation of French Canada is concerned, thirty years of social history will thus have had more effect than a century and half of political history" (Royal Commission of Inquiry on Constitutional Problems 1956, cited in Banting 1995, 284).

In India, power accrued to the national government largely as a legacy of the independence movement. As a result, there was general consensus among Indian policy makers that the nation-state was to be the engine of social and economic development. "Even before the planning system was established, the center took full control over the industrial sector by legislation, as permitted by the Constitution, since it was agreed on all sides that industrialisation would be at the heart of development and the necessary thrust could only be provided by the state operating through the central government" (Mozoomdar 1994, 99). The state was able to play such a large role without any contestation because of its historical role, which arose from the independence movement. As Chatterjee (1994, 55) notes, the emphasis on the nation-state emerged as a result of nationalism, and "the economic critique of colonialism . . . was the foundation from which a positive content was supplied for the independent national state: the new state represented the only legitimate form of exercise of power because it was a necessary condition for the development of the nation." The geopolitical situation at the end of World War II also encouraged this line of thinking. The key assumption was that national independence could be maintained through the attainment of economic power. In an increasingly industrialized world, economic power could be achieved through state-led industrialization. The rapid rise of the Soviet Union as an industrial and political power provided a model for policy makers in many developing countries.

State-led industrialization was seen as necessary for a number of reasons particular to the Indian situation, especially in the need for capital to build the industrial base required for sustained and diversified growth. In a poor country where savings rates were low the capital needed for development could only be mobilized by the state. Support for this expansive role of the state came from across the political spectrum. The left wanted all-India plans led by a National Planning Committee and "the National Planning Committee . . . [would be] the first real experience of the emerging state leadership of the Congress . . . with working out the idea of 'national planning.'" The centrist Congress also felt that "planning was not only a part of the anticipation of power by the state leadership of the Congress, it was also an anticipation of the concrete forms in which that power would be exercised within a national state" (Chatterjee 1994, 53). Meanwhile, the Bombay Plan, devised by leading industrialists, relied on planning by the state (Byres 1994). Hence, at independence and in the decade following, there was widespread political support for the notion that the Indian state was to be the architect and arbiter of economic development (Paranjape 1964; Hanson 1966; Rudolph and Rudolph 1987; Kaviraj 1991; Chakravarty 1987). The major period of centralization in India was during the regime of Indira Gandhi from 1971 through the 1980s. It is undoubtedly true that there was a political element to this centralization, namely the retention of power by Gandhi. It was personal aggrandizement that was the impetus behind this centralization, not party politics per se.

In the United States there have been two major periods of centralization—the Civil War and the New Deal. In both cases economic authority was shifted away from the states to the federal government. It would be a stretch to argue that the "federalization" of economic authority resulted from partisan politics, especially in the Civil War and the New Deal. In both cases, the federal government was responding to serious political (secession) or economic threats (depression). And even the other period of mild centralization, the beginning of the twentieth century, conforms to this pattern. The building of the American state in the end of the nineteenth century and the beginning of the twentieth century was less a result of partisan politics and was more of a response to economic conditions (Skowronek 1982).

In Britain, as in Canada and the United States, the role of the central government expanded during the war and with the rise of the welfare state. Major increases in the expenses of the British national government took place during World Wars I and II when government expenditures on goods and services expanded more dramatically than at other times in the twentieth century (Peacock and Wiseman 1961, 72). As for the welfare state, in Britain social policy was administered nationally and the largest proportion of government expenditures by the 1950s was on social services. The government was allocating over 40 percent of its total per-capita expenditures on social services in 1955 (84–85, 88). In 1890 local governments' share of total government expenditures on social services was almost 72 percent. In 1920 it was just over 50 percent, and after the depression in 1933 the local governments' share had dropped to 44 percent, and then it dropped to 38 percent in 1952 (106).

Provincialization is a little more complicated. Why would a national government decentralize if not faced with pressure from other political parties? Provincialization can occur for a variety of reasons. Based on our cases, when power goes to the states or provinces it is not because of the rise of state or provincial parties but due to the forces that give rise to state or provincial parties—local elites and voters feeling threatened by centralization and calling for diverting resources away from the central government. Even when provincial parties emerge, they do so after power has been given to the states or provinces.

In Canada, provincialization preceded the rise of regional parties and the periods when parties began to aggregate less effectively. In the two periods that characterized the emergence of regional parties (the 1920s and the 1980s) provincial governments had gained more authority and autonomy prior to the party system change. The first change in the party system in the 1920s followed (and did not precede) the increasing financial autonomy of provincial governments (Carty, Cross, and Young 2000). Until the early 1900s, provinces depended on the Dominion government for most of their resources, which were passed on as subsidies. In the 1910s, the economy expanded, and provincial governments began to tax their citizens to gather resources (Royal Commission on Dominion-Provincial Relations 1940). The regionalization of the party system in the 1920s followed this accrual of financial authority by the provincial governments.

Similarly, the increasing regionalization of the party system in the 1980s followed a period in the 1960s and 1970s during which provincial governments gained ever larger control over economic affairs in their geographic jurisdictions, according to scholars of Canadian political economy. One example comes from the growth of public enterprise during 1960s and 1970s. "In the 1970s, during which some 49 per cent of the existing corporations were created the left was in power in more jurisdictions than in any previous time" (Chandler 1982, 738).

> The coming to power of social democratic governments does not, however, explain the more general trend that in all provinces there has been an increase in the number of public corporations. The explanation probably lies in the general phenomenon of province-building. . . . Increased resources as well as a heightened consciousness of provincial interests have been the basis of a willingness to use state business as an element of industrial strategy. This has meant not only a continuation of the use of facilitative corporations but also an increase in the more intrusive nationalistic type. Since 1960 both the left and non-left have used public enterprise as an instru-

ment of nationalism. . . . The nationalistic crown corporation reflects the provinces' response to problems of economic development in vastly different economic and political milieux. (739)

In Quebec, for example, a white paper issued in March 1965 ensured a minimum standard of services for all citizens regardless of the locality in which they lived (Dyck 1986, 152). The provincial government consequently assumed control over education, social welfare, and health, and all assessment and tax collection were made provincial responsibility (153). The Quebec government also increased provincial involvement in the economic life of the citizens of the province through the creation of a number of public sectors corporations beginning with the 1960s, such as Hydro Quebec, Sidbec (the Quebec steel operation), and the Asbestos Corporation. The provincial government ran an auto insurance corporation, and the government was involved in mineral exploitation, petroleum, and forestry. Most important of all, the Caisse de Depot et Placement du Quebec, which managed funds collected by the Quebec pension plan and had assets worth $20 billion (Canadian), was "an important instrument of provincial economic policy" (194).

Likewise, all provinces in the 1960s revamped their civil services and expanded their administrative roles (as seen in the increase in the number of provincial employees: see Figure 5.2). The Keynesian expansion of the Canadian state in the 1960s gave the provinces a chance to increase their role in local economies, and this increased role of the provinces came before the regionalization of the party system that began in the 1960s and gathered momentum in the 1980s.

In India the situation is far clearer. As we noted in chapter 5, decentralization in India was adopted to deal with an economic crisis. The crisis required the central government to shed its shackles on the industrial economy. This also helped the central government deal with the fiscal crisis that was the main cause for reforming the economy (Ahluwalia 2002). The regionalization of the party system followed (see Figure 6.4). More importantly, in India, as in Canada, state governments gathered greater economic salience, ironically, during the period of centralization and in the 1980s when there was a large expansion in the activities of the national government. This expansion of the role of the state governments happened under the auspices of the Congress Party (see chapter 5) and in a period when party aggregation across states was not as major a concern as in the 1990s (Figure 6.4). Thus, once again, party system fragmentation followed increasing economic roles for state governments.

In Britain, devolution preceded the emergence of regional political parties as electoral forces. For instance, the Welsh parties emerged as politically salient only after measures decentralizing authority away from Whitehall had been initiated (Bogdanor 1999). One would be hard pressed to argue that the decentralization of the 1990s followed as a result of pressure from regional parties alone. The decentralization occurred for a more complex set of reasons (Bogdanor 1999).

To summarize, we acknowledge the possibility of reciprocal causation, that election results can lead to changes in political authority structures, which in turn affect election results. But in all four of our countries, party aggregation effects followed either a real migration of authority downward or upward, or they succeeded discussions about such migration of authority. Our focus has been on how voters think about supporting local versus national parties. Certainly voters understand that their actions can cause further changes in one direction or the other. Our evidence on the timing of events shows that voters—as revealed through their partisan choices—are responding to the changing nature of political authority in their countries more often than they are causing those changes through their partisan choices.

We now discuss several alternatives that might be offered to explain the difference between the United States case and the others. Most explanations for the United States party system, its two-partism in particular, are static. These explanations focus on institutional features, such as the presidency and the presidential election system, and single-member, simple-plurality elections for Congress. Some, however, focus attention on factors that change, such as the strength of the committee system in Congress, the prevalence of ballot access laws, and changes in civil service norms.

The committee system and rules of the lower house have been suggested as discriminating against third parties. One could argue that because of the weak committee systems in the Indian Lok Sabha, and in the British and Canadian Commons, there are more parties in those countries than in the United States. More floor action relative to committee action could mean less effective coordination among legislators on agenda control and voting. Although the committee systems are indeed different in these countries, this alone cannot explain the variance in the number of parties receiving votes in legislative elections in the United States as that variance differs from those in the other countries. In the late 1800s, for example, members of the Populist Party often complained that they were not given the chance to speak and that the two major parties essentially divided the House and the committee assignments between themselves. This was undoubtedly a complaint voiced by other minor-party legislators following the period of the strengthening of the committees in the 1880s. Yet this did not prevent the occurrence prior to the 1930s of either the emergence of third parties or voter support for minor parties that were locally but not nationally competitive.

Ballot access rules also can prevent minor parties from becoming competitive by raising the costs of running campaigns, hindering the mobilization of candidates, donors, and voters, and even outright intimidation of people attempting to organize. We do not have systematic comparative data on ballot access rules across our four countries, but it is almost certainly the case that the United States has the most onerous ballot access rules—at the state level—compared with those in the other three countries. These differences could go some way toward explaining why the United States has fewer parties than the other countries. These access rules can solidify two-partism both at the state and national level. We have found no concrete evidence, however, to support the idea that ballot access rules changed so dramatically in the United States in the 1930s that they caused the number of national parties to drop as it did. Most of these rules were established around the turn of the century, during the Progressive Era. One could argue that it took twenty years for those rules to have their effect, but we are doubtful. Nevertheless, this alternative raises interesting questions for further research.

The evolution of the United States party system has been linked directly by Shefter (1994) and indirectly by Skocpol (1995) to civil service reform. Although these authors do not explicitly address any influence that the emergence of a "national civil service" may have had on the number of national parties, their explanation suggests that a national bureaucracy and a two-party system go hand in hand. Civil service reform may lead to a nationalization of issues. Coleman (1996) makes a similar claim. Our argument is not entirely different, but the data from our other countries cast doubt on this as a definitive explanation. The Indian and British governments have had large national bureaucracies, yet the issues that currently dominate Indian elections and party politics are not national, whereas those in Britain typically are. It is not the existence of a national civil service but the functions it performs that determine whether national concerns will dominate local politics. Those functions are determined by the very factors that we focus on in this book. So, in the United States, the introduction of an income tax and the emergence of the welfare state were crucial to the nationalization of politics.

## AN EXTENSION TO OTHER ELECTORAL SYSTEMS

While this book has focused on the influence of political authority on party aggregation in four countries with single-member districts, it could be argued that, in principle, a larger role for the national government should make party systems more national regardless of the electoral system. The incentives for purely local candidates to contest and win elections should dissipate as the role of the national government in local areas increases. In contemporary western Europe, for example, there is hardly any area that is not touched by the actions of the national governments and, hence, the incentives for purely local candidates to contest elections are low. Does the role of the national government lower the number of parties more generally?

To assess whether this argument is correct, and to indicate some robustness for our claims, we build on the analysis and data provided by Amorim and Cox (1997) and reported again in Cox (1997). To determine the effective number of parties in fifty-one democracies in 1985 Amorim and Cox ran a series of statistical tests on cross-national data. They concluded that the specification that best explains the number of electoral parties (ENEP) in countries in the 1980s had four independent variables. UPPER specifies the "percentage of all assembly seats allocated to the upper tier(s) of the polity," and PROXIMITY represents whether legislative and presidential elections (in Presidential systems) are held concurrently, the idea being that concurrent elections could lower the number of parties (Cox 1997, 209, 210). They included an interaction term for the effective number of presidential candidates and Proximity (because the ability of presidential elections to lower the effective number of parties depends in part on the effective number of presidential candidates), and an interaction term of the effective number of ethnic groups and the logarithm of the median district magnitude in lower-house elections in the country.

For our purposes, it is not easy to come up with a measure that signifies the comparative role of the central government in these nation-states. Total government spending as a proportion of GDP can be useful but hides spending by local governments. Spending by local governments in relation to national governments hides whether that spending is discretionary or highly tethered to national government priorities.

The measure we use for this analysis is the proportion of total government wages that can be attributed to the central government. We think that it captures our key concept well—the role of the central government relative to other levels of government. This measure is also somewhat consistent with the proportion of central government employees to total government employees, which, as we saw in some of our discussion in chapter 5, is a reasonable measure of centralization for our four main countries. These data were available through the International Monetary Fund's *Government Financial Statistics*. The data were, however, not available for all fifty-one nations that Cox used in his analysis.

Table 8.1 reports the results of a regression analysis—using Amorim and Cox's data and their best specification—when we include the log of the proportion of wages of government employees attributable to the

TABLE 8.1
Predicting the Number of Parties

| Model | Unstandardized Coefficients | | Standardized Coefficients | | |
|---|---|---|---|---|---|
| | B | S.E. | Beta | t | Sig. |
| (Constant) | 8.067 | 1.407 | | 5.732 | .000 |
| RUPPER | 3.473 | 1.305 | 2.58 | 2.661 | .011 |
| PROXIMITY | −3.573 | .906 | −1.004 | −3.946 | .000 |
| PROXENP | 1.118 | .275 | 1.052 | 4.067 | .000 |
| NEWETH | .254 | .067 | .401 | 3.811 | .000 |
| LNCENTER | −1.269 | .325 | −.388 | −3.909 | .000 |

Dependent variable: ENEP = effective number of electoral parties
 $R^2 = 0.66$
 $N = 42$
 $F = 14.104$

central government (LNCENTER). The role of the central government does indeed lower the effective number of electoral parties in the country—the sign on the coefficient is negative and significant. Our claims are supported.

Our confidence in the results is increased by the fact that the sign and significance of the variables that Amorim and Cox found to be significant do not change. All the variables that Amorim and Cox found to influence the effective number of parties remain significant. The percentage of all seats allocated to the upper tier(s), the interaction of the effective number of ethnic groups and the median district size, and the proximity of the election to the presidential election interacted with the effective number of presidential candidates—each increases the effective number of parties. The proximity of the election to the presidential election still lowers the effective number of national parties. Cox and Knoll (2003) in a more extensive analysis with more cases observe that party-system inflation is indeed influenced by fiscal decentralization in addition to being affected by ethnic concentrations and favorable electoral rules.

While we consider this solid evidence in favor of our claims, and these results suggest the need for a broader examination of the relationship between multilevel political and economic authority and party systems, we take these results somewhat guardedly. On balance, we think that to understand party systems, it is necessary to study them over time and cross-nationally. Our emphasis in this book has been on over-time comparisons within countries. Perhaps the most important reason for our emphasis is that we wish to show that party systems do not stay constant and should not be studied at only one point in time. So, even the Amorim and Cox study, and our extension here, could be misleading in that they capture only snapshots of party systems that might be changing in response to changes in political authority across levels of government. In other words, to assume that the number of national parties is an equilibrium outcome for a given electoral system misses the power of other factors to shape party systems, factors that change over time much more frequently than electoral systems.

Two countries with electoral systems that are different than single-member, simple-plurality are Brazil and Russia, and recent political history in the countries conforms to our expectations. Both are federal nations in which the reach of the national party system is limited. In Brazil, as Jones and Mainwaring (2003, 150) observe, the "the national party system is a pastiche of state party systems" and that "state-level politics is very important, and regional and state differences in the party system have long been salient." This should be no surprise given that state governments in Brazil play a very important role in the economic life of the states in terms of the provision of public goods, government jobs, and the regulation of economic activity. Therefore, "Brazilian federalism generates incentives for legislators to pay *close attention to state-based issues and scant attention to national partisan issues*" (Samuels 2000, 2; emphasis added). In Russia, the reach of the national party system is also limited. The current federal arrangements are a result of individual negotiations between each province and the national government in Moscow (Stoner-Weiss 1999; Treisman 1999). The arrangements have given the provinces immense authority and limited the reach of the national party system. The national parties have little or no presence in the provinces, which are still controlled by provincial elites (McFaul 2001; Stoner-Weiss 2001).

## FINAL NOTE

We end this book with two thoughts. First, our data suggest there is nothing automatic about the American two-party system and its highly national parties. American two-partism has been stable for a long time. However, if recent trends in the devolution of fiscal authority to the states continues so that voters begin to pay much greater attention to state-level political economic issues, we may see more regionally competitive but nationally uncompetitive parties (i.e., uncompetitive for majority status) represented in Congress. If water issues become even more critical, for example, is it out of the question that a Western Party repre-

senting the southwestern states in the United States would seek representation and win votes and seats? By our argument, such a party would
most likely have to start in local and state-level election races. Federalism offers a space for such parties to begin. The arguments currently in
vogue in political science say that the American system of electing presidents would seem to mitigate against such an outcome. But that argument does not work in explaining nineteenth- and early twentieth-
century voting patterns, when presidential elections also gave incentives
for candidates and voters to stay in the major party fold, yet many did
not do so for House elections. Second, our argument relating the degree
of centralization and party aggregation is predicated on a key assumption that the legislatures, both national and provincial, across these four
nations have similar authority. Of course, it is possible that the legislatures may be playing a more far-reaching role in making policy in one
country, whereas the executives could be more significant in another.
This is a fruitful area of research as it would integrate several research
areas—legislative development, presidential systems, constitutional design, and party formation.

# APPENDIX

TABLE A.1 provides the sources for the tables and figures that include nonelectoral data. Sources for the electoral data are described below.

TABLE A.1
Data Sources for Figures and Tables

| Figure or Table Number | Sources |
| --- | --- |
| Table 2.2 | Data on effective number of groups from the 1971 national election study conducted by the Center for the Study of Developing Societies in Delhi, and data on the number of parties from Singh and Bose (1994) |
| Table 5.1 | Sylla (2000) |
| Figure 5.1 | Royal Commission on Dominion-Provincial Relations (1940); Historical Statistics of Canada, various editions; National Income and Expenditure Accounts for Canada, various editions |
| Figure 5.2 | Sutherland and Doren (1985) and the Canadian National Statistics web site, http://www.statcan.ca |
| Figure 5.3 | Banks (1976), Peters (1972), Mitchell (1998), Peacock and Wiseman (1961), Choucri (1976) |
| Figure 5.4 | India, Ministry of Finance, *Economic Survey*, various issues |
| Figure 5.5 | U.S. Department of Commerce (1975) |
| Table 7.1 | Data collected by Donna Barrie and made available to the authors |
| Table 7.2 | Indian National Survey conducted in 2001: principal investigators Pradeep Chhibber, Sandeep Shastri, and Richard Sisson |
| Figure 7.2 | Data collected by Donna Barrie and made available to the authors |
| Figure 7.5 | Indian national government, http://www.eci.gov.in |
| Table 8.1 | Data for Cox (1997), and the data on employment from the General Financial Statistics of the International Monetary Fund |

## Canadian Data

We are grateful to Brian Gaines for generously sharing his data set on riding-level Canadian election results. We supplemented his data by recording votes for some minor parties and by extending the results to later years. However, Gaines compiled most of the data, and without his generosity we could not have included Canada in this study.

We dropped the double-member ridings from the district-level measures of the number of parties. We also dropped ridings with missing vote totals for candidates or parties, or with missing party-label data for any candidate receiving more than 2 percent of the vote. We would also like to thank Donna Barrie for providing her data on Canadian members of parliament.

## U.S. Data

The election data from the United States were prepared by the Inter-University Consortium for Political and Social Research (1995). We then dropped nongeneral elections, contests with missing vote totals, and contests with more than one winner.

In some figures we distinguish between South and non-South. The southern states in the analysis are as follows: Alabama, Arkansas, Florida, Georgia, Louisiana, Mississippi, North Carolina, South Carolina, Tennessee, Texas, and Virginia.

In calculating the national-level and state-level measures of vote aggregation, if a candidate's party was coded as either missing or unidentified and the candidate received less than 2 percent of the vote, that candidate (but not necessarily the others in the contest) was dropped from the data set. If a candidate's party was coded as either missing or unidentified and the candidate received 2 or more percent of the vote, every candidate in the election (i.e., the entire contest) was dropped from the national measure. This presents virtually no problems for any of the four countries (few cases are dropped from any year), except for one year in the United States, 1806. For some reason the data on the party affiliation of candidates for that year are extremely thin. All candidates except those of the (Old) Republican Party in Vermont had missing party data (e.g., 266 candidates in New York had no party data). Thus, N for that year registers 1.0. This is the only year for which missing data on party affiliation is a major problem in any data set.

## Indian Data

The constituency-level and national measures of the effective number of parties in India were calculated using Indian election data prepared by Singh and Bose (1984; 1994) and India (1996b) and by our own research assistants for later election years from official Indian statistics available at the Election Commission of India website (www.eci.gov.in). The calculations used data for single-member constituencies in sixteen states: Andhra Pradesh, Assam, Bihar, Gujarat, Haryana, Himachal Pradesh, Karnataka, Kerala, Madhya Pradesh, Maharashtra, Orissa, Punjab, Rajasthan, Tamilnadu, Uttar Pradesh, and West Bengal. These 16 states account for over 95 percent of the country.

Our national-level, effective number of party results for India differ from those of Lijphart (1994) for two reasons. First, note that our data are not national-level data (as in Lijphart) but rather constituency-level data. To get the national measures, we aggregated across all districts. Our cutoff was 2 percent of total votes in each constituency,—that is, candidates receiving less than 2 percent in any constituency were dropped from the analysis (for reasons of efficiency). This could be a potential problem, especially if the proportion of votes received by minor parties in any given district aggregated to, say, 10 percent or more. In India, this procedure (eliminating all candidates with less than 2 percent of the vote) led to dropping of only 1.65 percent of the total vote for the average district (this varied little across election years). Because the proportion of votes dropped was so low, neither the district-level calculations or the national-level calculations were affected.

Our second, and most consequential, difference with Lijphart has to do with our treatment of independents. In Indian politics there are many independent candidates. In each electoral district (constituency), independents were included in the district calculations if they surpassed 2 percent of the vote in that district. In calculating the national N, each independent was included as a separate party. Lijphart, in contrast, includes these independents in his category "Other Parties," but leaves them out of the numerator, appropriately. However, he includes the number of independent votes in the denominator in calculating the proportion for each party.

Taagepera (1997) suggests several procedures for calculating N when there is incomplete data on which parties are included in the "Other Parties" category. Here, we have complete data, and these allow for the most accurate measure available for the effective number of parties (by including each independent as a single party).

## BRITISH DATA

The British electoral data come from Caramani (2000), supplemented with data on recent elections available from the British government.

### THE JONES AND MAINWARING (2003) NATIONALIZATION MEASURE

Computation of the Jones and Mainwaring measure of party nationalization involves using the vote share of the parties at two different aggregate levels. First, one would compute the Gini coefficient of each party across different states or provinces. Second, one would weight the Gini coefficients by corresponding national vote share of the parties. The reverse of this quantity (one minus this value) summarizes the level of nationalization of the party system for each election. The closer it is to unity, the more the party system is nationalized.

The first step to compute the Gini coefficient involves constructing a Lorenz curve of a ranked distribution and comparing it with that of a perfect equality. Let $G_i$ represent the Gini coefficient of party i where $i = 1, 2, \ldots, N$. Also denote $p_{ij}$ as party i's vote share in state j where $j = 1, 2, \ldots, M$. Rescale $p_{ij}$'s so that its sum across states for the party is unity and call it $q_{ij}$. Now rank $q_{ij}$'s in all the M states in ascending order and define $Q_{i(j)}$ as the cumulative sum of $q_{ij}$ in the first (j) states. This directly corresponds to the Lorenz curve.

The Gini coefficient for party i can then be expressed as[1]

$$G_i = \frac{2}{M} \sum_{(j)=1}^{M} \left| Q_{i(j)} - \frac{(j)}{M} \right|$$

Jones and Mainwaring's nationalization score (NS) can be defined as the reversal of the weighted average of each party's Gini coefficients by their respective national vote shares.

$$NS = 1 - \sum_{i=1}^{N} G_i p_i$$

where $p_i$ is party i's national vote share. As was mentioned in chapter 6, the measure we used for the analysis is the weighted average of the Gini coefficients rather than NS in the form shown here.

---

[1] Along with Jones and Mainwaring, we also used the STATA module, "ineqdec0" provided by Jenkins (see www.stata.com, accessed July 2003).

# BIBLIOGRAPHY

Abizadeh, Sohrab, and Mahmood Yousefi. 1988. "Growth of Government Expenditure: The Case of Canada." *Public Finance Quarterly* 16: 78–100.

Abramowitz, Alan. 1995. "It's Abortion, Stupid: Policy Voting in the 1992 Presidential Election." *Journal of Politics* 57: 176–86.

Adams, James. 2001. *Party Competition and Responsible Party Government.* Ann Arbor: University of Michigan Press.

Ahluwalia, Montek S. 2002. "Economic Reforms in India since 1991: Has Gradualism Worked?" *Journal of Economic Perspectives* 16 (3): 67–88.

Aldrich, John. 1995. *Why Parties? The Origin and Transformation of Party Politics in America.* Chicago: University of Chicago Press.

Alesina, Alberto, and Howard Rosenthal. 1995. *Partisan Politics, Divided Government, and the Economy.* New York: Cambridge University Press.

Alesina, Alberto, Nouriel Roubini, with Gerald D. Cohen. 1999. *Political Cycles and the Macroeconomy.* Cambridge, MA: MIT Press.

Alvarez, R. Michael, and Jonathan Nagler. 2000. "A New Approach for Modelling Strategic Voting in Multiparty Elections." *British Journal of Political Science* 30: 57–75.

Amorim, Octavio Neto, and Gary Cox. 1997. "Electoral Institutions, Cleavage Structures, and the Number of Parties." *American Journal of Political Science* 41: 149–74.

Argersinger, Peter H. 2001. "The Transformation of American Politics: Political Institutions and Public Policy, 1865–1910." In *Contesting Democracy: Substance and Structure in American Political History, 1775–2000,* ed. Byron E. Shafer and Anthony J. Badger. Lawrence: University Press of Kansas.

Armstrong, Christopher. 1981. *The Politics of Federalism: Ontario's Relations with the Federal Government, 1867–1942.* Toronto: University of Toronto Press.

Austen-Smith, David, and Jeffrey Banks. 1988. "Elections, Coalitions, and Legislative Outcomes." *American Political Science Review* 82: 405–22.

Bagchi, Amaresh. 1991. "India." In *Fiscal Decentralization and the Mobilization and Use of National Resources for Development: Issues, Experience and Policies in the ESCAP Region,* ed. Economic and Social Commission for Asia and the Pacific. Bangkok: ESCAP.

Bagchi, Amaresh, J. L. Bajaj, and William A Byrd, eds. 1992. *State Finances in India.* Delhi: Vikas Publishing.

Banfield, Edward C., and James Q. Wilson. 1963. *City Politics.* New York: Vintage.

Banks, Arthur. 1976. *Cross-National Time-Series Dataset.* Archive available at the Inter-University Consortium for Political and Social Research, Institute for Social Research, University of Michigan.

Banks, J. C. 1971. *Federal Britain?* London: George G. Harrap.

Banting, Keith G. 1995. "The Welfare State as Statecraft: Territorial Politics and Canadian Social Policy." In *European Social Policy: Between Fragmentation and Integration*, ed. Stephan Leibfried and Paul Pierson. Washington, DC: Brookings Institution Press.

Bardhan, Pranab. 2002. "Disjunctures in the Indian Reform Process," Paper presented at the Indian Economy Conference, Cornell University, April.

Baron, David, and John Ferejohn. 1989. "Bargaining in Legislatures." *American Political Science Review* 83: 1181–206.

Bartolini, Stefano. 2000. *The Political Mobilization of the European Left, 1860–1980*. Cambridge: Cambridge University Press.

Bartolini, Stefano, Daniele Caramani, and Simon Hug. 1998. *Parties and Party Systems. A Bibliographic Guide to the Literature on Parties and Party Systems in Europe since 1945*. London: Sage.

Bartolini, Stefano, and Peter Mair. 1990. *Identity, Competition, and Electoral Availability*. Cambridge: Cambridge University Press.

Bates, Stewart. 1939. *Financial History of Canadian Government: A Study Prepared for the Royal Commission on Dominion Provincial Relations*. Ottawa: Government of Canada.

Bawn, Kathleen. 1993. "The Logic of Institutional Preferences." *American Journal of Political Science* 37: 965–89.

Bawn, Kathleen, Gary Cox, and Frances Rosenbluth. 1999. "Measuring the Ties that Bind: Electoral Cohesiveness in Four Democracies." In *Elections in Japan, Korea, and Taiwan under the Single Non-transferable Vote*, ed. Bernard Grofman, Sung-Chull Lee, Edwin A. Winckler, and Brian Woodall. Ann Arbor: University of Michigan Press.

Bayly, Christopher. 1975. The *Local Roots of Indian Politics: Allahbad, 1880–1920*. Oxford: Clarendon Press.

Bednar, Jenna. 2001a. "Credit Assignment and Federal Encroachment." Department of Political Science, University of Michigan. Typescript.

———. 2001b. "Shirking and Stability in Federal Systems." Department of Political Science, University of Michigan. Typescript.

Bednar, Jenna, William Eskridge Jr., and John Ferejohn. 2001. "A Political Theory of Federalism." In *Constitutional Culture and Democratic Rule*, ed. John Ferejohn, Jonathan Riley, and Jack Rakove. New York: Cambridge University Press.

Bennett, Robert J. 1982. *Central Grants to Local Governments*. Cambridge: Cambridge University Press.

Benson, Lee, Allan Bogue, J. Rogers Hollingsworth, Thomas Pressly, and Joel Silbey, eds. 1974. *American Political Behavior: Historical Essays and Readings*. New York: Harper and Row.

Bermeo, Nancy. 2000. *Civil Society before Democracy: Lessons from Nineteenth-Century Europe*. Lanham, MD: Rowman & Littlefield.

Bernier, Gérald, and Daniel Salée. 1992. *The Shaping of Québec Politics and Society: Colonialism, Power, and the Transition to Capitalism in the 19th Century*. Washington, DC: Crane Russak.

Berrington, H. 1968. "Partisanship and Dissidence in the Nineteenth Century House of Commons." *Parliamentary Affairs* 21: 338–74.

Bibby, J. F. 1998. "Party Organization, 1946–1996." In *Partisan Approaches to Postwar American Politics*, ed. Bryon E. Shafer, 142–85. New York: Chatham House.

Bickerton, James. 1994. "Atlantic Canada: Regime Change in a Dependent Region." In *Canadian Politics*, James Bickerton and Alain-G. Gagnon. 2nd ed. Ontario: Broadview Press.

Bickerton, James, Munroe Eagles, Alain-G. Gagnon, and Patrick Smith. 1991. *The Almanac of Canadian Politics: Federal Constituencies and the 1988 General Election.* Peterborough, Ontario: Broadview Press.

Bickerton, James, and Alain-G. Gagnon. 1994. *Canadian Politics.* 2nd ed. Peterborough, Ontario: Broadview Press.

Bickerton James, Alain-G. Gagnon, and Patrick Smith. 1999. *Ties That Bind: Parties and Voters in Canada.* New York: Oxford University Press.

Birch, A. H. 1955. *Federalism, Finance, and Social Legislation in Canada, Australia, and the United States.* Oxford: Clarendon Press.

Black, Edwin R. 1965. "Federal Strains within a Canadian Party." *Dalhousie Review* 45: 307–23.

Black, Edwin R., and A. C. Cairns. 1966. "A Different Perspective on Canadian Federalism." *Canadian Public Administration* 9: 27–45.

Black, Jerome. 1978. "The Multicandidate Calculus of Voting: Application to Canadian Federal Elections." *American Journal of Political Science* 22: 609–37.

Blais, Andre. 1997. *Government, Party, and Public Sector Employees.* Pittsburgh: University of Pittsburgh Press.

Blais, Andre, and Agnieszka Dobrzynska. 1998. "Turnout in Electoral Democracies." *European Journal of Political Research* 33: 239–61.

Blais, Andre, and Richard Nadeau. 1993. "Explaining Election Outcomes in Canada: Economy and Politics." *Canadian Journal of Political Science* 26: 775–90.

Blake, Donald E. 1972. "The Measurement of Regionalism in Canadian Voting Patterns." *Canadian Journal of Political Science* 5: 55–81.

———. 1979. "1896 and All That: Critical Elections in Canada." *Canadian Journal of Political Science* 12: 259–79.

———. 1982. "The Consistency of Inconsistency: Party Identification in Federal and Provincial Politics." *Canadian Journal of Political Science* 15: 691–710.

———. 1985. *Two Political Worlds: Parties and Voting in British Columbia.* Vancouver: University of British Columbia Press.

Blake, Donald E., R. K. Carty, and Lynda Erickson. 1991. *Grassroots Politicians: Party Activists in British Columbia.* Vancouver: University of British Columbia Press.

Bogdanor, Vernon. 1999. *Devolution in the United Kingdom.* Oxford: Oxford University Press.

Boix, Carles. 1998. *Political Parties, Growth and Equality.* New York: Cambridge University Press.

Bowler, Shaun, David Lanoue, and Paul Savoie. 1994. "Electoral Systems, Party Competition, and Strength of Partisan Attachment: Evidence from Three Countries." *Journal of Politics* 56: 991–1007.

Brady, David. 1985. "A Reevaluation of Realignments in American Politics: Evidence from the House of Representatives." *American Political Science Review* 79: 28–49.

———. 1988. *Critical Elections and Public Policy Making*. Stanford, CA: Stanford University Press.

Brady, David, and Bernard Grofman. 1991. "Sectional Differences in Partisan Bias and Electoral Responsiveness in US House Elections, 1850–1980." *British Journal of Political Science* 21: 247–56.

Brass, Paul. 1965. *Factional Politics in an Indian State: The Congress Party in Uttar Pradesh*. Berkeley: University of California Press.

———. 1981. "Congress, the Lok Dal, and the Middle-Peasant Castes: An Analysis of the 1977 and 1980 Parliamentary Elections in Uttar Pradesh." *Pacific Affairs* 54: 5–41.

———. 1984. *Caste, Faction, and Party in Indian Politics*. Delhi: Chanakya Publications.

———. 1990. *The Politics of India since Independence*. New York: Cambridge University Press.

Brecher, Michael. 1966. *Succession in India: A Study in Decision-Making*. London: Oxford University Press.

Brownlee, Elliot W. 2000. "The Public Sector." In *The Cambridge Economic History of the United States*, vol. 3, *The Twentieth Century*, ed. Stanley L. Engerman and Robert E. Gallman. New York: Cambridge University Press.

Budge, Ian, and David McKay, eds. 1993. *The Developing British Political System in the 1990s*. 3rd ed. London: Longman.

Burnham, Walter Dean. 1970. *Critical Elections and the Mainsprings of American Politics*. New York: W. W. Norton.

Burns, Nancy, and Gerald Gamm. 1997. "Creatures of the State: State Politics and Local Government, 1871–1921." *Urban Affairs Review* 33: 59–96.

Burrows, Bernard, and Geoffrey Denton. 1980. *Devolution or Federalism?* London: Macmillan Press.

Butler, David, P. Roy, and A. Lahiri. 1996. *India Decides: Elections, 1952–1995*. Delhi: Living Media Books.

Butler, David, and Donald Stokes. 1970. *Political Change in Britain*. New York: St. Martin's.

Byres, Terence. 1994. "State, Class and Development Planning in India." In *The State, Development Planning and Liberalization in India*, ed. Terence Byres. New York: Oxford University Press.

Cain, Bruce. 1978. "Strategic Voting in Britain." *American Journal of Political Science* 22: 639–55.

Cairns, Alan. 1986. "The Embedded State: State-Society Relations in Canada." In *State and Society: Canada in Comparative Perspective*, ed. Keith Banting, 53–86. Toronto: University of Toronto Press.

Cameron, David. 1986. "The Growth of Government Spending: The Canadian Experience in Comparative Perspective." In *State and Society: Canada in Comparative Perspective*, ed. Keith Banting, 21–52. Toronto: University of Toronto Press.

Cameron, Duncan, ed. 1985. *Explorations in Canadian Economic History*. Ottawa: University of Ottawa Press.

Campbell, Angus, Philip E. Converse, Warren E. Miller, and Donald E. Stokes. 1960. *The American Voter*. Chicago: University of Chicago Press.

Campbell, Robert M. 1995. "Federalism and Economic Policy." In *New Trends in Canadian Federalism*, ed. François Rocher and Miriam Smith. Peterborough, Ontario: Broadview Press.

Canada. Royal Commission on Dominion-Provincial Relations. 1940. *Report of the Royal Commission on Dominion-Provincial Relations*. Book 1: *Canada, 1867–1939*. Ottawa: King's Printer.

Canada. Royal Commission of Inquiry on Constitutional Problems. 1956. *Report*. 3 vols. Quebec: Editeur Officiel.

Canada. Royal Commission on the Economic Union and Development Prospects for Canada. 1985. *Report*. 3 vols. Ottawa: Minister of Supply and Services.

———. 1986. "State and Society: Canada in Comparative Perspective." In *Collected Research Studies*, vol. 31, ed., Keith Banting. Toronto: University of Toronto Press.

Caramani, Daniele. 2000. *Elections in Western Europe since 1815: Electoral Results by Constituencies*. London: Macmillan Reference.

———. 2004. *The Nationalization of Elections*. Cambridge: Cambridge University Press.

Carmines, Edward, and James Stimson. 1989. *Issue Evolution: Race and the Transformation of American Politics*. Princeton, NJ: Princeton University Press.

Carroll, Barbara, and Ruth J. E. Jones. 2000. "The Road to Innovation, Governance, or Inertia: Devolution of Housing Policy in Canada." *Canadian Public Policy* 26: 277–94.

Carrothers, W. A. 1935. "Problems of the Canadian Federation." *Canadian Journal of Economics and Political Science* 1: 26–40.

Carty, R. Kenneth. 1991. *Canadian Political Parties in the Constituencies*. Toronto: Dundurn Press.

Carty, R. Kenneth, William Cross, and Lisa Young. 2000. *Rebuilding Canadian Party Politics*. Vancouver: University of British Columbia Press.

———. 2001. "Canadian Party Politics in the New Century." *Journal of Canadian Studies* 35 (4): 23–39.

Carty, R. Kenneth, and W. Peter Ward, eds. 1986. *National Politics and Community in Canada*. Vancouver: University of British Columbia Press.

Chakravarty, S. 1987. *Development Planning*. New Delhi: Oxford University Press.

Chambers, William Nisbett. 1974. "Party Development and Party Action." In *American Political Behavior: Historical Essays and Readings*, ed. Lee Benson, Allan Bogue, J. Rogers Hollingsworth, Thomas Pressly, and Joel Silbey. New York: Harper and Row.

Chandler, M. A. 1982. "State Enterprise and Partisanship in Provincial Politics." *Canadian Journal of Political Science* 15: 711–40.

Chandok, H. L. 1990. *India Database: The Economy*. New Delhi: Living Media.

Charlesworth, James. 1948. "Is Our Two-Party System Natural?" *Annals of the American Academy of Political and Social Science* 29: 1–9.

Chatterjee, Partha. 1994. "Development Planning and the Indian State." In *The*

*State, Development Planning and Liberalization in India*, ed. Terence Byres. New York: Oxford University Press.

Chhibber, Pradeep K. 1999. *Democracy without Associations*. Ann Arbor: University of Michigan Press.

Chhibber, Pradeep K., and Ken Kollman. 1998. "Party Aggregation and the Number of Parties in India and the United States." *American Political Science Review* 92: 329–42.

Chhibber, Pradeep K., and Irfan Nooruddin. 2004. "Do Party Systems Matter? The Number of Parties and Government Performance in the Indian States." *Comparative Political Studies* (April), forthcoming.

Chhibber, Pradeep K., and John Petrocik. 1989. "The Puzzle of Indian Politics: Social Cleavages and the Indian Party System." *British Journal of Political Science* 19: 191–210.

Chhibber, Pradeep K., and Mariano Torcal. 1997. "Elite Strategy, Social Cleavages, and Party Systems in a New Democracy." *Comparative Political Studies* 30 (1): 27–54.

Chorney, Harold, and Phillip Hansen. 1985. "Neo-Conservatism, Social Democracy and 'Province Building': The Experience of Manitoba." *Canadian Review of Sociology and Anthropology* 22: 1–29.

Chourcri, Nazli. 1976. *Nations in Conflict: Data on National Growth and International Violence*. Archive available at the Inter-University Consortium for Political and Social Research, Institute for Social Research, University of Michigan.

Claggett, William, William Flanigan, and Nancy Zingale. 1984. "Nationalization of the American Electorate." *American Political Science Review* 78: 77–91.

Clark, John F. 1997. "The Challenges of Political Reform in Sub-Saharan Africa: A Theoretical Overview." In *Political Reform in Francophone Africa*, ed. John F. Clark and David E. Gardinier. Boulder, CO: Westview Press.

Clarke, Harold. 1978. "The Ideological Self-Perceptions of Provincial Legislators." *Canadian Journal of Political Science* 11: 617–33.

Clarke, Harold, Richard G. Price, and Robert Krause. 1975. "Constituency Service among Canadian Provincial Legislators: A Test of Three Hypotheses." *Canadian Journal of Political Science* 8: 520–42.

Clarke, Harold, and Marianne Stewart. 1987. "Partisan Inconsistency and Partisan Change in Federal States: The Case of Canada." *American Journal of Political Science* 31: 383–407.

Clarke, Harold, and Gary Zuk. 1989. "The Dynamics of Third-Party Support: The British Liberals, 1951–79." *American Journal of Political Science* 33: 196–221.

Coleman, John J. 1996. *Party Decline in America: Policy, Politics, and the Fiscal State*. Princeton, NJ: Princeton University Press.

Converse, Philip E. 1964. "The Nature of Belief Systems in Mass Publics." In *Ideology and Discontent*, ed. David E. Apter. New York: Free Press.

Coppedge, Michael. 1997. "District Magnitude, Economic Performance, and Party-System Fragmentation in Five Latin American Countries." *Comparative Political Studies* 30: 156–85.

Corry, J. A. 1939. *The Growth of Government Activities since Confederation*.

A study prepared for the Royal Commission on Dominion-Provincial Relations. Ottawa: King's Printer.

Cotter, Cornelius P., and John F. Bibby. 1980. "Institutional Development of Parties and the Thesis of Party Decline." *Political Science Quarterly* 95: 1–27.

Cotter, Cornelius P., James L. Gibson, John F. Bibby, and Robert J. Huckshorn. 1984. *Party Organizations in American Politics*. New York: Praeger.

Cox, Gary. 1987a. *The Efficient Secret*. New York: Cambridge University Press.

———. 1987b. "Duverger's Law and Strategic Voting." Department of Political Science, University of California, San Diego. Typescript.

———. 1990. "Centripetal and Centrifugal Incentives in Electoral Systems." *American Journal of Political Science* 34: 903–35.

———. 1994. "Strategic Voting Equilibria under the Single Nontransferable Vote." *American Political Science Review* 88: 608–21.

———. 1997. *Making Votes Count*. New York: Cambridge University Press.

———. 1999. "Electoral Rules and Electoral Coordination." *Annual Review of Political Science* 2: 145–61.

Cox, Gary, and Jonathan Knoll. 2003. "Ethnes, Fiscs, and Electoral rules: The Determinants of Party-System Inflation." Paper presented at the annual meeting of the American Political Science Association, Philadelphia, September.

Cox, Gary, and Mathew McCubbins. 1993. *Legislative Leviathan*. Berkeley: University of California Press.

Cox, Gary, and Burt Monroe. 1995. "Strategic Voting Equilibria in Parliamentary Elections." Paper presented at the annual meeting of the American Political Science Association, Chicago, September.

Cox, Gary, and Michael Munger. 1989. "Closeness, Expenditure, and Turnout." *American Political Science Review* 83: 217–32.

Crewe, Ivor, Anthony Fox, and Neil Day, eds. 1995. *The British Electorate, 1963–1992: A Compendium of Data from the British Election Studies*. Cambridge: Cambridge University Press.

Crewe, Ivor, and Donald Searing. 1988. "Ideological Change in the British Conservative Party." *American Political Science Review* 82: 361–84.

Crewe, Ivor, and Katarina Thomson. 1999. "Party Loyalties: Dealignment or Realignment?" In *Critical Elections: British Parties and Voters in Long-Term Perspective*, ed. G. Evans and P. Norris. London: Sage.

Dalton, Russell J. 1984. "Cognitive Mobilization and Partisan Dealignment in Advanced Industrial Democracies." *Journal of Politics* 46: 264–84.

Dalton, Russell J., and Martin P. Wattenberg. 2000. *Parties without Partisans: Political Change in Advanced Industrial Societies*. Oxford: Oxford University Press.

Dasgupta, Jyotindra. 2001. "India's Federal Design and Multicultural National Construction." In *The Success of India's Democracy*, ed. Atul Kohli. Cambridge: Cambridge University Press.

Davis, Lance, E., and Robert J. Cull. 2000. "International Capital Movements, Domestic Capital Markets, and American Economic Growth, 1820–1914." In *The Cambridge Economic History of the United States,* vol. 2, *The Long Nineteenth Century*, ed. Stanley L. Engerman and Robert E. Gallman. New York: Cambridge University Press.

de Figueredo, Rui, and Barry Weingast. 1999. "Rationality of Fear: Political Opportunism and Ethnic Conflict." In *Military Intervention in Civil Wars*, ed. Jack Snyder and Barbara Walter. New York: Columbia University Press.

———. 2002. "Self-Enforcing Federalism." Department of Political Science, Stanford University. Typescript.

Dinkin, Robert J. 1977. *Voting in Provincial America: a Study of Elections in the Thirteen Colonies, 1689–1776*. Westport, CT: Greenwood Press.

———. 1982. *Voting in Revolutionary America*. Westport, CT: Greenwood Press.

Downs, Anthony. 1957. *Economic Theory of Democracy*. New York: Harper and Row.

Dreze, Jean, and Amartya Sen. 1998. *India: Economic Development and Social Opportunity*. Delhi: Oxford University Press.

Dunleavy, Patrick, and Christopher T. Husbands. 1985. *British Democracy at the Crossroads*. London: Allen & Unwin.

Duverger, Maurice. [1954] 1963. *Political Parties: Their Organization and Activity in the Modern State*. New York: John Wiley and Sons.

Dyck, Rand. 1986. *Provincial Politics in Canada*. Scarborough, Ontario: Prentice-Hall.

Eggleston, Stephen. 1993. "Parties and Parliaments: Political Development in Canada 1867–96." Ph.D. dissertation, Queens University.

Eggleston, Wilfrid, and C.T. Kraft. 1939. *Dominion-Provincial Subsidies and Grants*. A study prepared for the Royal Commission on Dominion-Provincial Relations. Ottawa: Government of Canada.

Elazar, Daniel. 1987. *Exploring Federalism*. Tuscaloosa: University of Alabama Press.

Eldersveld, Samuel J. 1964. *Political Parties: A Behavioral Analysis*. Chicago: Rand McNally.

———. 1982. *Political Parties in American Society*. New York: Basic Books.

Eldersveld, Samuel J., and Hanes Walton. 2000. *Political Parties in American Society*. 2nd ed. New York: St. Martin's.

Engerman, Stanley L. 2000. Preface to *The Cambridge Economic History of the United States*, vol. 3: *The Twentieth Century*, ed. Stanley L. Engerman and Robert Gallman. New York: Cambridge University Press.

Engstrom, Erik, and Samuel Kernell. 2000. "State Electoral Laws and the Impact of Presidential Elections on Party Control of the House of Representatives, 1840–1940." Department of Political Science, University of California, San Diego. Typescript.

Epstein, L. 1986. *Political Parties in the American Mold*. Madison: University of Wisconsin Press.

Erie, Steven. 1988. *Rainbow's End*. Berkeley: University of California Press.

Eskridge, William, and John Ferejohn. 1994. "The Elastic Commerce Clause: A Political Theory of American Federalism." *Vanderbilt Law Review* 47: 1355–1400.

Esping-Anderson, Gosta. 1985. *Politics against Markets: The Social Democratic Road to Power*. Princeton, NJ: Princeton University Press.

Farquharson, Robin. 1969. *Theory of Voting*. New Haven, CT: Yale University Press.

Farrell, David. M., and Paul D. Webb. 2000. "Political Parties as Campaign Organizations." In *Parties without Partisans: Political Change in Advanced Industrial Democracies*, ed. Russell J. Dalton and Martin P. Wattenberg, 102–28. Oxford: Oxford University Press.

Feddersen, Timothy. 1992. "A Voting Model Implying Duverger's Law and Positive Turnout." *American Journal of Political Science* 36: 938–62.

Fey, Mark. 1997. "Stability and Coordination in Duverger's Law: A Formal Model of Preelection Polls and Strategic Voting." *American Political Science Review* 91: 135–47.

Fickett, Lewis P. 1968. "The Major Socialist Parties of Indian in the 1967 Election." *Asian Survey* 8: 489–98.

Fieldhouse, Edward, and Andrew Russell. 2001. "Latent Liberalism? Sympathy and Support for the Liberal Democrats at the 1997 British General Election." *Party Politics* 7: 711–38.

Filippov, Mikhail, Peter Ordeshook, and Olga Shvetsova. 1997. "Party Fragmentation and Presidential Elections in Post-Communist Democracies." Department of Political Science, Washington University. Typescript.

———. 2004. *Designing Federalism: A Theory of Self-Sustainable Federal Institutions*. Cambridge: Cambridge University Press.

Finegold, Kenneth, and Theda Skocpol. 1995. *State and Party in America's New Deal*. Madison: University of Wisconsin Press.

Finer, Samuel E. 1980. *The Changing British Party System, 1945–79*. Washington, DC: American Enterprise Institute.

Fischer, David Hackett. 1974. "The Creation of the Federal Party." In *American Political Behavior: Historical Essays and Readings*, ed. Lee Benson, Allan Bogue, J. Rogers Hollingsworth, Thomas Pressly, and Joel Silbey. New York: Harper and Row.

Fisher, Steven. 1973. "The Wasted Vote Thesis." *Comparative Politics* 5: 293–99.

Fletcher, Martha. 1968. "Judicial Review and the Division of Powers in Canada." In *Canadian Federalism: Myth or Reality*, ed. J. Peter Meekison. Toronto: Methuen.

Foner, Eric. 2002. *Reconstruction: America's Unfinished Revolution, 1863–1877*. Perennial Classics. New York: Perennial Press.

Forsey, E. 1938. "Disallowance of Provincial Acts, Reservation of Provincial Bills, and Refusal of Assent by Lieutenant-Governors since 1867." *Canadian Journal of Economics and Political Science* 4 (1): 47–59.

Franda, Marcus F. 1962. "The Organizational Development of India's Congress Party." *Pacific Affairs* 35: 248–60.

———. 1968. *West Bengal and the Federalizing Process in India*. Princeton, NJ: Princeton University Press.

Frankel, Francine. 1978. *India's Political Economy, 1947–1977: The Gradual Revolution*. Princeton, NJ: Princeton University Press.

———. 1987. "Politics: The Failure to Rebuild Consensus." In *India Briefing, 1987*, ed. Marshall Bouton. Boulder, CO: Westview Press.

Franzese, Robert J., Jr. 2002. *Macroeconomic Policies of Developed Democracies*. Cambridge: Cambridge University Press.

Frendreis, John, James Gibson, and Laura Vertz. 1990. "Electoral Relevance of Local Party Organizations." *American Political Science Review* 48: 225–35.

Freyer, Tony A. 2000. "Business Law and American Economic History." In *The Cambridge Economic History of the United States,* vol. 2, *The Long Nineteenth Century,* ed. Stanley L. Engerman and Robert E. Gallman. New York: Cambridge University Press.

Frug, G. E. 1980. "The City as a Legal Concept." *Harvard Law Review* 93: 1057–154.

Gaines, Brian. 1997a. "Where to Count Parties." *Electoral Studies* 16: 49–58.

———. 1997b. "Duverger's Law and Canadian Exceptionalism." Department of Political Science, University of Illinois. Typescript.

———. 1999. "Duverger's Law and the Meaning of Canadian Exceptionalism." *Comparative Political Studies* 32: 835–61.

Galbraith, John, and Nicol Rae. 1989. "A Test of the Importance of Tactical Voting: Great Britain, 1987." *British Journal of Political Science* 19: 126–36.

Gallagher, John. 1973. "Congress in Decline: Bengal 1930 to 1939." In *Locality Province and Nation: Essays on Indian Politics 1870–1949,* ed. John Gallagher, Gordon Johnson, and Anil Seal. Cambridge: Cambridge University Press.

Gallagher, John, Gordon Johnson, and Anil Seal, eds. 1973. *Locality Province and Nation: Essays on Indian Politics, 1870–1940.* Cambridge: Cambridge University Press.

Gettys, Luella. 1938. *The Administration of Canadian Conditional Grants: A Study in Dominion-Provincial Relationships.* Chicago: Public Administration Service.

Gibson, Edward L. ed. 2003. *Federalism: Latin America in Comparative Perspective.* Baltimore: Johns Hopkins University Press.

Gienapp, William E. 1987. *The Origins of the Republican Party, 1852–1856.* New York: Oxford University Press.

Gimpel, James. 1996. *National Elections and the Autonomy of American State Party Systems.* Pittsburgh: University of Pittsburgh Press.

Golder, Matt. 2003. "Democratic Electoral Systems around the World, 1946–2000." Department of Political Science, New York University. Typescript. Paper presented at the Department of Political Science, University of Montreal.

Graham, Bruce. 1990. *Hindu Nationalism and Indian Politics.* New York: Cambridge University Press.

Griffith, J.A.G. 1966. *Central Departments and Local Authorities.* London: Allen & Unwin.

Grofman, Bernard. 1984. *Choosing an Electoral System: Issues and Alternatives.* New York: Praeger.

Grofman, Bernard, and Arend Lijphart, eds. 1986. *Electoral Laws and Their Political Consequences.* New York: Agathon Press.

Gulati, I. S., ed. 1987. *Centre-State Budgetary Transfers.* Bombay: Oxford University Press.

Gunn, J. A. 1971. *Factions No More: Attitudes to Party in Government and Opposition in Eighteenth-Century England.* London: Frank Cass.

Hanson, A. H. 1966. *The Process of Planning: A Study of India's Five-Year Plans, 1950–1965*. London: Oxford University Press.

Harrington, Joseph. 1990. "Power of the Proposal-Maker in a Model of Endogenous Agenda Formation." *Public Choice* 64: 1–20.

Harrison, Anthony. 1989. *The Control of Public Expenditure, 1979–1989*. New Brunswick, NJ: Transaction Books.

Hart, Henry C., ed. 1976. *Indira Gandhi's India: A Political System Reappraised*. Boulder, CO: Westview Press.

Hartz, Louis. 1955. *The Liberal Tradition in America*. New York: Harcourt, Brace.

Harvey, Anna. 1998. *Votes without Leverage: Women in American Electoral Politics, 1920–1970*. New York: Cambridge University Press.

Hawkins, Angus. 1998. *British Party Politics, 1852–1886*. London: Macmillan Press.

Hay, J. R. 1978. *The Development of the British Welfare State, 1880–1975*. London: Edward Arnold.

Haynes, George H. 1897. "The Causes of Know-Nothing Success in Massachusetts." *American Historical Review* 3 (1): 67–82.

Hennock, E. P. 1982. "Central/Local Government Relations in England: An Outline, 1800–1950." *Urban History Yearbook* 9:38–49.

Hibbs, Douglas. 1977. "Political Parties and Macroeconomic Policy." *American Political Science Review* 71: 1467–87.

Hill, Brian W. 1976. *The Growth of Parliamentary Parties, 1689–1742*. Hamden, CT: Anchon Books.

Hills, John, ed. 1990. *The State of Welfare*. Oxford: Oxford University Press.

Hirschman, Albert. 1970. *Exit, Voice, and Loyalty*. Cambridge, MA: Harvard University Press.

Hix, Simon. 1997. *Political Parties in the European Union*. New York: St. Martin's Press.

Hogwood, Brian. 1992. *Trends in British Public Policy*. Buckingham: Open University Press.

Hogwood, Brian, and Michael Keating. 1982. *Regional Government in England*. Oxford: Clarendon Press.

Holt, Michael. 1999. *The Rise and Decline of the American Whig Party: Jacksonian Politics and the Onset of the Civil War*. New York: Oxford University Press.

Hopkins, E. R. 1968. *Confederation at the Crossroads: The Canadian Constitution*. Toronto: McClelland and Stewart.

Hug, Simon. 2001. *Altering Party Systems: Strategic Behavior and the Emergence of New Political Parties in Western Democracies*. Ann Arbor: University of Michigan Press.

Hussain, Monirul. 2003. "Governance and Electoral Processes in India's North-East." *Economic and Political Weekly*, 8 March, 981–90.

Ickes, Harold. 1941. "Who Killed the Progressive Party?" *American Historical Review* 46: 306–37.

India. 1986. *Economic Survey*. New Delhi: Ministry of Finance.

———. 1989. *The Constitution (Sixty-Fourth Amendment) Bill, 1989.* New Delhi: Lok Sabha Secretariat.

———. 1992. *The Constitution (Seventy-third Amendment) Act, 1992 on the Panchayats.* New Delhi: Ministry of Rural Development.

———. 1996a. *Indian Public Finance Statistics: 1996.* New Delhi: Ministry of Finance, Department of Economic Affairs, Economic Division.

———. 1996b. *Statistical Report on General Elections, 1996 to the Eleventh Lok Sabha.* Vol. 3. New Delhi: Election Commission of India.

———. 1996c. *Economic Survey.* New Delhi: Ministry of Finance.

———. 2002. *Economic Survey.* New Delhi: Ministry of Finance.

India. Commission on Centre-State Relations. 1988. *Report.* Nasik: Government of India Press.

India. National Commission on Agriculture. 1976. *Report.* New Delhi: Ministry of Agriculture and Irrigation, Department of Agriculture.

Indian National Congress. 1954. *Report of the General Secretaries.* Allahabad and New Delhi: Indian National Congress.

Inglehart, Ronald. 1997. *Modernization and Postmodernization.* Princeton, NJ: Princeton University Press.

Inter-University Consortium for Political and Social Research. 1995. *Candidate and Constituency Statistics of Elections in the United States, 1788–1990* [computer file] (Study # 7757). 5th ICPSR ed. Ann Arbor, MI: Inter-University Consortium for Political and Social Research [producer and distributor].

Islam, Muhammed N. 1998. "Fiscal Illusion, Intergovernmental Grants and Local Spending." *Regional Studies* 32: 63–71.

Jackson, Matthew, and Boaz Moselle. 2002. "Coalition and Party Formation in a Legislative Voting Game." *Journal of Economic Theory* 103: 49–87.

Jaffrelot, Christophe. 1995. *The Hindu Nationalist Movement in India.* New York: Columbia University Press.

James, Scott C. 2000. *Presidents, Parties, and the State: A Party System Perspective on Democratic Regulatory Choice, 1884–1936.* New York: Cambridge University Press.

Jenkins, Rob. 1999. *Democratic Politics and Economic Reform in India.* Cambridge: Cambridge University Press.

Johnston, Richard. 2000. "Canadian Elections at the Millennium." *Choices* 6: 4–36.

Johnston, Richard. André Blais, Henry E Brady, and Jean Crête. 1992. *Letting the People Decide: Dynamics of a Canadian Election.* Stanford, CA: Stanford University Press.

Johnston, Richard, and C. J. Pattie. 1991. "Tactical Voting in Great Britain in 1983 and 1987." *British Journal of Political Science* 21: 95–108.

Jones, Kathleen. 1991. *The Making of Social Policy in Britain, 1830–1990.* London: Athlone.

Jones, Mark. 1994. "Presidential Election Laws and Multipartism in Latin America." *Political Research Quarterly* 47: 41–57.

Jones, Mark, and Scott Mainwaring. 2003. "The Nationalization of Parties and Party Systems: An Empirical Measure and an Application to the Americas." *Party Politics* 9: 139–66.

Jones-Luong, Pauline. 2002. *Institutional Change and Political Continuity in Post-Soviet Central Asia: Power, Perceptions, and Pacts*. New York: Cambridge University Press.

Kalyvas, Stathis N. 1996. *The Rise of Christian Democracy in Europe*. Ithaca, NY: Cornell University Press.

Katz, Richard. 1980. *A Theory of Parties and Electoral Systems*. Baltimore: Johns Hopkins University Press.

———. 1997. *Democracy and Elections*. New York: Oxford University Press.

Katz, Richard, and Peter Mair. 1992. *Party Organizations: A Data Handbook on Party Organizations in Western Democracies, 1960–1990*. London: Sage.

———. 1994. *How Parties Organize: Change and Adaptation in Party Organizations in Western Democracies*. London: Sage.

———. 1995. "Changing Models of Party Organization and Party Democracy: The Emergence of the Cartel Party." *Party Politics* 1: 5–28.

Kaviraj, S. 1991. "On State, Society and Discourse in India." In *Rethinking Third World Politics*, ed. James Manor. London: Longman.

Kawato, Sudafumi. 1987. "Nationalization and Partisan Realignment in Congressional Elections." *American Political Science Review* 81: 1235–50.

Keating, Michael. 1982. "The Debate on Regional Reform." In *Regional Government in England*, ed. Brian Hogwood and Michael Keating. Oxford: Clarendon Press.

———. 1989. "Regionalism, Devolution, and the State, 1969–1989." In *British Regionalism, 1900–2000*, ed. Patricia Garside and Michael Hebbert. London: Mansell.

Kedar, Orit. 2003. "Policy Balancing in Comparative Context." Ph.D. dissertation, Harvard University.

Kesselman, Mark. 1966. "French Local Politics: A Statistical Examination of Grass Roots Consensus." *American Political Science Review* 60: 963–73.

Key, V. O. 1949. *Southern Politics*. New York: Knopf.

Kiewit, D. Roderick, and Mathew McCubbins. 1991. *The Logic of Delegation*. Chicago: University of Chicago Press.

Kim, Heemin, and Richard Fording. 2001. "Does Tactical Voting Matter? The Political Impact of Tactical Voting in Recent British Elections." *Comparative Political Studies* 34: 294–311.

Kim, Jae-on, and Mahn-geum Ohn. 1992. "A Theory of Minor Party Persistence." *Social Forces* 70: 575–99.

King, David. 1973. *Financial and Economic Aspects of Regionalism and Separatism*. London: Her Majesty's Stationary Office (Commission on the Constitution).

King, Desmond, 1989. "Political Centralization and State Interests in Britain: The 1986 Abolition of the GLC and MCCs." *Comparative Political Studies* 21: 467–94.

King, Desmond, and Kenneth Janda. 1985. "Formalizing and Testing Duverger's Theories on Political Parties." *Comparative Political Studies* 18: 139–69.

Kirchheimer, O. 1966. "The Transformation of West European Party Systems." In *Political Parties and Political Development*, ed. J. LaPalombara and M. Weiner, 177–200. Princeton, NJ: Princeton University Press.

Kitschelt, Herbert. 1989. *Logics of Party Formation*. Ithaca, NY: Cornell University Press.

———. 1999. "Accounting for Outcomes of Post-Communist Regime Change: Causal Depth or Shallowness in Rival Explanations." Paper presented at the annual meeting of the American Political Science Association, Atlanta, September.

———. 2001. *Parties and Democracy*. Baltimore: Johns Hopkins University Press.

Kleppner, Paul. 1970. *The Cross of Culture*. New York: Free Press.

———. 1987. *Continuity and Change in Electoral Politics, 1893–1928*. New York: Greenwood.

Klingemann, Hans-Dieter, Richard I. Hofferbert, and Ian Budge. 1994. *Parties, Policy and Democracy*. Boulder, CO: Westview Press.

Kochanek, Stanley. 1968. *The Congress Party of India: The Dynamics of One-Party Democracy*. Princeton, NJ: Princeton University Press.

———. 1976. "Mrs. Gandhi's Pyramid: The New Congress." In *Indira Gandhi's India*, ed. Henry C. Hart. Boulder, CO: Westview Press.

Kohli, Atul. 1989. The *State and Poverty in India: The Politics of Reform*. New York: Cambridge University Press.

———. 1990. *Democracy and Discontent: India's Growing Crisis of Governability*. New York: Cambridge University Press.

———. 1994. "Centralization and Powerlessness: India's Democracy in a Comparative Perspective." In *State Power and Social Forces: Domination and Transformation in the Third World*, ed. Joel S. Migdal, Atul Kohli, and Vivienne Shue. New York: Cambridge University Press.

Kornberg, Allan, Harold Clarke, and Marianne Stewart. 1979. "Federalism and Fragmentation: Political Support in Canada." *Journal of Politics* 41: 889–906.

Kothari, Rajni. 1964. "The Congress 'System' in India." *Asian Survey* 4: 1161–73.

Kothari, Rajni, and G. Shah. 1965. "Caste Orientation of Political Factions: Modasa Constituency." In *Indian Voting Behaviour: Studies of the 1962 General Elections*, ed. Myron Weiner and Rajni Kothari. Calcutta: Firma K. L. Mukhopadhayay.

Laakso, Markku, and Rein Taagepera. 1979. " 'Effective' Number of Parties: A Measure with Application to West Europe." *Comparative Political Studies* 12: 3–27.

Lakdawala, D. T. 1991. "Inaugural Address." In *The Ninth Finance Commission: Issues and Recommendations*. New Delhi: National Institute of Public Finance and Policy.

———. 1993. "Issues before the Ninth Finance Commission." In *The Ninth Finance Commission: Issues and Recommendations*. New Delhi: National Institute of Public Finance and Policy.

Laver, Michael. 1987. "The Logic of Plurality Voting in Multi-Party Systems." In *The Logic of Multiparty Systems*, ed. M. J. Holler. Dordrecht, Netherlands: Martinus Nijhoff.

Lawson, Kay. 1980. *Political Parties and Linkage: A Comparative Analysis*. New Haven, CT: Yale University Press.

Lawson, Kay, and Peter H. Merkl, eds. 1988. *When Parties Fail: Emerging Alternative Organizations*. Princeton, NJ: Princeton University Press.

Leach, Richard H. 1988. "Canadian Federalism Revisited." In *Canadian Federalism: From Crisis to Constitution*, ed. Harold Waller, Filippo Sabetti, and Daniel Elazar. Lanham, MD: University Press of America.

LeDuc, Lawrence. 1985. "Partisan Change and Dealignment in Canada, Great Britain, and the United States." *Comparative Politics* 17: 379–98.

LeDuc, Lawrence, Harold D. Clarke, Jane Jenson, and Jon H. Pammett. 1980. "Partisanship, Voting Behavior, and Election Outcomes in Canada." *Comparative Politics* 12: 401–17.

———. 1984. "Partisan Instability in Canada: Evidence from a New Panel Study." *American Political Science Review* 78: 470–84.

Lees-Marshment, Jennifer. 2001. *Political Marketing and British Political Parties: The Party's Just Begun*. Manchester: Manchester University Press.

Leslie, P. M. 1987. *Federal State, National Economy*. Toronto: University of Toronto Press.

Levy, Gilat. 2004. "A Model of Political Parties." *Journal of Economic Theory*. Forthcoming.

Leys, Colin. 1959. "Models, Theories, and the Theory of Political Parties." *Political Studies* 7: 127–46.

Lijphart, Arend. 1994. *Electoral Systems and Party Systems*. New York: Oxford University Press.

Link, Arthur. 1959. "What Happened to the Progressive Movement in the 1920s?" *American Historical Review* 64: 833–51.

Lipset, Seymour M. 1954. "Democracy in Alberta." *Canadian Forum* (November–December 1954): 175–77, 196–98.

Lipset, Seymour M., and Stein Rokkan. 1967. "Cleavage Structures, Party Systems, and Voter Alignments: An Introduction." In *Party Systems and Voter Alignments*, ed. Seymour M. Lipset and Stein Rokkan. New York: Free Press.

Lipset, Seymour M., Martin A. Trow, and James S. Coleman. 1956. *Union Democracy: The Internal Politics of the International Typographical Union*. Glencoe, IL: Free Press.

Lloyd, Trevor. 1965. "Communication: Uncontested Seats in British General Elections, 1852–1910." *Historical Journal* 8: 260–65.

Loughlin, Martin. 1986. *Local Government in the Modern States*. London: Sweet & Maxwell.

Luetscher, George Daniel. 1903. "Early Political Machinery in the U.S." Ph.D. dissertation, University of Pennsylvania.

Mahler, G. S. 1987. *New Dimensions of Canadian Federalism: Canada in a Comparative Perspective*. Rutherford, NJ: Fairlegh Dickinson University Press.

Main, Jackson T. 1973. *Political Parties before the Constitution*. Chapel Hill: University of North Carolina Press.

Mainwairing, Scott. 1997. "Multipartism, Robust Federalism, and Presidentialism in Brazil." In *Presidentialism and Democracy in Latin America*, ed. Scott Mainwaring and Matthew S. Shugart. New York: Cambridge University Press.

Mainwaring, Scott, and Timothy Scully, eds. 1995. *Building Democratic Institutions*. Stanford, CA: Stanford University Press.

Mainwaring, Scott, and Matthew S. Shugart, eds. 1997. *Presidentialism and Democracy in Latin America*. New York: Cambridge University Press.

Mainwaring, Scott, and Mariano Torcal. 2003. "The Political Recrafting of the Social Bases of Party Competition: Chile, 1973–1995." *British Journal of Political Science* 33: 55–84

Mair, Peter. 1997. *Party System Change: Approaches and Interpretations*. Oxford: Oxford University Press.

Majumdar, R. C., H. C. Rayehaudhuri, and Kalikinkar Datta. 1956. *An Advanced History of India*. London: Macmillan.

Manor, James. 1988a. "Politics: Ambiguity, Disillusionment, and Ferment." In *India Briefing, 1988*, ed. Marshall Bouton and Philip Oldenburg. Boulder, CO: Westview Press.

———. 1988b. "Parties and the Party System." In *India's Democracy: An Analysis of Changing State-Society Relations*, ed. Atul Kohli. Princeton, NJ: Princeton University Press.

———. 1990. "How and Why Liberal and Representative Politics Emerged in India." *Political Studies* 38: 20–38.

———, ed. 1994. *Nehru to the Nineties: The Changing Office of the Prime Minister in India*. Vancouver: University of British Columbia Press.

Maravall, J. 1997. *Regimes, Politics, and Markets: Democratization and Economic Change in Southern and Eastern Europe*. New York: Oxford University Press.

March, Roman R. 1974. *The Myth of Parliament*. Scarborough, Ontario: Prentice-Hall.

Martin, J. 1974. *The Role and Place of Ontario in the Canadian Confederation*. Toronto: Ontario Economic Council.

Martin, Pugh. 1993. The *Making of Modern British Politics, 1867–1939*. Oxford: Blackwell.

Martin, R., and P. Tyler. 1992. "The Regional Legacy." In *The Economic Legacy, 1979–1992*, ed. Jonathan Michie. London: Academic Press.

Maxwell, J. A. 1936. "The Adjustment of Federal-Provincial Financial Relations." *Canadian Journal of Economics and Political Science* 2: 374–89.

Mayhew, David R. 1974. *Congress: The Electoral Connection*. New Haven, CT: Yale University Press.

McCormick, Richard P. 1975. "Political Development and the Second American Party System." In *The American Party Systems*, ed. William N. Chambers and Walter Dean Burnham. 2nd ed. New York: Oxford University Press.

McFaul, Michael. 2001. "Explaining Party Formation and Nonformation in Russia: Actors, Institutions, and Chance." *Comparative Political Studies* 34: 1159–87.

McInnis, Marvin. 2000. "The Economy of Canada in the Nineteenth Century." In *The Cambridge Economic History of the United States, vol. 2, the Long Nineteenth Century*, ed. Stanley L. Engerman and Robert E. Gallman. New York: Cambridge University Press.

McKelvey, Richard, and Richard Niemi. 1978. "A Multistage Representation of Sophisticated Voting for Binary Procedures." *Journal of Economic Theory* 18: 1–22.

Mclane, John R. 1989. "The Early Congress, Hindu Populism, and the Wider Society." In *Congress and Indian Nationalism: The Pre-independence Phase*, ed. Richard Sisson and Stanley Wolpert. Berkeley: University of California Press.

McLean, Iain. 1986. "Some Recent Work in Public Choice." *British Journal of Political Science* 16: 377–94.

Michie, Jonathan, ed. 1992. *The Economic Legacy, 1979–1992*. London: Academic Press.

Milkis, Sidney. 1993. *The President and the Parties: The Transformation of the American Party System since the New Deal*. New York: Oxford University Press.

Miller, Nicholas. 1980. "A New Solution Set for Tournaments and Majority Voting." *American Journal of Political Science* 24: 68–96.

Mitchell, Brian R. 1998. *International Historical Statistics: Europe, 1750–1993*. London: Macmillan Reference.

Mitra, Subrata Kumar. 1992. *Power, Protest, and Participation: Local Elites and the Politics of Development in India*. New York: Routledge.

Molinar, Juan. 1991. "Counting the Number of Parties: An Alternative Index." *American Political Science Review* 85: 1383–91.

Moore, B. 1992. "Taking on the Inner Cities." In *The Economic Legacy, 1979–1992*, ed. Jonathan Michie. London: Academic Press.

Morelli, Massimo. 1999. "Demand Competition and Policy Compromise in Legislative Bargaining." *American Political Science Review* 93: 809–20.

———. 2001. "Party Formation and Policy Outcomes under Different Electoral Systems." Department of Political Science, Ohio State University. Typescript.

Moscovitch, Allan, and Jim Albert, eds. 1987. *The Benevolent State: The Growth of Welfare in Canada*. Toronto: Garamond Press.

Mowry, George. 1983. *Reform and Reformers in the Progressive Era*. Westport, CT: Greenwood.

Mozoomdar, Ajit. 1994. "The Rise and Decline of Development Planning in India." In *The State and Development Planning in India*, ed. Terence Byres. Delhi: Oxford University Press.

Mughan, Anthony. 1986. *Party and Participation in British Elections*. London: Pinter.

Mullard, Maurice. 1987. *Politics of Public Expenditure*. London: Croom Helm.

Muller, Wolfgang. 1993. "The Relevance of the State for Party System Change." *Journal of Theoretical Politics* 5: 419–54.

Myerson, Roger, and Robert Weber. 1993. "A Theory of Voting Equilibria." *American Political Science Review* 87: 102–14.

Nardulli, Peter. 1995. "The Concept of a Critical Realignment, Electoral Behavior, and Political Change." *American Political Science Review* 89: 10–22.

Nayar, Baldev Raj. 1999. "Policy and Performance under Democratic Coalitions: India's United Front Government and Economic Reforms, 1996–98." *Journal of Commonwealth and Comparative Politics* 37 (2): 22–56.

Niemi, Richard, and John Fuh-sheng Hsieh. 2002. "Counting Candidates: An Alternative to the Effective N." *Party Politics* 8: 75–99.

Niemi, Richard, Guy Whitten, and Mark Franklin. 1992. "Constituency Characteristics, Individual Characteristics and Tactical Voting in the 1987 British General Election." *British Journal of Political Science* 22: 229–40.

———. 1993. "People Who Live in Glass Houses: A Response to Evans and Heath's Critique of Our Note on Tactical Voting." *British Journal of Political Science* 23: 549–53.

Nikolenyi, Csaba. 2000. "Party Aggregation in India." Department of Political Science, University of British Columbia. Typescript.

Noel, S. J. R. 1990. *Patrons, Clients, Brokers: Ontario Society and Politics, 1791–1896.* Toronto: University of Toronto Press.

North, Douglass C. 1990. *Institutions, Institutional Change, and Economic Performance.* New York: Cambridge University Press.

Olson, David. 1998. "Party Formation and Party System Consolidation in the New Democracies of Central Europe." *Political Studies* 46: 432–64.

Ordeshook, Peter, and Olga Shvetsova. 1994. "Ethnic Heterogeneity, District Magnitude, and the Number of Parties." *American Journal of Political Science* 38: 100–23.

Ostrogorski, M. 1902. *Democracy and the Organization of Political Parties.* Vol. 1. London: Macmillan.

Owen, Jonathan. 1989. "Regionalism and Local Government Reform, 1900–1960." In *British Regionalism, 1900–2000,* ed. Patricia Garside and Michael Hebbert. London: Mansell.

Palfrey, Thomas. 1989. "A Mathematical Proof of Duverger's Law." In *Models of Strategic Choice in Politics,* ed. Peter Ordeshook. Ann Arbor: University of Michigan Press.

Panebianco, A. 1988. *Political Parties: Organization and Power.* Cambridge: Cambridge University Press.

Panizza, Ugo. 1999. "On the Determinants of Fiscal Centralization: Theory and Evidence." *Journal of Public Economics* 74: 97–139.

Papachristou, G. 1968. "The Inter-play of Local and State Politics: The Rajasthan Case." In *The Fourth General Election in India,* vol. 1, ed. S. P. Varma and Iqbal Narain. Delhi: Orient Longmans.

Paranjape, H. K. 1964. *The Planning Commission: A Descriptive Account.* Delhi: Indian Institute of Public Administration.

Patterson, James. 1967. *Congressional Conservatism and the New Deal.* Lexington: University of Kentucky Press.

Peacock, A. T., and J. Wiseman. 1961. *The Growth of Public Expenditures in the United Kingdom.* London: George Allen & Unwin.

Pederson, M. 1979. "The Dynamics of European Party Systems: Changing Patterns of Electoral Volatility." *European Journal of Political Research* 7: 1–26.

Perry, David B. 1997. *Financing the Canadian Federation, 1867 to 1995.* Canadian Tax Paper no. 102. Toronto: Canadian Tax Foundation.

Persson, Torsten, and Guido Tabellini. 1999. "The Size and Scope of Government: Comparative Politics with Rational Politicians." *European Economic Review* 43: 699–735.

———. 2003. *The Economic Effects of Constitutions*. Cambridge, MA: MIT Press.

Peters, B. Guy. 1972. *Political Systems Performance Dataset*. Archive available at the Inter-University Consortium for Political and Social Research, Institute for Social Research, University of Michigan.

Petrocik, J. 1981. *Party Coalitions: Realignments and the Decline of the New Deal Party System*. Chicago: University of Chicago Press.

Philip, Alan Butt. 1975. The *Welsh Question: Nationalism in Welsh Politics, 1945–1970*. Cardiff: University of Wales Press.

Powell, G. Bingham. 2000. *Elections as Instruments of Democracy*. New Haven, CT: Yale University Press.

Pugh, Martin. 1993. *The Making of Modern British Politics, 1867–1939*. Oxford: Blackwell Publishers.

Pulzer, Peter. 1988. "When Parties Fail: Ethnic Protest in Britain in the 1970s." In *When Parties Fail*, ed. Kay Lawson and Peter Merkl. Princeton, NJ: Princeton University Press.

Rae, Douglas. 1971. *The Political Consequences of Electoral Laws*. 2nd ed. New Haven, CT: Yale University Press.

Rae, Nicole. 1994. *Southern Democrats*. New York: Oxford University Press.

Rand, Dyck. 1986. *Provincial Politics in Canada*. Scarborough, Ontario: Prentice-Hall.

Ranney, Austin. 1962. *The Doctrine of Responsible Party Government*. Urbana: University of Illinois Press.

Rao, M. G., and S. Mundle. 1992. "An Analysis of Changes in State Government Subsidies: 1977–87." In *State Finances in India*, ed. A. Bagchi, J. L. Bajaj, and W. A. Byrd. Vikas. New Delhi.

Rayside, David M. 1978. "Federalism and the Party System: Provincial and Federal Liberals in the Province of Quebec." *Canadian Journal of Political Science* 11: 499–528.

Reddy, Ram G., and G. Haragopal. 1985. "The Pyraveekar: 'The Fixer' in Rural India." *Asian Survey* 25: 1148–62.

Reid, Escott M. 1932. "The Rise of National Parties in Canada." In *Papers and Proceedings of the Annual Meeting of the Canadian Political Science Associations*, 187–200. Kingston, Ontario: Canadian Political Science Associations.

Rice, J. J., and M. J. Prince. 2000. *Changing Politics of Canadian Social Policy*. Toronto: University of Toronto Press.

Richards, James O. 1972. *Party Propaganda under Queen Anne: The General Elections of 1702–1713*. Athens: University of Georgia Press.

Richter, William L. 1977. "Electoral Patterns in Post-Princely India." In *Studies in Electoral Politics in the Indian States*, vol. 2, *Electoral Politics in the Indian States: Three Disadvantaged Sectors*, ed. Myron Weiner and John Osgood Field. New Delhi: Manohar Book Service.

Riker, William. 1964. *Federalism*. Boston: Little, Brown.

———. 1976. "The Number of Political Parties: A Reexamination of Duverger's Law." *Comparative Politics* 9: 93–106.

———. 1982. "The Two-Party System and Duverger's Law." *American Political Science Review* 76: 753–66.

————. 1986. *The Art of Political Manipulation*. New Haven, CT: Yale University Press.

————, ed. 1993. *Agenda Formation*. Ann Arbor: University of Michigan Press.

Robins, Robert. 1979. "Votes, Seats and the Critical Election of 1967." *Journal of Commonwealth and Comparative Politics* 27: 247–62.

Robinson, James. 2002. "Political Origins of Dictatorship and Democracy." Department of Political Science, University of California, Berkeley. Unpublished manuscript.

Rohrschneider, Robert. 1993. "New Parties versus Old Left Realignments: Environmental Attitudes, Party Policies, and Partisan Affiliations in Four West European Countries." *Journal of Politics* 55: 682–701.

Rose, Richard. 1974a. *Politics in England: An Interpretation*. Boston: Little, Brown.

————, ed. 1974b. *Electoral Behavior*. New York: Free Press.

————. 1980. *Do Parties Make a Difference?* London: Macmillan.

Rosenstone, Steven J. 1983. *Forecasting Presidential Elections*. New Haven, CT: Yale University Press.

Rosenstone, Steven J., Edward H. Lazarus, and Roy L. Behr. 1994. *Third Parties in America: Citizen Response to Major Party Failure*. Princeton, NJ: Princeton University Press.

Roy, Ramashray. 1969. "Two Patterns in India's Mid-Term Elections." *Asian Survey* 2 (4): 287–302.

Rudig, Wolfgang. 1990. *Green Politics One*. Edinburgh: Edinburgh University Press.

Rudolph, Lloyd I. 1989. "The Faltering Novitate: Rajiv at Home and Abroad in 1988." In *India Briefing, 1989*, ed. Marshall Bouton and Philip Oldenberg. Boulder, CO: Westview.

Rudolph, Lloyd I., and Susanne H. Rudolph. 1987. *In Pursuit of Lakshmi: The Political Economy of the Indian State*. Chicago: University of Chicago Press.

Russell, Peter, Rainer Knopff, and Ted Morton. 1993. *Federalism and the Charter*. Ottawa: Carleton University Press.

Saez, Lawrence. 2002. *Federalism without a Centre: The Impact of Political and Economic Reform on India's Federal System*. New Delhi: Sage.

Samuels, David. 2000. "Concurrent Elections, Discordant Results: Presidentialism, Federalism, and Governance in Brazil." *Comparative Politics* 33: 1–20.

————. 2002. "Presidentialized Parties: The Separation of Powers and Party Organization and Behavior." *Comparative Political Studies* 35: 461–83.

Sartori, Giovanni. 1976. *Parties and Party Systems*. Cambridge: Cambridge University Press.

————. 1986. "The Influence of Electoral Systems: Faulty Laws or Faulty Method?" In *Electoral Laws and Their Political Consequences*, ed. Bernard Grofman and Arend Lijphart. New York: Agathon Press.

Savoie, D. J. 1981. *Federal-Provincial Collaboration: The Canada-New Brunswick General Development Agreement*. Montreal: McGill-Queen's University Press.

————. 1999. *Governing from the Centre: The Concentration of Power in Canadian Politics*. Toronto: University of Toronto Press.

Sayers, A. M. 1999. *Parties, Candidates and Constituency Campaigns in Canadian Elections*. Vancouver: UBC Press.

Scarrow, S. 1996. *Parties and Their Members*. Oxford: Clarendon Press.

Schattschneider, E. E. [1960] 1975. *The Semisovereign People*. Hinsdale, IL: Dryden Press.

Schlesinger, Joseph. 1991. *Political Parties and the Winning of Office*. Ann Arbor: University of Michigan Press.

Schultz, S. K. 1989. *Constructing Urban Culture: American Cities and City Planning, 1800–1920*. Philadelphia: Temple University Press.

Schwartz, Mildred. 1974. "Canadian Voting Behavior." In *Electoral Behavior*, ed. Richard Rose. New York: Free Press.

Schwartz, Thomas. 1989. "Why Parties?" Department of Political Science, University of California, Los Angeles. Typescript.

Sen, Amartya, and Jean Dreze. 1998. *India; Economic Development and Social Opportunity*. New Delhi: Oxford University Press.

Shachar, Ron, and Barry Nalebuff. 1999. "Follow the Leader: Theory and Evidence on Political Participation." *American Economic Review* 89: 525–47.

Shafer, Byron, and Anthony Badger, eds. 2001. *Contesting Democracy: Substance and Structure in American Political History, 1775–2000*. Lawrence: University Press of Kansas.

Sharpe, L. J., and K. Newton. 1984. *Does Politics Matter? The Determinants of Public Policy*. Oxford: Clarendon Press.

Shefter, Martin. 1994. *Political Parties and the State: The American Historical Experience*. Princeton, NJ: Princeton University Press.

Shively, W. Phillips. 1982. "The Electoral Impact of Party Loyalists and the 'Floating Vote': A New Measure and a New Perspective." *Journal of Politics* 44: 679–91.

———. 1992. "From Differential Abstention to Conversion: A Change in Electoral Change, 1864–1988." *American Journal of Political Science* 36: 309–30.

Shugart, Matthew, and John Carey. 1992. *Presidents and Assemblies: Constitutional Design and Electoral Dynamics*. New York: Cambridge University Press.

Shvetsova, Olga. 1996. "The Duverger Law without Two-Partism." Department of Political Science, Washington University. Typescript.

Simeon, Richard. 1972. *Federal-Provincial Diplomacy: The Making of Recent Policy in Canada*. Toronto: University of Toronto Press.

Simeon, Richard, and David J. Elkins. 1974. "Regional Political Cultures in Canada." *Canadian Journal of Political Science* 7: 397–437.

Singh, V. B., and Shankar Bose. 1984. *Elections in India: Data Handbook on LokSabha Elections, 1952–80*. New Delhi: Sage.

———. 1994. *Elections in India: Data Handbook on Lok Sabha Elections, 1986–1994*. New Delhi: Sage.

Sinha, R. K. 2003. *Understanding Poverty*. Anamika Publishers & Distributors.

Sisson, Richard. 1972. *The Congress Party in Rajasthan: Political Integration and Institution Building in an Indian State*. Berkeley: University of California Press.

Sklar, Richard, and C. S. Whitaker Jr. 1964. "Nigeria." In *Political Parties and*

*National Integration in Tropical Africa*, ed. James S. Coleman and Carl Rosberg. Berkeley: University of California Press.

Skocpol, Theda. 1992. *Protecting Soldiers and Mothers*. Cambridge, MA: Harvard University Press.

———. 1995. *Social Policy in the United States: Future Possibilities in Historical Perspective*. Princeton, NJ: Princeton University Press.

Skowronek, Stephen. 1982. *Building a New American State: The Expansion of National Administrative Capacities*. New York: Cambridge University Press.

Smiley, Donald V. 1988. "Public Sector Politics, Modernization and Federalism: The Canadian and American Experiences." In *Canadian Federalism: From Crisis to Constitution*, ed. Harold Waller, Filippo Sabetti, and Daniel Elazar. Lanham, MD: University Press of America.

Stern, Robert. 2001. *Democracy and Dictatorship in South Asia: Dominant Classes and Political Outcomes in India, Pakistan, and Bangladesh*. Westport, CT: Praeger.

Stewart, Gordon T. 1986. *The Origins of Canadian Politics: A Comparative Approach*. Vancouver: UBC Press.

Stewart, Ian. 1986. "Friends at Court: Federalism and Provincial Elections on Prince Edward Island." *Canadian Journal of Political Science* 19: 127–50.

Stokes, Donald. 1963. "Spatial Models of Party Competition." *American Political Science Review* 57: 368–77.

Stoner-Weiss, Kathryn. 1999. "Central Weakness and Provincial Autonomy: Observations on the Devolution Process in Russia." *Post-Soviet Affairs* 15 (1): 87–106.

———. 2001. "The Limited Reach of Russia's Party System: Underinstitutionalization in Dual Transitions." *Politics and Society* 29: 385–414.

Sullivan, Michael. 1996. *The Development of the British Welfare State*. London: Prentice-Hall.

Sundquist, James. 1973. *Dynamics of the Party System: Alignment and Realignment of Political Parties in the United States*. Washington, DC: Brookings Institution.

———. 1983. *Dynamics of the Party System: Alignment and Realignment of Political Parties in the United States*. Rev. ed. Washington, DC: Brookings Institution.

Sutherland, Sharon, and G. Bruce Doren. 1985. *Bureaucracy and Control in Canada: Control and Reform*. Toronto: University of Toronto Press.

Sylla, Richard. 2000. "Experimental Federalism: The Economics of American Government, 1789–1914." In *The Cambridge Economic History of the United States,* vol. 2, *The Long Nineteenth Century*, ed. Stanley L. Engerman and Robert E Gallman. New York: Cambridge University Press.

Taagepera, Rein. 1997. "Effective Number of Parties for Incomplete Data." *Electoral Studies* 16: 145–51.

Taagepera, Rein, and Matthew Shugart. 1989. *Seats and Votes: The Effects and Determinants of Electoral Systems*. New Haven, CT: Yale University Press.

———. 1993. "Predicting the Number of Parties: A Quantitative Model of Duverger's Mechanical Effect." *American Political Science Review* 87: 455–64.

Teaford, Jon C. 2002. *The Rise of the States: Evolution of American State Government*. Baltimore: Johns Hopkins University Press.

Thain, Colin, and Maurice Wright. 1995. *The Treasury and Whitehall*. Oxford: Clarendon Press.

Tomlinson, B. R. 1976. *The Indian National Congress and the Raj, 1929–1942*. London: Macmillan.

Torcal, Mariano, and Scott Mainwaring. 2001. "The Political Re-crafting of Social Bases of Party Competition: The Case of Chile, 1973–1995." *British Journal of Political Science* 31: 1157–95.

Treisman, Daniel. 1999. *After the Deluge: Regional Crises and Political Consolidation in Russia*. Ann Arbor: University of Michigan Press.

Truman, David. 1954. *The Governmental Process*. New York: Alfred Knopf.

Tsbelis, George. 1986. "Notes and Comments: A General Model of Tactical and Inverse Tactical Voting." *British Journal of Political Science* 16: 395–404.

Ullman, Stephen H. 1983. "Political Development and Party Change in Quebec, 1980–1983." *American Review of Canadian Studies* 13 (2): 29–41.

Underhill, Frank. 1935. "The Development of National Political Parties in Canada." *Canadian Historical Review* 16: 367–87.

U.S. Department of Commerce, Bureau of the Census. 1975. *Historical Statistics of the United States*. Washington, DC: Department of Commerce.

Vanderbok, William. 1990. "The Tiger Triumphant: The Mobilization and Alignment of the Indian Electorate." *British Journal of Political Science* 20: 237–61.

Vietor, Richard H. K. 2000. "Government Regulation of Business." *In The Cambridge Economic History of the United States*, vol. 3, *The Twentieth Century*, ed. Stanley L. Engerman and Robert E Gallman. New York: Cambridge University Press.

Wagner, A. 1958. "Three Extracts on Public Finance." In *Classics in the Theory of Public Finance*, ed. R. A. Musgrave and A. P. Peacock. London: Macmillan.

Wallace, P. 2000. "India's 1998 Election: Hindutva, the Tail Wags the Elephant, and Pokhran." In *Indian Politics and the 1998 Election: Regionalism, Hindutva, and State Politics*, ed. Ramashray Roy and Paul Wallace. Thousand Oaks, CA: Sage.

Waller, Harold, Filippo Sabetti, and Daniel Elazar, eds. 1988. *Canadian Federalism: From Crisis to Constitution*. Lanham, MD: University Press of America.

Wallis, John Joseph. 1991. "The Political Economy of New Deal Fiscal Federalism." *Economic Inquiry* 29: 510–24.

Walton, Hanes. 1969. *The Negro in Third Party Politics*. Philadelphia: Dorrance.

———. 1972. *Black Political Parties*. New York: Free Press.

Ward, Stephen. 1988. *The Geography of Interwar Britain: The State and Uneven Development*. New York: Routledge..

Ware, Alan. 1987. *Citizens, Parties and the State*. Oxford: Polity Press.

———. 1996. *Political Parties and Party Systems*. New York: Oxford University Press.

Washbrook, David. 1973. "Country Politics: Madras 1880 to 1930." In *Locality Province and Nation: Essays on Indian Politics, 1870–1940*, ed. John Gallagher, Gordon Johnson, and Anil Seal. Cambridge: Cambridge University Press.

———. 1976. *The Emergence of Provincial Politics: The Madras Presidency, 1870–1920*. New York: Cambridge University Press.

Wasson, Ellis Archer. 1991. "The House of Commons, 1660–1945: Parliamentary Families and the Political Elite." *English Historical Review* 106: 635–51.

Wattenberg, M. P. 1991. *The Rise of Candidate-Centered Politics*. Cambridge, MA: Harvard University Press.

Wearing, Joesph. 1981. *The L-Shaped Party: The Liberal Party of Canada, 1958–1980*. Toronto: McGraw-Hill Ryerson Limited.

Webb, P. D. 2000. *The Modern British Party System*. London: Sage.

Weber, Max. 1946. "Politics as a Vocation." In *From Max Weber: Essays in Sociology* , ed. H. H. Gerth and C. Wright Mills. New York: Oxford University Press.

Weiner, Myron. 1957. *Party Politics in India*. Princeton, NJ: Princeton University Press.

———. 1962. *The Politics of Scarcity: Public Pressure and Political Response in India*. Chicago: University of Chicago Press.

———. 1967. *Party Building in a New Nation: The Indian National Congress*. Chicago: University of Chicago Press.

———. 1987. "Rajiv Gandhi: A Midterm Assessment." In *India Briefing, 1987*, ed. Marshall Bouton. Boulder, CO: Westview Press.

———. 1989. *The Indian Paradox: Essays in Indian Politics*. Newbury Park, CA: Sage.

———. 1996. "The Regionalization of Indian Politics and Its Implications for Reform." Paper presented at the Conference on India's Economic Reforms, Harvard University.

Weingast, Barry. 1995. "The Economic Role of Political Institutions." *Journal of Law, Economics, and Organization* 11: 1–31.

Widner, Jennifer. 1997. "Political Parties and Civil Societies in Sub-Saharan Africa." In *Democracy in Africa: The Hard Road Ahead*, ed. Marina O'Harvey. Boulder, CO: L. Rienner.

Wildavsky, Aaron. 1959. "A Methodological Critique of Duverger's Political Parties." *Journal of Politics* 21: 303–18.

———. 1984. *The Politics of the Budgetary Process*. Boston: Little, Brown.

Willey, Joseph. 1998. "Institutional Arrangements and the Success of New Parties in Old Democracies." *Political Studies* 46: 651–68.

Wilson, James Q. 1973. *Political Organizations*. New York: Basic Books.

Wilson, John, and David Hoffman. 1970. "The Liberal Party in Contemporary Ontario Politics." *Canadian Journal of Political Science* 3: 177–204.

Yadav, Yogendra. 1996. "Reconfiguration in Indian Politics: State Assembly Elections, 1993–95." *Economic and Political Weekly* 31 (2, 3): 95–104.

Young, James Sterling. 1974. "Community and Society." In *American Political Behavior: Historical Essays and Readings*, ed. Lee Benson, Allan Bogue, J.

Rogers Hollingsworth, Thomas Pressly, and Joel Silbey. New York: Harper and Row.

Young, L. 1998. "Party, State and Political Competition in Canada: The Cartel Argument Revisited." *Canadian Journal of Political Science* 31: 339–58.

Young, R. A., Phillipe Faucher, and Andre Blais. 1984. "The Concept of Province-Building: A Critique." *Canadian Journal of Political Science* 17: 783–818.

# INDEX